THE ARTS OF THAILAND

AN INTRODUCTION TO

THE ARTS OF THAILAND

Steve Van Beek

Luca Invernizzi Tettoni

Contents

Endpapers: Detail of a lacquered panel dating from the Ayutthaya period. (M.C. Piya Rangsit collection.)
Opposite: Buddha descends from Tavatimsa heaven on a ladder made of nagas and jewels. On his left is a golden ladder for Indra and on his right is a silver ladder for Brahma, the two gods who accompanied him back to earth after he preached to his mother and the gods for three months. (Buddhaisawan Chapel, Bangkok)

Published 1985. Third edition 1988
Copyright © 1988 by Steve Van Beek.
Photographs © 1988 by Luca Invernizzi Tettoni.

ISBN: 962-7088-18-8

Printed in Hong Kong by
Toppan Printing Co. (HK) Ltd.
Book design by Werner Hahn, Grapho Ltd.
Drawings by Angkarn Kalayanapongsa
Published by Travel Publishing Asia Limited,
16/F Capitol Centre,
5-19 Jardine's Bazaar,
Causeway Bay,
Hong Kong.

Preface and Acknowledgements

On first encounter, Art in Thailand appears to be a straight-forward subject. In fact, it is an enormously complex field whose scholars hold widely varying opinions on how its periods should be divided and named, the dates or provenance of particular pieces, and the best representative pieces of each school. The difficulty arises in part from the multiplicity of styles and influences to which the country has been exposed, the fact that numerous schools with diverse styles were functioning during any one period, and that the smaller schools often straddled two periods. To confound discussion, there is a paucity of evidence to give conclusive support to any single interpretation.

To avoid confusing the general reader, the author has chosen those interpretations which accord with a general academic consensus or tradition. Where possible, alternative theories are noted, but such an approach will not satisfy everyone. It is for that reason that the author acknowledges a debt of deep gratitude to the following eminent art historians and experts who in correcting the text overlooked interpretations often contrary to their own to ensure as closely as possible the factual accuracy of this book.

Chin You-di
Alfred Pawlin
Penpane Damrongsiri
Piriya Krairiksh
Prayoon Ulushata
Mira Kim Prachabarn
Peter Skilling
M.C. Subhadradis Diskul
Sumet Jumsai
Uab Sanasen

Following pages: *This reclining Buddha, created in Sukhothai in the 14th or 15 century and placed in Sukhothai's Wat Phra Pai Luang, was moved to Bangkok early in the 19th century. It now occupies an honored place in Bangkok's Wat Bovornivet. Made of bronze and 3.5 meters long, the image is attended by a mural of disciples, painted in the second half of the 19th century.*

The photographer wishes to express his gratitude to Mrs. Penpane Damrongsiri, Curator of the National Museum, Bangkok for her generous assistance which made the book possible, overcoming all sorts of bureaucratic and practical obstacles; to Mrs. Chira Chongkol, Director of The National Museum, Bangkok, and to Mr. Taveesak Senanarong, Director General, Department of Fine Arts, for providing the necessary permissions; to H.R.H. Princess Chumbhot of Nagor Svarga, patron of arts who opened the doors of Suan Pakaad Palace, to M.C. Piya Rangsit who allowed us to reproduce the superb works of art of The Rangsit Collection, to Praku Knanumsommanajara and to Mr. Surat Osathanugrah who also agreed to have their beautiful collections photographed. Greatly absent in a book which aims at covering the best of Thai art is the collection of H.R.H. Prince Bhanubandhu Yugala, which at the last moment became impossible to photograph for personal reasons. We are nevertheless grateful to the Prince for his enthusiastic sympathy and his help, and we hope to be able to include some pieces from his outstanding collection in a future edition.

The warmest thanks to the painters and friends Angkarn Kalayana-pongsa, Uab Sanasen, Thawan Duchanee, Preecha Thaothong, Chalermchai Kositpipat, Panya Vijinthanasarn, Arunothai, Somsakul, Chakrabhand Posayakrit, Pichai Narand, Pratuang Emjaroen, Surasit Souakong, to Alfred Pawlin of the Visual Dhamma Gallery and to Diethard Ande of The White Lotus Co., Ltd. and to the owners of the Hamilton King Collection.

Above all, the photographer acknowledges his debt to Cindy Caldwell who helped him throughout all stages of preparation of the book, to Alberto Cassio whose technical advice was needed in many occasions, and last but not least to Prof. Jean Boisselier, from whom he learnt to understand and to appreciate the art of South East Asia.

Guide to spelling

Where possible, I have used the Thai terms and have noted where necessary the equivalents in Pali or Sanskrit. These are the pronunciations of key Thai letters:

BH   An aspirated B as in bhumisparsa pronouned as "boom"

DH   An aspirated D as in dhyani pronounced as "dye"

DV   Pronounced "dawa" as in Dvaravati

K   A G sound as in Kanprien pronounced as "gun"

KH   An aspirated K as in Khon, pronounced as "cone"

NG   As in Phangnga, pronounced as the "ng" in "singer"

P   A hard P as in Phetchaburi, pronounced "pet"

PH   An aspirated P as in Phitsanulok, pronounced "pit"

SR   An S sound as in Srivijaya, pronounced as "sea"

SV   Pronounced "sawa" as in Avalokitesvara

T   A hard T as in Tavatimsa, pronounced as "tea"

TH   An aspirated T as in Sukhothai, not a diphthong as in the English word "the" but as in the word "tie"

V   Pronounced as a W as in vihan or "we"

The spelling of Thai place names is based on the system devised by the Thai Royal Institute, but the reader should be aware that there is more than one system of Romanized Thai, and differences in spelling will be found even in names of major cities.

What is Thai Art?

Down the centuries, Thailand has seen the emergence and extinction of a number of widely varying art styles. These have been brought unaltered from foreign lands, been developed by the indigenous populations or, in most instances, have resulted from a fusion of several modes, alien and native, to create one which is entirely new. Until the 13th century, art forms were heavily influenced by those of neighboring countries notably India, Sri Lanka, and Kampuchea. With the founding of Sukhothai in the mid-13th century, a style emerges which is uniquely Thai. To comprehend the vast body of art which comes under the heading of "Thailand," however, one must explore the various ingredients that went into the creative cauldron.

With its rich land, abundant rainfall and ample sunshine, the country has always been an inviting place for settlement. From early times, its fertility has attracted a variety of foreign ethnic groups who blended with indigenous populations. Together they farmed the country's valleys and plains, using the resultant prosperity to fuel the creation of art.

Some 4,000 years ago, Thailand's northeastern region was the home of a Bronze Age culture of advanced social organization and artistic attainments. By the 1st century A.D. Indian merchants were traversing Thailand's central region and southern peninsula bringing new concepts which, more than those of any other culture, would profoundly shape the country's religion, literature, art, and politics.

By the third century, Chinese annals were recording the existence of numerous autonomous kingdoms along the Gulf of Siam coastline. In the central Chao Phya River Valley, thriving towns were gaining recognition as centers of religion and learning. Pilgrims from India, and later Sri Lanka, brought Theravada Buddhism which supplanted the Hinduism and the Mahayana Buddhism professed by the majority of the country's peoples. Through the end of the first millennium, waves of Khmers, Indonesians and others made their contributions to the cultural mix.

In the 13th century, the focus of activity shifted to the upper reaches of the Chao Phya Valley. At Chiang Mai there arose the Lanna kingdoms, which dominated the northern region between Burma and Laos. Just to the south, the first Thai nation was established at Sukhothai. It was once thought that the Thais migrated from China, but recent research has suggested that they had lived from early times along both sides of the border with China but until the 13th century were not powerful enough to assert their independence. With the waning of Khmer influence early in the 13th century, the Thai principalities formed a confederation which, though it would have several capitals, has functioned as a sovereign nation down to the present day. Strictly speaking, Thai history begins from this point.

The appellation "Thai" has created confusion and controversy among those trying to describe precisely the history and compass of the country because it denotes only one race among many, some of which had been established long before the Thais made their appearance. Until World War II, the country was known as "Siam". Some scholars feel the term more accurately describes the country as a geographical and political entity, and have clamored to have it reinstated. Popular usage, however, has decreed the retention of "Thailand" and "Thai" and it is these names which are used in this book.

In 1350, Ayutthaya became Thailand's capital. For 400 years, Ayutthaya reigned supreme in the politics of the region, growing enormously rich on trade and embellishing its capital with monuments to reflect its pre-eminent position. In 1767, however, it was overrun and destroyed by Burmese armies. The remnants of the population moved downriver to Thon Buri and, in 1782, to Bangkok where they established the capital that serves the kingdom today.

Until the present century, Thailand was governed by an absolute monarchy. In 1932, following a revolution, it became a constitutional monarchy. For the past 700 years, 90% of its people have professed Theravada Buddhism as their religion. These two potent forces have been at the base of Thailand's art and culture, with kings providing the patronage, and the glorification of Buddhism being the principal theme addressed by its artists.

The division of Thailand's art into periods or schools was undertaken in the 1920s, and the system devised has been followed with little modification since then. It has been contested, on the grounds that its divisions are somewhat arbitrary, that it clouds comprehension by assigning names to periods based on specific cities or kingdoms (about which there is often little concrete information) rather than broader geographical areas or schools, that it fails to cover adequately all the divergences from the set norm for a particular school, and that it does not allow for evidence discovered in the past half-century. In response, a phalanx of new art historians has formulated several new classification systems but has made slow progress in seeing them adopted.

This is the system generally followed and by which pieces in Thailand's museums are identified:

Prehistoric	Up to the 1st century A.D.
Indianized (Hindu)	1st to 6th centuries A.D.
Dvaravati (Mon)	6th to 11th centuries A.D.
Srivijaya	8th to 13th centuries A.D.
Lop Buri	10th to 14th centuries A.D.
Sukhothai	13th to 15th centuries A.D.
Lanna (Chiengsaen)	13th to 16th centuries A.D.
Ayutthaya	1350 to 1767
Thon Buri	1767 to 1782
Bangkok (Ratanakosin)	1782 to present

Major Kings of Thailand

Sukhothai:
Intradit (1238 — 1270?)
Ramkamhaeng (1279 — 1299 or 1316)
Lu Thai (1317 — 1347)
Li Thai (Thammaraja) (1347 — 1368)

Lanna:
Mengrai (? — 1311 or 1317)
Tiloka (1442 — 1488)

Ayutthaya:
Ramathibodi (U Thong) (1350 — 1369)
Boromaraja I (1370 — 1388)
Ramesuan (1369 and 1388 — 1395)
Boromaraja II (1424 — 1448)
Boroma Trailokanat (1448 — 1488)
Ramathibodi II (1492 — 1529)
Chakraphat (1549 — 1565)
Naresuan (1590 — 1605)
Prasat Thong (1630 — 1656)
Narai (1657 — 1688)
Phra Petraja (1688 — 1703)
Boromakot (1733 — 1758)

Thon Buri:
Taksin (1767 — 1782)

Bangkok (Chakri dynasty):
Rama I (Phra Phutta Yot Fa) (1782 — 1809)
Rama II (1809 — 1824)
Rama III (1824 — 1851)
Rama IV (Mongkut) (1851 — 1868)
Rama V (Chulalongkorn) (1868 — 1910)
Rama VI (Vajiravudh) (1910 — 1925)
Prajadhipok (1925 — 1935)
Ananda (1935 — 1946)
Bhumibol (1946 —)

Opposite: *Ayutthaya's Wat Phra Ram, built in 1369 is an excellent example of the prang-centered wat developed by Khmer architects and adopted in Sukhothai and Ayutthaya. The central prang is framed by smaller chedis at each of the four corners and an outer wall aligned according to the cardinal points. A vihan has been set to the east so its Buddha image will face the rising sun.*

Above: *Plan of Ayutthaya drawn by a 17th century European artist. (Courtesy of White Lotus, Bangkok)*

The Classical Arts

Architecture

As with other branches of Thai art, Thailand's architecture is an amalgam of ideas borrowed from other sources, notably Indian, Sri Lankan and Kampuchean, but blended in the alembic of Thai architects' genius to evolve an architectural aesthetic and the language to express it. The elements they created were not employed according to decorative merit but had symbolic intent which Thai architects sought to interpret in the most beautiful ways possible. It is well to remember that nearly every component, decorative piece or painting in a Thai religious structure (which constitutes 95% of classical Thai architecture) is there to symbolize a particular aspect of Thai Theravada Buddhism.

Many symbolic elements began their lives as Hindu concepts. Just as the Christians found it expedient to adopt pagan celebrations and symbols as their own, Buddhists modified many of the Hindu concepts of India (where Buddhism is regarded as an offshoot of Hinduism rather than as a separate religion) to fit their own needs. This is evident in town planning, in the layout of religious complexes and the juxtaposition of their various buildings and in the architectural elements of the buildings themselves. Despite the antecedents, what emerged by the 17th century was an architectural approach which was uniquely Thai and without parallel elsewhere.

City Planning

Sukhothai and Si Satchanalai, the earliest cities with enough buildings remaining to allow reconstruction of a town plan, were not planned cities in the manner of Angkor Wat or Angkor Thom, but a number of Khmer concepts of building alignment and composition of individual components were employed in their construction. Angkor Wat and Baphuon had been designed as embodiments in stone of the Hindu cosmology. At the center was a massive tower meant to represent Mount Meru, the city of Brahma and the home of the gods. Its upper portion was divided into seven major levels and subdivided into 33 lesser tiers to symbolize the 33 heavens. At the summit in the 33rd heaven sat Indra, who presided over the universe. By its very height, the central tower pierced the sky, becoming one with the heavens themselves.

Below: *The prang of Prasat Hin Phimai, a late 11th, early 12th century Khmer structure. Though the exterior is Hindu, the interior lintels suggest it was built as a Tantric Buddhist structure. Jayavarman VII converted it to Mahayana Buddhism and built a second sanctuary.*

In legend, the tower was surrounded by 13 concentric circles: seven oceans and six mountain ranges, the last dropping into the great primordial ocean. In Angkor, architects contented themselves with fewer than 13 rings but did not stint in creating grandeur on a scale worthy of heaven's giants: the outer wall of Angkor Thom is 12 kilometers on a side.

Beyond the wall was a huge moat meant to signify the primordial ocean in whose midst were four islands, one of which was inhabited by men. Thus, the temple served as a tangible link between the world of men and the world of the gods. The symbolism was carried one step further in the bridges that spanned the moat. The bridge piers were surmounted by representations of Indra recalling the myth of Indra's bow made of nagas, a Hindu euphemism for a rainbow, the cosmological causeway spanning the two worlds. In small temples, this motif was often represented by an arch over the entrance gate lintel in the shape of twin nagas, themselves water symbols and a link between heaven and earth. Passing the threshold of the outer gate one was, in effect, crossing a rainbow and entering heaven.

Sukhothai's Theravada Buddhist architects adopted the Hindu concepts, altering key details to suit their own purposes. The central tower or prang became the 33 heavens through which man must evolve life by life to reach perfection. It also came to represent the spiritual epicenter of a city, the point from which all blessings flowed from the heavens to the city's inhabitants. In Sukhothai this purpose was served by Wat Mahathat and in Ayutthaya by a wat of the same name. By the Bangkok period, the concept of the prang-centered wat was no longer employed by architects.

The Khmer mode particularly suited a water-based culture like that of the Thais. From the idea that a religious building must be surrounded by water in emulation of heavens contained by the primordial ocean, came the Sukhothai concept that a wat must be ringed by ponds. In city planning, water took on practical considerations. In a country dependent on rivers and canals for transportation and communication, it was only natural that cities would be surrounded by defensive moats. Thus both Ayutthaya and Bangkok were designed as islands protected by rivers and canals, at a stroke serving both symbolic and practical purposes.

The cylindrical or pyramidal shapes of Mount Meru are found everywhere in Thai architecture. The prangs, stupas and chedis, the royal parasols, the crowns worn by kings, on the masks drama players wear, the upper portions of balustrades and posts, are all representations of a hierarchy of perfection. The technique of dividing structures into tiers could give religious buildings a very horizontal, squat look but this tendency is countered in several ways. One, evident on prangs, is the use of redented corners which score the structure with vertical lines but avoid giving it a grid-like look. The other mitigating factor is a Thai abhorrence for straight lines and true perpendiculars. The outline of a chedi doesn't climb in a steep unvarying line to the finial but describes a parabolic arc, giving the monument structural stability, grace, and a sense of height. Similarly, the columns of chapels taper as they rise and are set to tilt

Below: The Phra Vihan Yot in Wat Phra Kaew was built by Rama III in the Chinese style, that was in great vogue during the period. Ceramic tiles decorate its tall pilasters and the mongkut that crowns it. Guarding it is a pair of tantimas.
Bottom: A 19th century engraving of a meru for a deceased member of the royal family.

16

Below: The bot of Wat Na Phramane built in the mid-15th century is a stellar example of later Ayutthayan wat architecture.
Bottom: The bot of Bangkok's Wat Phra Chetupon (Wat Po) is set on a platform and surrounded by a phra rabieng with four vihan thits set at the cardinal points to serve as entrances. The courtyard beyond is demarcated by four L-shaped vihan khots at the corners.

inwards. The walls, doors and window frames are constructed as trapezoids, broader at the bottom than at the top. Viewed from the end, the overlapping roofs of a chapel flow in a parabolic arc mimicking the chedi's lines. From the side, the roof line rises at either end rather than describing a straight line perfectly perpendicular to the ground. The overall effect is one of soft sinuosity which belies the basic blockiness dictated both by its primary shape — that of a triangle set on a rectangle — and its building materials which require construction of thick, heavy walls and columns.

The Hindu concepts that dictated alignment and placement of buildings within a large complex were applied by the Thais both to the complex itself and to individual buildings within it. In Ayutthaya, this included siting buildings according to the cardinal points of the compass and generally along an east-west axis. In the Ayutthayan period this meant establishing the prang as the principal monument, surrounding it with walls and secondary prangs but aligning additional buildings behind and before it along a line connecting the rising and setting sun. In the Bangkok period, the prang was replaced by the bot ubosot as the principal building. It, too, was located according to the cardinal points and the other buildings in the complex were set within the same grid, but instead of being placed directly in front or behind it, were to one side or the other.

Building Design

A Thai Buddhist religious complex is defined as a "Wat," a difficult word to translate directly into English. It can be used to mean a temple or a monastery but as neither English term in itself adequately describes it, the term "wat" is employed throughout this book when referring to a Thai Buddhist temple complex. It denotes a single entity comprising several buildings which lie within a single compound or in close proximity to it. The wat serves as a place of worship, of meeting, of education. The monks who inhabit it, or quarters nearby, are regarded as upholders and interpreters of the religion, as teachers of lay subjects (until this century, monks were responsible for all secular education), as arbiters in village disputes, as counselors and as medical practitioners of herbal remedies. Thus, the wat is the focal point of village and city life. The construction costs for a wat are borne by the local community or by a single patron. A wat is erected as an act of merit which will redound to the donor's credit in a future life allowing him or her to be reborn as a higher being. A wat can also be erected in memory of a great event, such as a victory in war.

Thai architects of each period of history have been guided by a universal aesthetic peculiar to that period and modified by regional constraints, but never as an expression of individual genius. Architects, like artists, were employees or servants retained by royal houses or were monks attached to particular wats. They might be rewarded for jobs well done by being conferred with honors or elevated in rank, but in general they were anonymous.

Architects and artists were also highly-prized items of war booty.

After King Mengrai of Chiang Mai defeated the Mon king of Pegu in 1288, he returned to Chiang Mai with 500 carpenters and craftsmen who built Wat Kathom, named for the architect who designed it, a rare honor then or today.

It is often possible to discern the motivation or importance of a wat by examining its name. A "Wat Luang" or "royal wat" is one constructed or restored by royal patronage and will often have the word "Rat", "Raja", or "Racha" in its name, such as "Ratburana" or "Rajapradit". Wats may be named for the rulers who built them, such as Wat Chamatewi in Lamphun, named for the Mon princess who decreed its erection in the 7th century, or like Ayutthaya's Wat Phra Ram, named for the founder of the city, King Ramathibodi.

Wats are often named for important images they contain. The Vihan Phra Monkon Bopit in Ayutthaya, Wat Phra Singh in Chiang Mai, and Wat Phra Keo in Bangkok all house the famous Buddha images contained in their names. The word "Phra" is an honorific for a Buddha image and is often the key word identifying a wat containing one. In many cases, the chedi was the first structure built and other buildings were added later to make it a wat. The complete wat may then carry the name of the original chedi as at Wat Phra Chedi Si Samphet, the "Phra" in this case used as an honorific for the word "Chedi" which follows it. Those wats that contain an important relic of the Buddha are entitled "Maha" (Great) "That" (Relic) and are generally the principal wats in a town. There are nine major Wat Mahathats in Thailand, one each in Chiang Rai, Chai Nat, Sukhothai, Phitsanulok, Ayutthaya, Bangkok, Yasothon, Phetchaburi and Nakhon Si Thammarat.

In many instances, tracing the lineage of a wat is difficult because of the practice of renaming a wat after it has been rebuilt. This is particularly true with the wats of Bangkok, many of which were originally Ayutthayan structures that were renovated by kings of the present dynasty. Thus, Wat Salek became Wat Mahathat, Wat Bodharam became Wat Chetupon (or as it is popularly known, Wat Po) and Wat Benjabopit (Five Princes) became Wat Benjamabopit (King of the Fifth reign i.e. King Rama V).

The buildings and monuments enclosed within a wat wall are described at length further on but for purposes of comparison are enumerated here. The main building in a wat is the Bot (or Ubosot). It holds a Buddha image and serves as a congregation and ordination hall for monks only. There is only one bot in each wat. A Vihan holds the principal Buddha image and serves as the general sermon hall for monks and worshipers. A wat may have one, none or more than one vihan but it is secondary in importance to the bot except in instances where a wat does not possess a bot. In structure, the vihan is virtually identical to the bot.

A wat may also have a Prasad reserved for royal use, a Library, and a symbolic library set on stilts called a "Ho Trai". Its courtyard will contain one or more stupas, chedis or prangs containing ashes or relics. One note: Thai wats, especially in the later periods, were seldom planned as entire

Below: Detail of a Khmer lintel providing details of Khmer architectural design. This lintel, 57 cm. high by 69 cm. wide, was found at Wat Pranyat, Baan Narai province of Chanthaburi and is now in the National Museum, Prachin Buri.
Bottom: 18th century wooden model of a vihan. (Wat Matchimawat Museum, Songkhla)

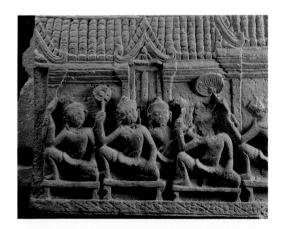

Below: *Ceiling of the vihan of Wat Mahathat in Nakhon Si Thammarat, decorated with lotus blooms and stars, 18th century.*

units, so there is a certain disjointed quality to them. In many cases, too many buildings are packed into too small a space and views are often obstructed. There is little of the grand concept of Angkor, where one's eye is led up to the summit and each element is related to the other. Doors which could frame spectacular views are often too low or are blocked by objects immediately beyond them. Thus, to appreciate a wat's beauty one must look at its individual components rather than the overall impact.

The principal building materials have varied with the ages. Khmer and Lop Buri architects built in stone and laterite; Sukhothai and Lanna builders constructed their monuments in laterite and brick. Lacking a suitable durable building material and wanting one which would be portable, Ayutthaya and Bangkok architects opted for brick cemented by mortar and covered with one or more coats of stucco. Lack of engineering technology and a strong mortar compelled Ayutthayan architects to build their walls and columns very thick in order to counteract the lateral thrust of the very heavy roofs. Walls as much as 1.6 meters thick were not uncommon. As binding materials and construction techniques improved, the walls became thinner.

The outer walls of bots and vihans are either whitewashed or are highly decorated. The concept of elaborate decoration stems not only from a Thai love for bright color but from a Hindu and Khmer credo that a temple is more than a repository for a Buddha image, it is the transposition to earth of a heavenly world. Porcelain mosaic pieces, patterned ceramic tiles (as at Wat Rajabopit), porcelain plates (Wat Arun), gold leaf, paint, faience (the vihans of Wat Arun and Wat Rajapradit), mirrored tiles (Wat Phra Kaew), marble (Wat Rajapradit and Wat Benjamabopit bots) and other materials have been employed to beautify architectural surfaces. They lend a glittering, fairy-like aspect to Thai wats which classical purists find abhorrent but which are a source of delight for most observers. Despite the seeming jumble of contrasting shapes and decorative patterns, there is to Thai wats a harmony and grace that transcends the over-exuberance displayed by its individual components.

Thai architectural credo dictates that the bot and vihan should face water because Buddha is said to have sat under a Bodhi tree facing a river when he attained Enlightenment. If the site lacks a natural body of water, the monks may dig a pond. If no water whatever is available, the bot and vihan together with the images they contain should face the rising sun. The importance of water was carried still further during the Ayutthaya period by Mahayana Buddhist belief, which likened a religious building to a boat carrying Buddhist pilgrims to salvation. In the late Ayutthaya and early Bangkok periods this was represented by a curved line along the building's base corresponding to the deck line of a boat. Such structures are called "Thawng samphao" or "ship's hull" bots or vihans.

No particular shape is described for a bot but it is usually a rectangle with a ratio of length to width of 2:1. It may also be cruciform as with the bot of Wat Benjamabopit in Bangkok. The rectangular bot is made up of

Left: A pair of Dvarapala (guardians) decorate the inner surfaces of the doors to the bot of Wat Yai Suwannaram, built in the late 17th-early 18th century in Phetchaburi. Painted on wood, the deities are typical of those found in many Ayutthayan wats.
Below: Different styles of window decoration.

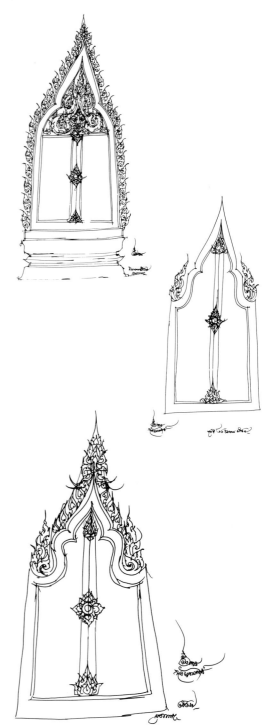

Below: *Various styles of column capital decoration with the water lily type at the top and the lotus bud capital below.*

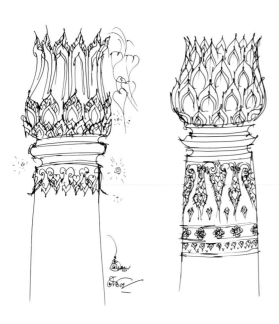

solid walls or of twin rows of columns bound together by walls and by two rows at either end perpendicular to them comprising the end walls. Parallel to and outside the walls may be a second row of columns which hold up the roof eaves. The columns, like the walls, may be whitewashed or covered in colored materials. They are surmounted by capitals in the shape of lotus buds or water lilies. In the Bangkok period, the water lily capital was used to the complete exclusion of the lotus bud. In many bots and vihans, especially those whose floors are raised above ground level, the columns will be tied together with a low balustrade. In large bots, there will be two or more rows of interior columns to support the roof and leave the central area unobstructed.

During the early Ayutthaya period, wat interiors were illuminated by the light passing through vertical slits in the walls, a somewhat unsatisfactory method which was partly a holdover from Khmer architectural tradition and in part stemmed from the inherent weakness of the walls which did not allow wide windows. In the Bangkok period, the slits were replaced by proper windows set below wide lintels which supported the upper portions of the brick walls. There are usually five, seven, or nine windows on a side in accordance with a Thai preference for odd numbers. The entrance doors are in the end wall facing the Buddha image; narrower doors may flank the entrance door. Each door is comprised of a pair of leaves set in a frame which rests directly on the threshold of the building.

Window shutters and door leaves may be decorated in a variety of ways. They may be carved in relief and covered with gold leaf like those at Wat Phra Kaew. They may be carved and inset with mirrored tiles as those of Wat Rakang, be covered in mythical scenes rendered in mother-of-pearl such as the doors of Wat Chetupon's bot, or done in lacquer and gold as the windows of Wat Chetupon's vihan. During the late Sukhothai and early Ayutthayan periods, the principal subjects of the door leaves were a pair of deva, or angels with swords, who served as guardians of the wat. In the middle and late Ayutthayan period, they were either covered in intricate floral patterns or featured the earth with devas at the base from which vines sprang upwards and among whose tendrils animals and birds frolicked. In the middle Ayutthayan period, the Himaphan (Himalayan) forest with its wealth of animals was depicted below a sky with flying garudas. In the north the doors were set in elaborate frames flanked by the door guardians. These were crowned by equally elaborate pediments depicting peacocks with twin nagas on either side of the pediment, their tails intertwined over its top to form a triangular frame.

The roof, covered in glazed clay tiles (or wooden shakes in the North), is generally made up of three overlapping sections, with the lower roofs set at gentle slopes, increasing to a topmost roof with a pitch of 60 degrees. Ayutthayan roofs were generally covered with brown glazed tiles framed by blue or green, while roofs of the present period are normally orange with yellow and blue or green borders. Some, like Wat Chetupon, may be cobalt blue with yellow and orange borders. Supporting the lower edges of the roofs are eave brackets usually in the form of a naga either with its head at the bottom of the bracket or, a later development, with the head at the top. In the North, the eave bracket is a triangular piece with the naga's head at the top and the tail curving back on the body to end at the wall; the lower portion of the bracket is a filigree of foliage. Along the eaves of many bot and vihan roofs is a row of small brass bells with clappers attached to thin brass pieces shaped like Bodhi tree leaves which the wind sets moving to produce a pleasant sound.

The gables or pediments of bots and vihans are canvases for a rich variety of ornate decoration. The gables of Ayutthayan wats were highly-decorated with reliefs covered in paint, gilt or mirrored tiles, a treatment followed in the Bangkok period. Wats of the past two centuries usually depict Phra Narai (progenitor of the deity Rama with which the present dynasty identifies) mounted on a garuda and surrounded by attendant theps hovering amidst vines and foliage. Early in the 19th century there was a vogue to depict a thep riding on a heavenly chariot, and during the reign of King Rama III, Chinese pottery was formed into decorative flowers, those of Wat Chalerm Phra Kiat and Wat Raja Oros in Thon Buri being the best known.

At both extremities of the roof peak is a curious figure known as a Chofa, which literally translates as "bunch of sky". The chofa is generally seen to represent a garuda which grasps two nagas in its claws and may have been an attempt to appeal to Vishnuite Hindus. In some instances, the chofa is the head of a naga. It is used atop bots, vihans and sala kanprien, none of these buildings being regarded as consecrated until the chofa has been fixed in place. It may also be found at the roof peak of palace buildings. Running along both bargeboards from the chofa to the roof eaves is a pair of nagas. Nagas also cap stairway railings as at Chiang Mai's Doi Suthep, may pass through wat buildings as at Wat Phumin in Nan, or serve as an entranceway from the road to a bot entrance such as those at Wat Phra That Chae Heng, also in Nan.

The ceiling of a bot or a vihan may be plain or ornamented with lotus or star cluster motifs. In northern bots, one can see the exposed framework of beams, rafters and queen posts supporting the roof, an intricate system using short rather than long pieces of wood. The interior walls are covered floor to ceiling with paintings of the life or previous lives of the Buddha. At the end of the hall farthest from the entrance door is the Buddha image. If there is more than one image, the one in front, called the "presiding image", is generally more important. Around the image may be eight disciples in attitudes of worship. Up to the end of the Ayutthaya period, the ashes of dead kings were placed in chedis. After the late Ayutthayan period, the practice arose of placing the ashes in the Choranam, the space between the Buddha image and the back wall. Some of the ashes of King Rama IV (Mongkut), for example, were sealed into the choranam of Wat Rajapradit while some of King Rama V's ashes now rest in the choranam behind the

Below: *Different styles of eave brackets which support the lower edges of the roofs.*

22

Below: *Stone bai sema, the boundary stone that defines the consecrated ground, at Ayutthaya's 18th century Wat Suwandararam.*
Bottom: *A sketch of a bai sema.*

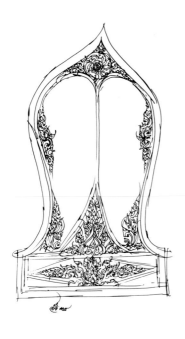

replica of the Phra Buddha Jinnarat image at Wat Benjamabopit.

Surrounding a bot is a series of galleries known as the Phra Rabieng or cloister. Those of Wat Po, Wat Arun, Wat Benjamabopit and the vihan of Wat Suthat, all in Bangkok, hold rows of Buddha images. The Phra Rabieng of Wat Phra Kaew is decorated with painted scenes from the Thai literary classic, the Ramakien. These galleries are intended as quiet zones for meditation. They are colonnaded with one side open to face the bot. When there is no phra rabieng, the wat will be surrounded by a Kampaeng Keo or "jeweled wall". It is often entered through an elaborate gate such as those seen in Angkor Wat, notably those with the saddle roofs at Ban Serai representing Indra's bow. A good example of this type of gate is found at Wat Benjamabopit. Such a gate may also be crowned with a mongkut spire as at Wat Phra Kaew.

The principal difference between a vihan and a bot is that the latter is surrounded by eight bai sema or boundary stones which define consecrated ground. These are placed at the four corners and at the axes of the four cardinal points. Eight luk nimit or stone spheres and, often, gold and jewelry, are placed in holes dug at these points and covered with earth. A ninth luk nimit will be buried at the place the main Buddha image is to be sited. Over the eight luk nimit are erected boundary stones (bai sema) shaped like leaves and carved in intricate reliefs. The subjects of the reliefs may be intertwined nagas, pictures of the gods Vishnu, Siva or, with older bai sema, the faces of Brahma or Indra. In the Bangkok period, the bai sema may appear as pairs of thin slabs placed back to back with a narrow space separating them. The bai sema denote where all earthly power ends; not even a king may issue orders within their bounds.

It is not essential for a wat to have a vihan, and the rules attending its design and orientation are not as strict as for a bot. For example, it may have an even number of windows and may face any direction. The vihan also has a number of variations. Four Vihan Thits placed at right angles to the vihan or bot at the four cardinal points may take the place of gateways as is the case at Wat Chetupon and Wat Arun. Four Vihan Khots, L-shaped rooms, may be set at the corners of the courtyard wall as at Wat Saket and again at Wat Chetupon.

Wats may have a Sala Kanprien, a building which looks like a bot but lacks walls between its columns and may have a small open hall or sala at one end or located nearby. Here, the monks say prayers between noon and 1 p.m. for pious Buddhists to hear. A wat courtyard may also contain a Sala, an open-walled structure with a decorated roof where monks take their midday meals which have been brought to them by worshipers. The sala may serve as an overnight shelter for travelers. The Prasad, a cruciform building with a prang or mongkut at the meeting point of its four roof peaks, is normally reserved solely for use by royalty. A wat may have a Library resembling a vihan or a separate Ho Trai, a building set on stilts and very elaborately decorated as befits a structure holding holy scriptures. The same courtyard may contain a number of bell towers, slender structures containing one bell or several bells like that at Thon Buri's Wat Rakang. The bells toll the hours or warn in times of emergency. The tower will often be ornately decorated like that at Wat Chetupon.

A Mondop is a square building which serves as a reliquary container or a library. It may have plain walls or be girt by columns. The roof can be cruciform as at Wat Mahathat or be square and stepped like the mondop at Wat Phra Kaew, a variation of the circular mongkut.

One of the oldest and most important monumental structures is the Prang. It arrived in Thailand from India via Angkor Wat and first found favor in Khmer temples of the Northeast. As a Khmer structure such as those at the Bayon, its upper portion was decorated with four faces of Brahma facing the four cardinal directions. Adopted by the Buddhists, it was altered to contain niches for images as can be seen at Wat Arun, Wat Po and Wat Phra Kaew. It originally held relics of Buddha but in later times was used to hold the ashes and relics of kings, holy men, and important personages.

Some see the prang as a closed lotus bud, others, as a modified form of Siva's lingam. In whatever form, it is a powerful symbol of potency which was appreciated by Ayutthayan builders who made it the centerpiece of their wats. The prang resembles an ear of corn or a cucumber stood on end and pointing at the sky. Like the Hindu prang, the Buddhist prang has six tiers on its upper portion, the seventh, the topmost, being a depiction of Nibhan or Nirvana, the most exalted heaven. The entire structure is crowned by a "nophasun" equivalent to the Hindu vajra or thunderbolt. Around the base of the lowest tier is a ring of demon guardians who protect the deities from the inhabitants of earth and hell. Those of Wat Arun are good examples of this type of decoration. Prangs were also used to crown royal buildings such as the royal pantheon. Here, their presence symbolizes that the building is the abode of living deities, a belief which stems from the deva-raja (god-king) concept adopted during the Ayutthayan period.

The chedi, one of the most beautiful of all Thai architectural forms, was also derived from India via Sri Lanka. It originally held relics of Buddha and later his scriptures. By the Ayutthayan period it had come to mark the site of the cremation of a well-known king or the abbot of a wat. Today, anyone with sufficient money can build one as a receptacle for his or her ashes. Stouter versions of the chedi were originally called stupas but today the terms are used interchangeably with "chedi" given almost exclusive preference over "stupa" in Thai terminology.

At one time, chedis were placed in the forest far from habitation. Much later, they were incorporated into wat compounds as key architectural elements. The base of the chedi is composed of three platforms representing the three worlds: hell, earth and heaven. The top spire has up to 33 rings representing the 33 Buddhist heavens. While Sukhothai architects adopted the Sri Lankan bell-shaped chedi virtually unchanged, Ayutthayan architects modified it to its square form, redenting the corners and enhancing its natural grace. The best Ayutthayan chedis

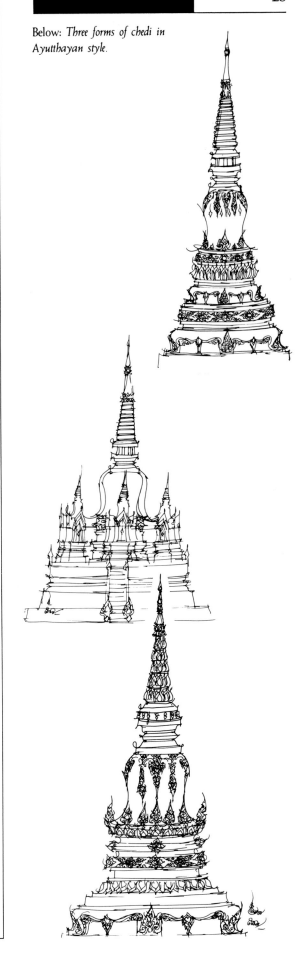

Below: *Three forms of chedi in Ayutthayan style.*

are at Wat Phu Khao Thong and Wat Phra Si Suriyothai.

The Mongkut is the chedi equivalent of the prang which caps the roof of a building. The mongkut is a delicate structure of seven circular tiers which correspond to the six major levels of heaven with the spire forming the seventh level. It is also used to denote royal buildings and has an exact counterpart in the crown worn by Rama IV and subsequent kings.

The living quarters for monks are plain by contrast to the ornate buildings within the wat compound. The monks dwell outside the walls either in dormitories or in individual meditation cells or Kutis raised off the ground on stilts. In the past, the quarters were usually placed to the south of the wat or on the right side if the wat faced water. This orientation came from a belief that if the monks slept directly in front of the Buddha image, they would die young. If they slept at its left side, they would be violently ill; if behind, there would be discord in the monk community. Today, these strictures regarding monks' quarters placement are no longer heeded.

A royal structure which has no religious significance but which incorporates all the elements of wat architecture is the Meru, named after Mount Meru. Merus were constructed as towers in which dead kings and senior members of the royal family were cremated. Though not incinerated like Balinese cremation towers, they were elaborate structures often requiring months of construction time only to be disassembled once the cremation rites had taken place. The tallest recorded meru was built in Ayutthaya to a height of 102.75 meters and took 11 months to complete. In 1824, a meru was erected for the cremation of King Rama II. It stood 80 meters tall and was surrounded by eight 40 meter tall towers known as Meru Thits. Building it required 896 large teak tree trunks, 5,500 other logs, 2,800 sheets of bamboo slats, and 400,000 bamboo poles. Because of their great expense, the last great meru was built in 1869 for King Rama IV's cremation.

Sculpture

When one speaks of Thai art he is generally referring to sculpture and to its principal manifestation, the creation of images of Buddha, and to a lesser extent, of Hindu deities.

The creation of an image of a deity suggests idolatry to a Western observer but the devout Buddhist has no such qualms, recognizing in the image not a man, but a reminder of a set of precepts by which one can chart the course of his life and of his individual actions. Buddhist tradition relates that as the Buddha was dying, there was great consternation among his disciples who were apprehensive about carrying on without their teacher. One in particular, Ananda, asked how the disciples might recall the memory of their leader. Buddha replied that it was not he they should remember but his doctrine. Pressed further, he replied that they might heap up a mound of earth and place a relic of his body after cremation — a hair, a tooth, ashes — in it as a reminder. The mound of earth eventually evolved into a stupa, becoming higher and narrower as the years passed.

Opposite: *This Sukhothai period Buddha Sassada was originally placed in Wat Phra Si Ratana Mahathat, and is now in the vihan of Si Sassada in Bangkok's Wat Bovornivet.*
Below: *This superbly-carved five-headed stone naga is one of a pair guarding the entrance to the main sanctuary of Prasat Phanom Rung.*
Bottom: *A sketch of a naga, that decorates the edge of the roof.*

Later adherents, however, were not satisfied. They required a more concrete reminder, one to which worshipers of Hindu images and spirits in trees and stones could relate. From their need came the Buddha image as we know it.

The image is regarded as a personification of a philosophical abstract. Buddha is seen not as a man but as the Doctrine in human form. On viewing the image, one perceives the principles of behavior which its progenitor embodied and preached. The earliest images, created in India, date from approximately 2,000 years ago and were important in spreading the Doctrine and winning converts.

To the artist and his patron, the image is never a mere work of art but a sacred object to be revered. The donor gains merit for his act but does not put his name on the image nor is he identified in any way with it. Similarly, no works are signed by the artist. The image must be blessed by Buddhist priests when it is made and again when moved or placed in a new setting. In the past, heavy punishment was exacted for damaging an image. If it were accidentally damaged beyond repair, it continued to be considered worthy of respect and was placed in the base of a new chedi. When an enormous Buddha image from Ayutthaya's Wat Si Sanphet was destroyed by the Burmese in 1767, King Rama I incorporated its fragments into a famous chedi at Bangkok's Wat Chetupon (Wat Po).

The question arises: How did the sculptor know which physical features to give to the image? Legend says that the only statue of Buddha created during his lifetime was made when he went to preach to his mother in Tavatimsa Heaven. The King of Kosala, missing his teacher, caused his sculptors to carve an image out of sandalwood, relying on their memories to recreate his features. When Buddha returned, the image is said to have arisen and moved toward him to pay him honor. Buddha, however, held up his hand, commanding the image to remain where and as it was in order to serve as a model for future devotees and sculptors.

A more likely explanation is that sculptors relied on ancient texts which outlined the lakshanas or characteristics by which sages would be able to recognize future Buddhas. One set of these comprised clichés from Sanskrit poetry used to describe deities and heroes. These highly evocative descriptions included legs like a deer's, thighs like the trunk of a banana tree, arms smooth and rounded like the trunk of an elephant, hands like lotus flowers just beginning to bloom with the fingertips turned back like petals, a head shaped like an egg, a chin like a mango stone, a nose like a parrot's beak, eyebrows like drawn bows and hair like the stings of scorpions.

The more commonly used source, however, was a series of 32 lakshanas from Pali religious texts. They included feet with 108 auspicious signs (which served as the model for numerous Buddha Footprints, recalling an incident in his life when sages examined the feet of an ascetic sleeping in the forest and discovered them to have all 108 signs indicating he was a Boddhisatta or Buddha-to-be), wedged-shaped heels, long fingers and toes of equal length, legs like an antelope, arms long enough that he could touch either knee without bending, skin so smooth that dust would not adhere to it, body thick like a banyan tree, long eyelashes like those of a cow, 40 teeth, a hairy white mole between his eyebrows (urna), a protuberance (ushnisha) on the top of his head (either a turban, a topknot or a bump on his skull), and deep blue eyes. To these, sculptors added ear lobes elongated by heavy earrings worn in his youth, a reference to his royal upbringing and a flame atop the ushnisha to signify the fiery energy of his intellect.

Different ages and schools in various lands have chosen to interpret these characteristics in different ways, but within each school, each artist adhered to his school's interpretation without injecting his own personality into it. In early Indian bas reliefs, Buddha was depicted in symbolic terms, such as a tree, a serpent, a pair of footprints or a stupa. Later sculptors began depicting him as a personage, a composite of the various lakshanas. In Thai art, it reached its height of literal interpretation with Sukhothai sculptors portraying him with fingers and toes of equal length and with exaggeratedly long arms. Sculptors in the periods following Sukhothai returned to a more realistic depiction.

A Buddha image can be found in any size ranging from a few centimeters to massive, like the 45 meter long reclining Buddha at Bangkok's Wat Chetupon. Tradition decrees four positions for the Buddha image: Seated (the Maravijaya or Victory over Mara, being the most common), Standing, Walking (rare, generally confined to the Sukhothai period and in one or two instances to the Ayutthaya period), and Reclining (as the Buddha was at his death). Seated images are depicted with their feet in the Vajrasena or "adamantine" position with both soles pointing upwards, the Virasana or "hero" pose with one leg atop the sole of the other foot, or seated in the so-called "European fashion" on a throne with his feet placed firmly on the ground. Only three periods, the Dvaravati, Srivijaya and Ayutthaya, have produced the latter style and only in a few instances. The Buddha wears a robe (in reality a long piece of cloth worn like a sari) which covers either the left only or both shoulders. This mode as well as the form and length of the robe end which falls over his left shoulder and down his chest often provides the key to identifying the school of its creation.

Buddhist iconography calls for Buddha's hands to be placed in gestures representing various events in his lifetime. These gestures or mudras are of Indian origin, but sometime during the reign of King Rama III (1824-1851) a list of 40 of the most common were prepared. The six most often seen are the Vitarka Mudra (Argumentation or Preaching), Varada Mudra (Bestowing Charity), Bhumisparsa Mudra (Calling the Earth to Witness), Dhammachakra Mudra (Setting in Motion the Wheel of the Law or the Buddhist Doctrine), Dhyani or Samadhi Mudra (Meditation), and the Abhaya Mudra (Calming or Dispelling Fear).

The Buddha either sits flush with the ground or on a base which may

Below: *A meditating Buddha displaying the samadhi mudra; this 21 cm. tall statue was found in Sathing Phra district, Songkla, and dates from the late 6th century.* Bottom: *Sketch of the bhumisparsa mudra.*

Below: *Standing gilt red sandstone Buddha displaying the abhaya mudra. Found at Wat Phra Mahathat in Chaiya, it stands 1.85 meters tall and dates from the 13th-15th centuries. (Wat Phra Boromathat Museum, Chaiya)*

be in the shape of a lotus (Chiengsaen, U Thong and Ayutthaya periods). The base may also be decorated with the signs of the zodiac or with a single zodiac sign indicating the year in which the image was cast (Bangkok period). Alternatively, it may be decorated with numerous three-dimensional figures such as Mara's demons in the late Ayutthayan statue of Buddha in meditation or ghoulish figures from hell as in the depiction of the monk Phra Malai in the Bangkok-period "Phra Malai Visits Hell". Buddhas seated in the "European fashion" generally discourse from a throne.

Some images were painted, though those which have survived from earlier ages bear no traces of pigment other than a few smudges of color. Images were often decorated with jewelry or were clothed. In the present day, the Emerald Buddha, the realm's most sacred image, wears a different set of clothes for each season. In a holy ceremony at Wat Phra Kaew presided over by the King, the image's clothes are changed at the beginning of the hot, the rainy and the cold seasons. Buddha images are said to have personalities and/or voices. Tradition relates that the Emerald Buddha caused the elephant carrying it to veer away from the town to which it was headed because it did not want to reside there. An old legend says that the Emerald Buddha and the Phra Bang, now in Luang Prabang, Laos, cannot be placed in the same town because of antipathy between them. Non-observance of this prohibition is said to lead to disaster for the town. The Buddha image in Sukhothai's Wat Si Chum is said to have spoken on several occasions, though it is more likely the voice was that of a man hidden in the stairway concealed in the wall behind the image. The crystal Phra Sak Tang Khamani carved in late Chiengsaen style is said to bring rain and is carried in a procession in Chiang Mai each April 1. The Phra Buddha Jinnarat in Phitsanulok was said to have wept tears of blood when the town was captured by Ayutthaya early in the 14th century. Similarly, the Phra Chao Phananchoeng image in the wat of the same name in Ayutthaya is reported to have cried watery tears when the city was overrun and sacked by the Burmese in 1767.

Not only do images have personalities, they have names such as the Phra Kaew Morakot (Emerald Buddha), the Phra Buddha Sihing, and the Phra Mongkol Bopit. Moreover, wats are often named for the image which rests in their principal bot or vihan.

Studying the various schools of Thai sculpture is often difficult because art historians are unable to come to an agreement on how each school or period is to be defined. Various classification systems have been introduced but despite their merits each has a deficiency. Where one satisfies by establishing a chronology, it ignores geographical differences. Another attempts to differentiate by region or school but is unable to encompass the various influences which were at work at a given moment or to accommodate the combinations of styles tempered by local aesthetics. It may also fail to account for the possibility that artisans imported from a different country were laboring in a school, while in the next valley a different group from another locality was at work. In the end, one can only establish general descriptions and allow expandable limits to encompass those sculptures which do not fit neatly into the category. The sketches on these pages are intended for comparisons so one may distinguish the chief features of each period.

Thai sculptors produced a number of Adorned Buddhas or images wearing jewelry and crowns. Popular since the 15th century, these images have caused iconographists a number of problems since they seem a contradiction to the contention that the Buddha was an ascetic who had forsworn all accouterments and material possessions. This stylistic aberration has been explained as symbolizing the power of his doctrine and his victory over Mara or is seen as a reference to his royal upbringing. Alternatively, it could be an oblique reference to the choice put to him before his birth of becoming the Buddha or becoming a Chakravartin, a Universal Monarch, another avenue by which he could have brought peace to mankind. The adorning may also refer to an incident in the Life of Buddha when he was confronted by the proud Emperor Jambupati. To convince the monarch of the emptiness of earthly power, Buddha clothed himself in the raiment of a king and, after impressing Jambupati with his magnificence, calmly told him such displays meant nothing. Jambupati was convinced and converted to Buddhism. No single all-encompassing explanation has yet been devised, however. These adorned Buddhas are recognized by their ushnishas and by the lakshanas they display and the mudras they perform.

The Adorned Buddhas are not to be confused with another category of images: the Boddhisatvas and Boddhisattas. In Mahayana Buddhism, a Boddhisatva is an emanation of the five Dhyani Buddhas — four of the cardinal points and one of the zenith — identified in the Mahayanan sutras. Of these emanations, the Avalokitesvara, related to the Amithaba Buddha of the west, was the most popular among sculptors of the Srivijaya and late Lop Buri periods. The Boddhisatva Avalokitesvara may be portrayed with four arms (the usual number) or as many as 11 heads and 22 arms. He has a heavily ornamented body, and may have an antelope skin flung over his left shoulder or a tiger skin tied at his waist. The key identifying mark is his hair which is tied in a chignon (Jatamukuta) and decorated with an image of Amithaba meaning "infinite light", a reference to his transcendental nature. Alternatively, he may be portrayed as an ascetic. Another popular Boddhisatva was the Maitreya, the future Buddha who will be born in 2,400 years.

Theravada Buddhism, the school that Thailand ultimately adopted, recognizes the Boddhisattas, the Buddhas-to-be identified in the Chadok Tales. These are more difficult to distinguish because they lack precise identifying marks; but, then, Thai sculptors produced very few of them. The most noted was a series of 500 Boddhisattas sculpted in the 15th century.

Two other popular subjects were the Dhammachakra or Wheel of

Below: A 13th century late Lop Buri standing Buddha displays the vitarka mudra. Fifty centimeters tall, the bronze image was found in the crypt of Ayutthaya's Wat Ratburana. (Chao Sam Phraya National Museum, Ayutthaya)

Below: *The seated Buddha in the 14th century Wat Phra Si Ratana Mahathat in Chalieng, is typical of many of the huge brick and stucco images produced in situ to occupy Sukhothai wats.*

the Law and the Buddhapada or Buddha's Footprint. The Wheel of the Law is a device meant to represent Buddha's Doctrine and is the object referred to in the mudra for "Setting the Wheel of Law in Motion". It was first devised in India during the reign of the 3rd century B.C. Buddhist ruler Asoka. As a subject for sculpture, it was popular in Thailand only among Mon artists. The Buddha's Footprint was popular because Buddhist lore suggests that during his lifetime, the Buddha flew to Thailand and implanted his foot on a mountaintop leaving behind the 108 auspicious signs in the whorls and lines of its imprint. Buddha Footprints were especially popular among the sculptors of Ayutthaya but enjoyed limited popularity in the Bangkok period, notably the mother-of-pearl footprints of Wat Chetupon's Reclining Buddha and Saraburi's Bangkok period Wat Phra Buddha Bhat, built solely to encase a footprint said to have been discovered in the jungle by a hunter.

Until the 16th century and to a limited extent into the 19th century, Thai sculptors produced numerous images of the trinity of Hindu deities. Though images of Brahma the Creator are rare, there are dozens of statues of Vishnu the Preserver and of Siva the Destroyer. Vishnu was especially popular because his avatar, Rama, was the hero of the literary classic, the Ramakien. Several rulers of Sukhothai (Ramkamhaeng) and Ayutthaya (Ramathibodi and Ramesuan) incorporated his name into their own and the kings of the present dynasty have all adopted his name (Rama I, II, III...) Another avatar of Vishnu, Narayana (Phra Narai in Thai) has enjoyed great popularity in Thailand and in the Bangkok period has been portrayed riding Vishnu's vehicle, the garuda, in the pediments of its major wats. In statues carved in-the-round, Vishnu is portrayed with a smooth, unadorned body and standing with his four arms outstretched. Prior to the 8th century A.D., Vishnus wore cylindrical miters or hats; those after that date wore crowns.

Statues of Siva are somewhat rarer. The Hindu deity was portrayed in the standing position with a smooth unadorned body bearing several pairs of arms but wearing a tall chignon with an ornament instead of a miter like Vishnu. Both images were produced by the schools of art prior to the 12th century and generally stand in the triple flexion stance. Siva's face is also carved on Srivijayan and pre-Angkorian linga, also referred to as a Mukhalinga. Other subjects include the Rusis, the Brahman hermits whom Buddha converted in large numbers, and mythical animals.

Sculptors have also produced intaglios and engraved seals as well as votive tablets (Phra pim). The creation of votive tablets stems from a belief that Buddhism and all evidence of its existence would disappear after the arrival of the Maitreya, 2,400 years from now. It was felt that the life of the religion could be extended by creating votive tablets which would survive long after the wats, images, sculptures, scriptures and other physical evidence had disappeared. By depicting the Buddha and including a few cryptic inscriptions, future generations would know that a great man and his doctrine had existed and would be prompted to explore further.

Left: This stone Vishnu, 128 cm. tall, was found at Ayutthaya; though of unknown origin, it bears close resemblance to the Vishnu statues found in the South, dating from 6th century. It is supported by a stone plate backing it and holds a club in its lower left hand, a globe of the earth on a stand in the lower right, a chakra in the upper right hand and a conch shell in the upper left. (Bangkok National Museum)

Above: A bronze Vishnu, 2.67 m. tall, cast in Sukhothai in the 14th century. (Bangkok National Museum)

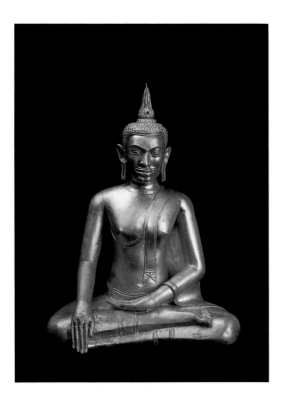

Below: *One of the many gold images found in the Wat Ratburana crypt in Ayutthaya. The 18 cm. U Thong B image sits in the Maravijaya position and displays the bhumisparsa mudra. (Chao Sam Phraya National Museum, Ayutthaya)*

Theravada votive tablets were generally made of metal, terracotta or clay. Mahayana votive tablets were made of clay which was often mixed with the ashes of dead holy persons. The latter were dried in the sun rather than baked in the belief that having been created by fire, human ashes should not be burned a second time. The clay tablets were produced from metal or stone molds intricately crafted by artisans for use by ordinary people to make their own votive tablets. These would then be buried beneath chedis.

Thai artists have also created amulets which Buddhist devotees wear around their necks in veneration of a particular monk or of the Buddha himself. These have certain cabalistic significance not in strict keeping with Buddhist tenets. They are said to ward off sickness, evil spirits and even knife or bullet wounds.

Thai sculptors have created images in stone, wood, gold, silver, ivory, gemstones, stucco, terracotta and ceramics but by far the most popular material has been bronze, with Thai artists producing more bronze images than sculptors of any other Southeast Asian country. Since ancient times, the technique used to cast images has been the "lost wax" process. Solid bronze pieces were created but it was more common to cast hollow core images. For the latter, a core of clay and sand was shaped to the rough contours of the finished piece. A mixture of beeswax and shellac was applied to the desired thickness of the completed image, a skin which could vary from several millimeters to several centimeters depending on the size of the image. Into this malleable surface was etched the features of the face and the ornamentation. The wax was then brushed with a solution of cow dung and mud to ensure every crevice was filled. Finally, it was covered with a thick layer of clay. On larger pieces, vents would be molded in the clay cover to allow the escape of air and melted wax and the entry of bronze.

The entire piece was then placed in a kiln where it was baked for several hours. The heated wax melted and ran out the vents, often into collection cups for later re-use. When cooled, the clay mold was filled with molten bronze which occupied the areas vacated by the melted wax. When the bronze had hardened, the mold was broken away and discarded. Large pieces were usually cast in segments and assembled. The largest known is the 14th century, eight-meter-tall seated Phra Sri Sakyamuni Buddha image created in Sukhothai and moved from that city's Wat Mahathat to Bangkok's Wat Suthat by King Rama I.

Many early bronze Buddhas were covered in gold leaf. In the Lop Buri period, the image's eyes were fashioned of metal while in the Lanna and Bangkok periods, colored gemstones or enamel were used for the eyes.

Good stone is scarce in Thailand but there are several pieces, notably of Hindu figures, which testify to the skill of the Thai sculptors in carving the material into statues of great beauty. The limestone found in Thailand is of a schistic variety which cracks easily and required sculptors to modify their normal styles to accommodate its weaknesses. In those rare instances when carvers were bold enough to venture beyond the safer closed figures they created images with outstretched arms, only to have them break and fall off at a later date. Limestone was more workable but was available in insufficient quantity to allow wide use. It was employed by sculptors of the Dvaravati period to create the Wheels of the Law. The same sculptors also experimented with the very hard quartzite, creating a number of intriguing monumental images of the Buddha.

Sculptors also carved in wood, but despite the durability of teak few statues have survived weathering and attacks by insects. Two superb examples of standing images can be found just in front of the Phra Buddha Sihing image in Bangkok's Buddhaisawan Chapel.

Stucco was employed for sculpture and for wat decoration. The material used differed slightly from European stucco in that it was composed of lime and sand and often blended with rice husks. The wet substance was either shaped by hand or pressed into molds. Sukhothai sculptors expanded its usefulness by applying it in layers thereby allowing the creation of large pieces. The material was usually shaped over a framework of bamboo, wood or, in some cases, thin tin rods which formed an armature. Large free-standing images were generally made of brick or laterite and covered with stucco. The finished images were nearly always painted but the colors on the surviving examples have faded to the point that they give little indication of how the images or decorations originally looked. The skin areas of many stucco Buddha images were covered in gold leaf and Mon sculptors introduced the innovation of inlaying the stucco with colored stones, bits of ceramic or mother-of-pearl.

Terracotta has been used in Thailand since Neolithic times mainly for figures and in a few instances for architectural decoration. Like stucco it was shaped by hand or in a mold. The molds themselves are marvels of craftsmanship, painstakingly created so that the finished pieces are of supreme beauty. Terracotta is a difficult material to work, but Thai sculptors achieved high skill in shaping it to a variety of purposes. Big pieces presented special challenges because they were difficult to fire. For that reason, the hollow core was generally adopted and in many instances, the image was fired in sections and assembled later. By this method the sculptors were able to produce statues as tall as 1.3 meters. The terracotta was also used to make votive tablets of fine detail and compelling beauty.

Ceramics have occupied a major place in Thai sculpture especially during the Sukhothai period when numerous decorative figures were crafted. Those of Wat Mangkon provide good examples of the art; some were 1.5 meters tall and fired in one piece and coated in gray or off-white glazes. Ceramic plates formed the basis of a thriving export industry in Sukhothai and Si Satchanalai.

Below: A *Lop Buri* votive tablet with its plaster impression dating from the 12th-13th centuries. This tablet is of the type known as a *Trailokayarijaya mandala.* (Bangkok National Museum)

Below: A mural in Wat Bovornivet, Bangkok (2nd half of the 19th century) shows the various steps in creating a "lost wax" image.

Identifying features of Thai sculpture:

Indianized *5th-8th c.*
Vishnus: Standing: broad shoulders, wasp-waisted, heavily-ornamented, stiff poses with shoulders thrown back, four arms, upper two hold vajra, conch, lotus, etc., lower rest on club and globe on a stand which with feet give five points to anchor statue to base. Vishnus with belt set at a diagonal and with a huge ribbon: Suratthani. Vishnus with belt straight across waist: Dong Si Mahaphot. Vishnus with no pleats down the front: Takua Pa. Face with full cheeks, gently curving eyebrows, finely sculpted lips, often with Adam's apple, the miter is tall, cylindrical, and without decoration.

6th c. (Peninsula)
Buddha: Standing: Gupta influence, no pleating of robe, right shoulder bare, left hand grasps end of robe. Flat curls, thick lips.

6th c. (Valley)
Buddha: Standing: Amaravati influence, pronounced pleating of the robe, narrow waist, barest hint of robe. Square head, very large hair curls, small ushnisha, narrow eyes.

Dvaravati
6th-11th c.
Heavy, thick features. Look like real people.
Buddha: Standing: Full frontal pose as wide at top as at bottom, pleatless robe covers both shoulders, falls to base, front hem forms a deep "U" from one wrist almost to ankles and up to other wrist, slight bulge at waist indicating belt. Asexual bodies, often outsized hands, thick fingers, usually vitarka mudra with right hand but may display with both hands. Featureless back.
Seated: Knees wide apart, virasana position, several layers of robe over left shoulder fall to chest.
Seated on a throne "European Fashion". Head with thick, heavy curls. Cone-shaped or hemispherical ushnisha often ending in small flame or knob. Corpulent faces, flat noses, thick lips, single thick unbroken flat arch eyebrows, deepset narrow eyes, sometimes an urna.

Srivijaya *8th-13th c.*
All surfaces carved, sandstone or bronze, lightness and grace.
Avalokitesvara: Standing: tribunga body, often four arms, sarong tied at waist with belt, strand of jewels from left shoulder to right hip, may have antelope skin on left shoulder, tiger skin tied at waist. Up tilted head, hair in tall chignon and

ornamented by Amithaba, full cheeks, eyes often with pupils. Buddha: Usually seated: vajrasena, torso tilted back, usually bhumisparsa mudra, robe end falls over shoulder in flat pleated mat ending at chest or navel, sometimes Muchalinda. Medium to narrow face, ushnisha spherical and smooth and with curls, sharply ridged nose. In late Srivijaya, there are no curls.

Si Thep *7th-12th c.*
Usually Vishnu: Standing: long and lithe, tribunga, brief loincloth, no ornaments. Effeminate face, slightly puffy, tall miter.

Lop Buri *Early (8th-10th c.)*
Avalokitesvara and Maitreya: Usually standing: vitarka mudra, often four arms, slight flexion of body, short shirt-like robe, no ornaments. Thin mustache, high, full chignon almost as wide as head.

Middle (11th-13th c.)
Adorned Buddha: Standing: abhaya mudra, robe covers both shoulders, ornamented belt. Conical ushnisha, diadem may have flame points.

Late (13th-14th c.)
Buddha: Seated: often Muchalinda, sometimes abhaya, vitarka, or dhyani mudra, detailed belts and frontal pleats. Highly-stylized faces, somewhat dull eyes, band separating hair from forehead, conical knob on ushnisha, may have Bayon-patterned mukutas with high points.

Sukhothai *Early (13th-14th c.)*
Buddha: All four attitudes, loose interpretation of lakshanas, very smooth, liquid skin.
Usually seated: Bhumisparsa mudra, prominent chest, broad hips, broad shoulders, robe flap ends at navel in distinctive scalloped pattern.
Standing: abhaya mudra, ornamented belt, robe often with bottom of inner garment visible beneath lower robe hem.
Walking; vitarka or abhaya mudra. Weight on left foot, mudra with left hand, robe indicated by thin line, strap-like robe end falls over shoulder to navel, no belt, "hooks" on robe hem. Oval face, brows arch and drop down either side of nose in unbroken curve, curls of head dip into forehead to give face heart shape, flame ushnisha.

Later (15th c.)
Buddha: Strict interpretation of lakshanas with long arms, wedge-shaped heels, fingers and toes of equal length.

Haripunchai *(7th ? — 14th c.)*
Buddha (no Hindu images): More often standing than seated but seated with robe on both shoulders, vajrasana pose. Thick lips, wide nose, triple-curve eyebrows, low ushnisha, proportionally largest curls of any period.

Lanna *Early (up to 13th c.)*
Buddha: Seated: Thick, solid but supple body, square look, torso exactly perpendicular to ground, vajrasena, bhumis-parsa mudra.Robe open, right shoulder bare, robe end falls like strap to above nipple. Round face, large curls, arched eyebrows, prominent eyes, prominent chin marked by lines, smooth lotus bud ushnisha.

Late Chiengsaen (14th-16th c.)
Buddha: Seated: thick, solid body, virasana, but a few vajarasena, bhumisparsa mudra, robe open, robe end falls in stylized pattern to waist, right shoulder bare, date often imprinted on base. Small mouth, thick lips, nose with flared nostrils, separated eyebrows, flame finial though still some lotus bud finials.

Post-16th c.
Adorned Buddha: Seated: on lotus, bhumisparsa mudra, bare torso, strands of jewels. Diadem with ribbons falling to shoulders, sometimes tall arrowhead finial.

U Thong
Buddha: Usually seated: maravijaya, virasana, robe is thick-ened line, right shoulder bare, robe end like strap falls to navel, scallop at waist to suggest belt. Small curls, small band separates hair from forehead.
From U Thong A to U Thong C the body shape progresses from solid and square to tall and narrow. The finial progresses from a knob to a flame.

U Thong A:
Broad face, wide mouth, thick lips, band separates hair from forehead, knob on ushnisha, single unbroken eyebrow.

U Thong B:
More refined face, very small curls, small flame set in cup.

U Thong C:
Tall and narrow, tall flame, exaggerated proportions in attempt to emulate Sukhothai sculpture.

Ayutthaya
14th-15th c. (Sukhothai influence)
16th-17th c. (Less humane, more remote)
18th c. (Detailed decoration on robe, faces somewhat insipid)
Buddha: Seated: marvijaya, virasana, dhyani mudra, robe covers only the left shoulder, strap falls over left shoulder. Also a few seated "European fashion". Bases may include other figures.
Standing: Both shoulders covered, roll of pleats down front, "hook" on robe hem.
Walking: Weight on right foot, mudra displayed with right hand. Broad, ovoid faces, flat arch eyebrows, prominent eyes half closed, medium-sized mouth, defining line around lips, on sandstone there may be a thin mustache, strong chin with incised line to define and another line passing from nose through lips. Small curls, ushnisha is part of head, flame finial.

Bangkok *18th-mid 19th c.*
Adorned Buddha: Standing: heavily ornamented, new postures and mudras not seen before. Faces narrow and somewhat bland, tall flame finials.

Mid 19th-20th c.
Buddha: New realism, look like real people, ushnisha not pronounced, robe falls naturally.

North since 16th c.
Buddha: Seated and standing, round faces of Lanna but Lao influence of pointed, bat-like ears.

Painting

Painting ranks as one of Thailand's greatest cultural achievements. Though confined to a rather narrow range of subjects and treatments, the genre was explored to the fullest. What emerged was aesthetically pleasing, revealing of the culture and its literature, and displaying a vivid imagination, even wit, in its portrayal of the entire spectrum of Thai society.

Like sculpture, classical painting was concerned with religion and morality. It was meant to be decorative, instructional and, in itself, to serve as an act of devotion by the artist who gained merit by his creation and by the observers who were guided by the moral precepts it illustrated. Its predominant medium was the murals that cover the interior walls of bots and vihans. Paint was also applied to wood, principally to portray the wat guardians on the fronts and/or backs of door leaves, the figures on window shutters and, to a lesser extent, the scenes on the side and back surfaces of manuscript cabinets not covered by black lacquer and gold leaf art. Cloth banners, few examples of which have survived, were hung on wat walls as supreme examples of artistry, usually depicting Buddha descending from Tavatimsa Heaven or standing flanked by two of his disciples.

Painting was also combined with ornate calligraphy in religious manuscripts which, like the illuminated manuscripts of medieval Europe were considered both sacred text and works of art. The final category, lacquer and gold appliqué, is often classified as painting, but as a different technique is employed, it and the illustrated manuscripts are treated in the Minor Arts chapter.

Painting has undoubtedly been pursued as long as architecture and sculpture but unlike them has lacked durability. Its principal enemies have been fire, water, and the technique employed in its creation. The priming method has been adequate but the tempera paint, applied to a dry rather than wet surface as in fresco painting, has failed to adhere to the wall. The humid air, rising damp and rainwater seeping through leaky roofs has worked between primer and paint and within a few decades caused the paint to wash off or to crack, flake and fall off. Art historians know of paintings in Mon structures from later inscriptions relating to them and of Sukhothai paintings from stone slabs etched with portrait outlines, but only the paintings of the Ayutthaya and Bangkok periods have survived to the present day and there are few of those indeed.

The painting process began with the preparation of the wall. As the bricks of the wall and the stucco covering them were made of soils containing salts which would alter the hues of the pigments, the wall had to be brushed several times with a special neutralizing solution made by boiling the leaves of the cassia tree. The stucco surface was then smoothed by applying several coats of limewash mixed with fine sand and plant saps. Finally, the artist brushed on several coats of a primer made of white chalk blended with boiled and crushed tamarind seeds which acted as a binder. Each coat had to dry completely before the next one could be applied, a

Opposite: *A scene from the murals at Wat Ko Keo Suttharam is typical of Ayutthayan painting in its use of a cream-colored background and its extreme spaciousness in contrast to the compactness of Bangkok period paintings. Depicted here are the various levels of Mount Meru and a paradise with floating theps and animals.*

Above: *The interior of Wat Ko Keo Suttharam in Phetchaburi. Painted in 1734, the murals are unusual in that the Battle with Mara is behind the Buddha rather than on the front wall and the scenes on the side walls have been compartmentalized in diamond-shaped frames.*

38

Below: *A hapless foreigner appears in a painting of the Battle with Mara painted during Rama III's reign on the walls of Thon Buri's Wat Suwannaram.*

time-consuming process which might take several weeks.

Early artists had to content themselves with a very limited range of colors made from available materials. Red ochre, yellow ochre and white were obtained from local minerals while black was produced from crushed charcoal. By the 15th century, cinnebar vermilion was being imported in powder form from China; the crypt of Wat Ratburana in Ayutthaya displays a liberal use of this bright color. Greens were produced either from earth greens or vegetable matter; by the 18th century, malachite from China was being employed to produce a much brighter green. The crushed colors were combined with the resin of the "ma khwit" tree which served as a binder.

The pigments were applied to the dry surface with brushes made from the fibers of tree and vine roots. These somewhat stiff brushes give a pencil-like quality to the strokes, a line of unvarying width far removed from the expanding and contracting line of Chinese painters. For fine details, animal hair brushes were used, those made of the hair taken from the inside of a cow's ear being the most highly prized.

Like architecture and sculpture, the paintings were created at the behest of patrons, usually royalty, who considered them to be acts of merit-making. These patrons often set two schools in competition to spur them to produce their best work. Yet despite the royal patronage and the development of a classical school, the paintings were easily accessible to members of every stratum of society. These were the texts illiterate people could "read" without help. One needed no formal education; he only needed to remember the tales he had heard long ago at his mother's knee. He could swiftly decipher the murals because though they contained royal palaces, realms, personages and deities beyond his ken, the paintings were of the society and times in which he lived, with elements and people from everyday life. In short, the paintings related to him because they were "Thai" in every nuance and manifestation. In the Bangkok period, he was aided by brief bits of text written in the mural near the action described. The murals of Wat No in Suphan Buri provide an example of this technique.

The murals of Ayutthaya and Bangkok dealt with the Tosachat, the Life of Buddha, the Ramakien, and the Traiphum (Three Worlds) often with two or more subjects decorating the walls of a single bot or vihan. In some instances, the stories were of local personalities such as the adventures of a monk who traveled to Sri Lanka for religious instruction. In a departure from the norm, the walls of Wat Rajapradit are covered with depictions of the main royal festival which occurs in each of the 12 months of the year. Of the Tosachat, the story of Vessandan, Buddha's next to last incarnation, is the most popular, often covering one wall of a bot with the other nine chadoks being required to share the opposite wall among themselves, as at Thon Buri's Wat Suwannaran.

While the subjects varied, there was a consistency in the way the paintings were laid out in a temple. The main story — the Buddha's Life or the Tosachat — occupied the panels between the windows, the most accessible to the viewer's vantage point. Above the windows were several rows of deities, theps, or other celestial beings in worshipful attitudes arranged so they faced the far end of the building where the Buddha image was situated. The wall behind the image might be covered with the three worlds of the Traiphum (Heaven, Earth and Hell) or with spillovers from the Tosachat that didn't fit the side walls.

The wall facing the Buddha image was almost always reserved for the Battle with Mara, a cataclysmic encounter attacked with gusto by the painters resulting in a furious motion at variance with the peaceful scenes gracing the other walls. It was here that the artist gave vent to his emotions and imagination, producing works of grand proportions.

Thai classical painting was characterized by a two-dimensional approach devoid of perspective in the Western sense and without a vanishing point. The figures were rendered without modelling and without the play of light and shadow that would give the overall picture a feeling of depth. There was an economy of line and a tendency to use colors in blocks rather than in graduated tones between one hue and the next.

The artist of old began by sketching the composition on paper. As with the technique for decorating lacquerware, pins were used to make holes in the paper along the outlines of the principal figures. The paper was placed on the wall and a porous sack of fine ashes was lightly struck against the paper so the white powder passed through the pin holes. The color would be applied between the dotted lines left on the wall. This technique is thought to arise from the practice of having a master make the preliminary sketch and then direct his apprentices to flesh out the figures by adding color. Each figure and its principal features was further emphasized by black outlines drawn around key features. During the Bangkok period gold leaf was usually used to highlight jewelry and architectural ornaments.

Within each panel between the windows is an entire story or several episodes of a story laid out in somewhat random order. One must know the story beforehand since the elements are not arranged like a comic strip moving from left to right and descending row by row. It may begin in the middle and run clockwise or counterclockwise or it may zigzag back and forth. A single palace or a meandering river may serve as a stage set for three or four episodes or an entire story. Once the viewer has identified the key actor, he can follow him through his exploits. When viewed in this manner, it quickly becomes apparent that instead of a single scene populated by dozens of actors, the panel contains several scenes each with nearly the same handful of characters.

Each panel is a set piece complete in its own and is placed, not for ease of storytelling, but as the artist elects. Where it is necessary to separate one scene from another, he erects a zigzag fence or a screen of trees to create a forest glade. He may alter perspective and proportion in order to fit in a

Below: *This detail of a cloth wall banner depicts Buddha's victory over Mara. Created in the 19th century.*
Bottom: *Mythical elephants in the heaven of the Pahcekha Buddhas, a Rama III period painting in the bot of Bangkok's Wat Suthat.*

Opposite: *The marriage of Buddha's father and mother, Suddhodana and Mahamaya in the life of Buddha murals at the Buddhaisawan Chapel. The murals painted in the reign of Rama I make extensive use of the zigzag line to compartmentalize individual scenes within the episode.*

desired element. In the end, there is no perceivable composition, only an abundance of detail and energy spilling in all directions, an arrangement which pleases by its sheer vitality and by the excellence of its execution.

The figures look quite un-Thai. The models that artists followed are not known but it has been suggested that they were inspired by the Indian-influenced figures on Nang Yai (Giant Figure) shadow puppets or the masks used in Khon dramas because of their somewhat static features and the aureolae or nimbi which surround them. The assertion has equally energetically been challenged on the grounds that the figures' faces do not resemble those on the shadow puppets and that any connection between the two is purely coincidental. The figures are dressed in sumptuous garments which cover the lower body but leave the upper torso bare except for strands of jewelry. The women's melon-like breasts are either bare or covered by diaphanous veils which do little to hide them from curious eyes. Except for the bare or scantily-veiled breasts, the fashions reflect those followed up to the late-19th century, when Western clothes were adopted.

One of the more appealing aspects of Thai painting is the artists' penchant for filling "off-stage" areas with scenes of ordinary life. These little spaces tucked into corners or behind buildings or walls seem to provide the artists respite from the formalism of the main subject. While in the same precise style, one finds here the common people in their daily pursuits, be it watching a shadow play, amorous dalliance, children's games, even a robbery and opium smoking. In a very real way then, the paintings become microcosms of Thai life and society.

The backgrounds of Ayutthayan murals were generally painted in light hues with no attempts to create landscapes per se. By the Bangkok period, artists were filling every available space with figures, buildings and foliage.

One would expect that in a tropical country like Thailand the landscape in paintings would be bright green accented by the beautiful flowers and plants which abound in nature. Instead, the landscape is somber, an apparent attempt to avoid interfering with the scenes being played out against it. Natural elements like trees and rocks are placed like props. Trees are thickly planted in groves whose individual members are only wispily hinted at. Though the seas off Thailand's shore are tame with only a hint of rolling breakers, the seas in Thai paintings are massive. They are rendered as an imbrication of alternating rows of white-capped waves like fish scales or disks, and are undoubtedly a convention borrowed from Chinese painting.

The areas above the windows in Wat Buddhaisawan are occupied by bands of Buddhas, of worshiping disciples or other subjects. Repeated endlessly, they cover all four walls from the tops of the windows to the ceiling.

While most of the mural paintings have long since disappeared, a few remain that provide a very good idea of the genre as a whole.

Buddhism and The Life of Buddha

There is much of the miraculous about the events in Buddha's life, most of them undoubtedly added long after his death by overzealous writers and/or disciples trying to appeal to a broad audience steeped in Hindu mythology or spirit worship. In attempting to relate Buddha's life and at the same time shed some light on the episodes which appear in paintings, lintels and votive tablets, it is necessary to include several of these somewhat fantastic elements, many of which are found only in Thailand.

Buddhist doctrine, adapted in part from Hindu beliefs, contends that each man and woman is condemned to die and be reborn endlessly in a quest to become perfect. The good or bad one does in this life determines whether he or she will be reborn as a higher or lower being. In Buddhist belief, good can be accumulated and even transferred, as when a dutiful child performs acts of merit to aid a dead parent to be reborn as a higher being. If one is successful in evolving life by life into a better person, he eventually reaches perfection whereupon he breaks this cycle of rebirths and passes into nibhan (nirvana), an ethereal state of eternal bliss.

In Theravada Buddhist belief professed by Thais, the man known to the world as "Buddha" was the fourth of five Great Teacher Buddhas (there are numerous other, Pacheka, Buddhas who do not preach). This Buddha, Gautama Buddha, died in 543 B.C. Buddhist tradition holds that the fifth and final Great Buddha, the Maitreya, will appear on earth 5,000 years after Gautama Buddha, or in the year 4457 A.D.

Gautama Buddha was the final, 500th incarnation of a single being. Each of these incarnations has been recounted in a body of works known as the Chadok (Jataka) Tales, the last ten, collected in a work titled the Tosachat (Dasajati), being the most important.

Buddha was born Prince Siddhartha of the Sakya clan in the city of Lumbini in present-day Nepal. His greatness was portended in a dream his mother had wherein she was carried to the Himalayan forests by heavenly deities where a white elephant circled her bed three times and entered her body through the right side to become the embryonic Buddha.

Standing upright and with one hand holding a tree branch, the queen gave birth to her child. Astrologers predicted that the boy would one day become a Buddha or a Chakravartin, a Universal Monarch. One sage, Asita, swore the boy would become a Buddha at

which, miraculously, the Buddha appeared on top of Asita's head as verification of the truth of the old sage's words.

Prince Siddhartha married at the age of 16 years and the couple settled down to a life of luxury in the palace, secluded from the world outside. His elongated earlobes, distended by the weight of heavy earrings, are references to this period in his life. One day, when he was 29 years old, the prince ventured for the first time beyond the palace walls and was confronted by the harsh reality of life as it is lived by ordinary men. As he traveled along a country road, he encountered an old man, a sick man, a dead man and a holy man. Shocked and saddened by what he saw, he returned to the palace and began pondering the question of why man was condemned to suffer such torment. Unable to gain a satisfactory answer from the wise men of the court, he determined to find out for himself. Recalling the serene light which shone on the face of the holy man, he decided that by emulating his life he might find the answer he was seeking. As he was pondering leaving his luxurious life, it was announced that his wife had given birth to a son. The news momentarily dissuaded him from his quest but after more thought he decided to sever his links with his past. One night, he left his family, never to return.

Prince Siddhartha traveled deep into the forest and at the side of a stream cut off his hair, donned a plain robe, took up an alms bowl and became a wandering Hindu ascetic. For the next six years, he starved himself and inflicted all forms of abuse on his body in the hope that self-abnegation and pain would reveal an answer. It led him nowhere, and he realized that instead of pursuing extremes he should seek a Middle Way. On emerging from his fast, a nobleman's daughter named Sujata prepared him a delicious soup in a golden bowl. When he finished, Sujata gave Gautama the bowl which he placed in a brook asking that it float upstream as a sign that he was destined to become the Buddha. It did.

He began meditating on the causes of human suffering and at last, beneath a tree, Buddha at the age of 35 found the answer he had been seeking: Man suffers because of discontent, lust and craving for what are, in the end, ephemeral goals and materialistic objects. Life is impermanent, and things of this world cannot protect one from unhappiness or from the inevitable: death and rebirth. Only by extinguishing desire and attachment to material objects or to other human beings can one find peace.

While wrestling with the ramifications of this revelation, he was assailed by the forces of darkness in the form of Mara's three lascivious daughters and myriad other temptations set loose to veer him from his path. Through force of mind and the merit he had accumulated in past lives, he was able to withstand their onslaught. When Mara asked him, "Who can vouch for your goodness?" Gautama pointed his right hand towards the ground and said, "The earth shall be my witness". At that moment, the earth goddess, Toranee, appeared and wrung from her hair a torrent of water which washed away Mara, his daughters and all other evils and temptations. Gautama continued to meditate through the night and at dawn was suffused with the pure light of supreme understanding.

In the seven weeks following his Enlightenment, Buddha meditated at seven locations in the vicinity of Bodhgaya. In the fifth week, while seated at the edge of Lake Muchalinda, a terrible storm arose causing the waters of the lake to rise. Seeing that Buddha was lost in thought, the naga king Muchalinda slipped his coils under Buddha's body, lifting him above the threatening flood. At the same time he spread the hoods of his seven heads to shelter him from the driving rain.

Buddha contemplated entering nibhan immediately or remaining on earth to preach his new-found wisdom. Brahma and other deities descended to earth to plead with him to remain as a teacher. He envisioned a marshy pond of lotuses with some blossoms immersed in mire, some floating on its surface and others rising above it. Those deep in the water were like people sunk in evil; for them no help was possible. Those which had risen far above it had no need of help. Those persons trying to rise above evil but uncertain about how their souls might ascend needed aid to reach salvation. It was then that Buddha elected to remain on earth.

His first sermon was preached at Deer Park in Sarnath to the five monks who had traveled with him during his six years as an ascetic. To them he explained his doctrine, sending it whirling like a wheel into the world, an act referred to by the Dhammachakra mudra or "Setting the Wheel of the Law in Motion". He then began traveling, seeking new converts to his doctrine. Buddhist texts in Southeast Asia include an episode not found in the Sanskrit or Pali originals. In it, Buddha is confronted by the proud Emperor Jambupati, who refuses to listen to the words of an insignificant teacher. Buddha causes a splendid palace to appear and adorns himself with a crown and jewelry. In this guise, he invites Jambupati to visit him. The emperor is impressed by this display of magnificence. Buddha, however, rebukes him by pointing out that earthly glory is an empty achievement. Perceiving the lesson, Jambupati abandons his throne and becomes a monk. It is thought that this story is the explanation for the Adorned Buddhas which Southeast Asian Theravada sculptors created in great numbers.

Buddha also acted as a mediator in a dispute between two clans — the Sakya who were related to his father and the Koliyas related to his mother — over the division of irrigation water. He displayed the "Calming the Relatives" mudra and then, listening quietly to both sides, resolved the dispute to their mutual satisfaction. In another instance, Buddha was challenged by those who sought to discredit him. He announced that a miracle would take place by a mango tree. His

detractors countered by buying all the mango orchards and cutting down the trees and then erected a platform to perform magical tricks. Buddha responded by asking a gardener to plant a mango seed which when it touched the earth sprang up as a full-grown tree heavy with fruit. At the same moment, Indra let loose a bolt of lightning which toppled the heretics' platform. The episode is referred to as the Miracle at Savatthi and has been depicted in several murals and reliefs.

Seven days after Buddha's birth, his mother had died and gone to heaven as a deity. Buddha ascended to the Tavatimsa Heaven (the Heaven of the Thirty-Three Gods) and spent one monsoon season preaching his doctrine to her and others. His descent to earth on a trio of ladders accompanied by Brahma and Indra is the subject of stucco reliefs in several Sukhothai wats, and of numerous mural paintings and cloth banners.

Buddha's last convert was Supatra, who became a novice. Buddha converted many other people in his lifetime and on reaching his 80th birthday was tempted once again by Mara to forget mankind and enter nibhan immediately. Buddha resisted in order to prepare the monks to carry on after him. He gathered them together, announcing that he would pass into nibhan in three months' time and that there was much to be accomplished before then. He spent the next three months preaching. One day, he was served a piece of pork by a blacksmith named Chunda. Realizing that the meat was tainted, he ate it and asked Chunda to bury the rest. He then became very ill. His disciples were angry with Chunda, but Buddha calmed them noting that just as Sujata's meal had enabled him to reach Enlightenment, so Chunda's meal would enable him to pass into nibhan. Though ill, Buddha traveled with his disciples to Kusinara. At the bank of a river, he asked his chief disciple, Ananda, to prepare a bed between two trees. After answering many doctrinal questions and giving one last sermon, he lay on his side, his upper body supported on his elbow and his head resting on his hand, and calmly passed from existence.

In the following centuries, a dichotomy appeared in the interpretation of his teachings, a division which eventually led to the formation of two schools of thought. The earlier, the Theravada "Doctrine of the Elders" in Thailand, Laos, Burma, Kampuchea, Sri Lanka and India preached that if a person had progressed to the point where he had extinguished all desire, there would be little or nothing to hold him to earth and he would pass on to nibhan unhindered. About the 1st century B.C., a new school which would later be professed in Japan, China, Korea, Nepal and Tibet contended that it was a man's duty to postpone his enlightenment to help others reach spiritual perfection. This new sect styled itself the Mahayana or Greater Vehicle, derisively dubbing the Theravadans "Hinayana" or Lesser Vehicle. In the main, however, the two schools are in agreement on the principal points of doctrine, and there has never been serious conflict between them.

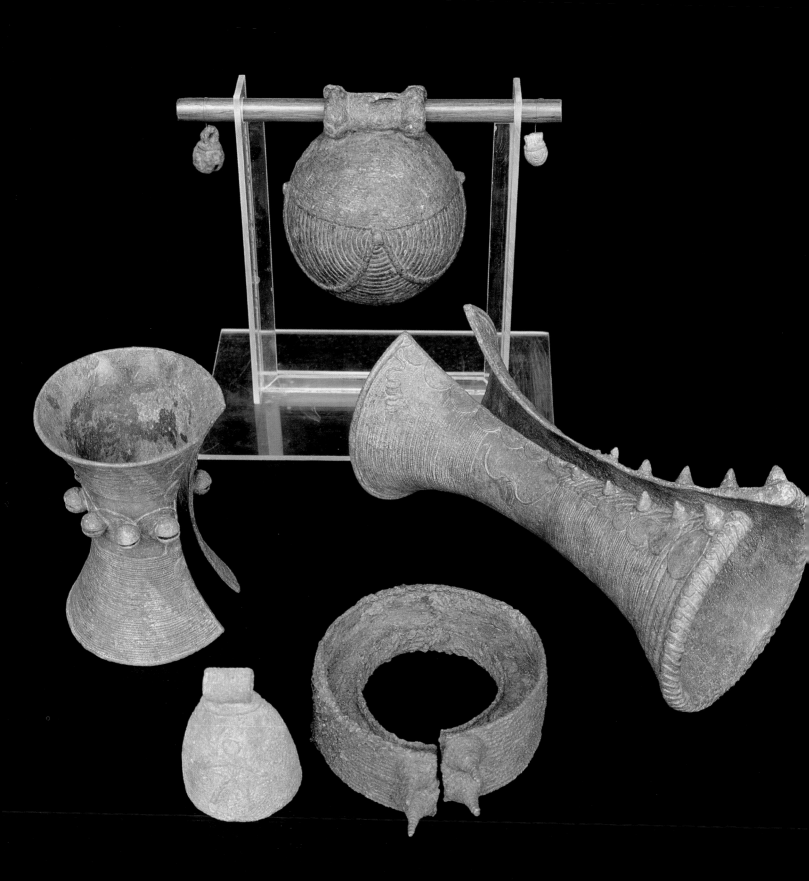

Prehistory

Thailand's first museums of modern art were a number of caves in such widely dispersed locations as Udon Thani province in Thailand's Northeast; Uthai Thani, 500 kilometers north of Bangkok; and Koh Khian in Phangnga and Tham Sin in the South. On limestone walls, Stone Age artists drew ochre and black stick figures as well as full-bodied humans and animals cavorting in empty space. In these primitive landscapes, birds, tortoises, frogs and herds of cattle appear at random, often overlapping one another without regard to the others' right of prior domain. Perhaps the artists drew in light so dim they could not discern the outlines of figures previously sketched there.

Scattered across the walls of a representative example at Uthai Thani are drawings of men wearing thick bracelets and leading cows whose sides are covered in intricate geometric designs. There is a certain whimsy to the depictions; their creators may have been prehistoric graffiti artists waiting out a monsoon storm before resuming work. It may have been that the man-and-cow figures had shamanistic connotations designed to increase the size of one's herd and, with it, the owner's prosperity.

With this paucity of definitive evidence, it is little wonder that until recently archeologists had characterized Thailand as a backwater, a latecomer in technological and artistic development that didn't begin to bloom until the 6th or 7th centuries. In treatises on prehistoric periods, Thailand was described as a bog of thick jungles and marshy lowlands populated by primitive hunters and gatherers, technology borrowers without any drive or inventive genius.

In the 1950s it had been postulated that conditions in prehistoric Thailand had been ideal for the cultivation of rice and other crops, but little evidence had been found to support the contention. In 1965 an American archeologist exploring a cave in the North discovered a large cache of pebble tools, ground stone tools, animal bones and several shards that appeared to date from 7000 B.C. More important he discovered, in the excavation trenches, seeds and plant husks whose structures suggested that these early cave dwellers had planted and harvested crops rather than gathered food from the wild.

About the same time, Thai and American archeologists at the small northeastern Thailand village of Non Nok Tha began finding bronze

Previous pages: Paintings on the walls of a limestone cave on Koh Khian Island in Phangnga Bay are thought to date from prehistoric times. They are devoted to figures, animals and abstract patterns. Opposite: Bronze bracelets and other ornaments from various periods of the Ban Chieng era are displayed at Bangkok's Suan Pakaad Palace. (H.R.H. Princess Chumbhot collection).

Above: Socketed ax head and pick points made of bronze at Ban Chieng and thought to date from 2000 B.C. (H.R.H. Princess Chumbhot collection)

Right: *Baked clay Ban Chieng pots with whorl designs made between 300 B.C. and 200 A.D. (H.R.H. Princess Chumbhot collection)*

implements and artifacts in large burial mounds. It was initially assumed that these tools had been imported from an important bronze-working center in northern Vietnam or perhaps had found their way south from a bronze culture in the north of China.

The discovery of their true importance came almost by accident; and by a non-archeologist. In 1966, a young American sociologist was doing research in Ban Chieng 130 kilometers northeast of Non Nok Tha, when he literally tripped over the key which opened a new era in archeology and art history. While walking along a village path, he stumbled over the root of a kapok tree and landed among a number of clay circles which he recognized to be the rims of buried jars. Thinking it an odd place to discard old jars, he surmised that the constant erosion to which the Northeast is subject could have worn away the soil covering an old archeological site.

He alerted the Thai Fine Arts Department, which formed a team to dig at the site. Several pots were meanwhile sent to the University of Pennsylvania laboratories for thermoluminescence testing to determine their ages. Before the results came back, excavation at Ban Chieng revealed numerous bronze objects, many of sophisticated design.

In Pennsylvania, researchers were dumbfounded. The clay pots were found to date from perhaps 3000 B.C. What it suggested was that the bronze artifacts buried with them would have to be of nearly equal antiquity. If it were true, it meant that Thailand, not the Middle East, had opened the Bronze Age — 700 years before Mesopotamia, until then regarded as the cradle of civilization.

Chronometric dating of the bronze objects showed them to be at least 5,300 years and perhaps 6,000 years old. The question then arose of whether they had been created at Ban Chieng or imported from elsewhere. Smelting bronze is a highly technical undertaking for a primitive society. It requires heating a cauldron to 1,000 degrees C. (cooking fires are only 600-800 degrees C.), removing the oxygen for a proper bonding of bronze and tin, and molding the molten bronze into tools and decorative objects using equipment produced specifically for the purpose, itself a very technical task. Further excavation at Ban Chieng unearthed clay molds, crucibles and splashes of bronze suggesting spills during the pouring process, conclusive evidence that the artifacts had been cast at the site where they were found.

For art historians, the most exciting finds were the bronze bracelets and pins, the glass beads and clay pots found in the burial mounds. In general, they have been categorized into three periods:

Early (3000 — 1000 B.C.): The plateau that holds Ban Chieng and other Bronze Age sites today gives no hint that it once supported an affluent culture. The tableland between the Korat mountain range and the Mekong River is, like most of northeastern Thailand, flat, barren and poor.

It is not certain if the first inhabitants were indigenous or migrated from elsewhere. What they occupied, however, was a fertile, forested land which allowed them to develop an advanced form of rice cultivation and to domesticate cattle, pigs, chickens and dogs for their own use. Post holes at the site suggest their houses were raised off the ground, perhaps little different from the wood and thatch houses in which northeasterners live today.

The clay pots were found at the feet or head of bodies buried in the grave sites. Also found were jewelry, tools, weapons and hard, baked clay balls of the kind fired from "pellet" bows which shot projectiles rather than arrows. The bronze spearpoints were socketed to fit on wooden shafts. Their points had been bent double, a primitive practice found in several other parts of the world which served to "kill" the spirit of the weapon when it was placed with the body. Also found were tigers' teeth and bronze hairpins with holes drilled in them.

Different types and numbers of objects were buried with each body suggesting early social stratification. Infants were buried in special jars somewhat larger than those placed at the head and feet of adults.

The pots evolved through a series of distinctive shapes:

Early 3000 — 2500 B.C.: Tall and broad with a circular base and incised designs were moulded on the shoulders.

2500 — 2000 B.C.: Infant burial jars with deeply incised designs appeared for the first time.

2000 — 1500 B.C.: Straight-sided jars, the so-called "beaker" jars, were introduced as were round pots with long necks. The outer surfaces were cord-marked giving them a rough look.

1500 — 1000 B.C.: Globular cord-mark pots, frequently incised on the shoulder and often painted, appear for the first time.

Middle (1000 — 300 B.C.): The settlements were more prosperous with farmers practicing advanced wet rice cultivation. By this point water buffaloes had been domesticated and trained to pull wooden plows possibly fitted with iron tips. Infant burial seems to have ceased by this point as no evidence of the practice has been found at Ban Chieng.

Below: *A black and white urn with deeply-incised design and made of baked clay is thought to date from the early Ban Chieng period (3000-2000 B.C.). (H.R.H. Princess Chumbhot collection)*
Bottom: *Ban Chieng urn on a stand and decorated in a geometric design. This 25 cm. tall baked clay piece dates from the late Ban Chieng period. (H.R.H. Princess Chumbhot collection)*

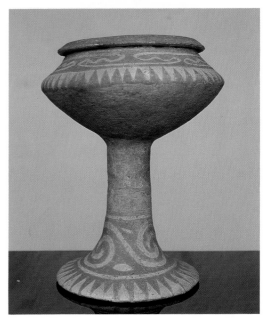

The pottery buried with the body was first broken into small pieces. These shards were then placed in sheets under and over the body, a practice of unknown origin. The jars reassembled from the shards reveal a more complex design than previously displayed. Elegant white or brick-colored pottery was incised with designs on the shoulders and painted.

By this period, bronze bracelets had become more elaborate and were worn by greater numbers of people. Spear points were made of iron or bi-metallic alloys.

Late (300 B.C.-200 A.D.): This was the apogee of the Ban Chieng culture and the height of bronze technology. Found in the upper levels of the burial mounds were wire necklaces of highly refined bronze with up to 20% tin content. The necklaces suggest a high level of technology because making this type of wire requires drawing it while hot, tempering it and re-heating it before drawing it again. The necklaces also suggest a highly-evolved economy with ample wealth and time to devote to the creation of objects made purely for decorative purposes. By this point, bronze was used exclusively for ornaments; tools were made of iron.

Pots of the late period are highly-decorated with rust-colored geometric patterns on beige grounds. Also found are ceramic carved rollers in a variety of designs. Their purpose is unknown, but it has been suggested they were inked and used to print cloth. Numerous glass beads were also found, usually in children's graves.

This burst of creativity marked the culmination of this glorious culture. No one knows why it died out or what became of its people. Today, farmers till the soil seemingly oblivious to the creative ferment that once bubbled in their small villages.

Collections of pots in Bangkok's Suan Pakaad Palace and the National Museum reveal a fabulous wealth of imagination. The pots are highly decorated far more than would be required for what are essentially kitchen utensils. What gives the pots their charm is the highly-individualistic nature of the artists who felt no need to conform to a particular style, a trait which frustrates archeologists trying to classify them into precise categories.

The potters are thought to have shaped their pots with the paddle and anvil technique used in the Northeast today. The wet clay was molded with the hands to form an open-ended cylinder. The cylinder was placed on a stand and the fingers were wrapped around a wet leaf which was used to smooth and shape the rim. Once complete, the clay anvil was held against the inner walls of the jar while a paddle was struck against the outer wall until the jar assumed its final contour. At this time, the designs were incised and the decoration painted. If required, a foot was added. Some middle period pots, particularly the carinated or ridged pots, may have had their bottom parts paddled over molds and a top part added later. The pot was then dried in the sun for two days and fired in an open fire for 30 minutes using rice straw as the fuel. Rounded bases were common but handles and spouts or other attachments were rare. The early pots had both simple and complex geometric scrolls plus geometric motifs. The middle period pots were incised and painted while the late period pots were only painted. Geometric spirals and whorls predominated; there were few animal or human figures.

Pots often have rough, cord-marked surfaces, a decorative technique which developed early. Potters used one of two methods: one was to beat the outer surface with a cord-wrapped paddle. The other was to wrap a cylinder with cord and roll it around the outer surface. Sometimes both methods were used together. Other decorative techniques include rocker stamping, comb-pricking, appliqué, free-hand painting, incising and burnishing. Often, two or more of these techniques were used together.

Most bronze artifacts were formed by beating the cold metal with a heavy object. Later, molten bronze was poured into clay molds. There is also evidence the lost-wax process was used (see the Sculpture chapter).

In the middle period, bracelets acquired a beauty and elegance one doesn't normally associate with primitive peoples. The most popular was a flanged T-section shape, a form that was also rendered in marble. Spirals, rings, "C" and "D" shaped and flat bracelets of striking design were also found. Bracelets with scalloped outer rims were often produced in sets of three. Bronze beads and bells with incised designs were also found.

Don Tha Phet

In 1976, archeologists excavating in the village of Don Tha Phet in Kanchanaburi province, 30 km. northeast of the River Kwai, found numerous very thin bronze vessels and etched beads made of agate or cornelian and iron tools similar to those in Ban Chieng. The objects date from around 1000 B.C. and the etched beads show Indian influence. Also found were small bronze animals including a lovely peacock. The find led archeologists to postulate that the artisans might have been descendants of Ban Chieng people who migrated west and mixed with a proto-Malay people coming from the south.

Ban Kao

Excavations in the River Kwai Valley near the village of Ban Kao in 1960-1962 turned up a series of clay and terracotta pots of intriguing design including a few without precedent. The colors range from black through gray to brown depending on the clay or clay composition used in their making. Three types have been identified. Two include a container without support and a second with a ring support. It is the third, of which a dozen examples have been found, that has elicited the most interest. It is a terracotta container that stands on three legs which taper to points and whose use can only be conjectured. It may have been designed as a cooking pot which could stand over a fire unsupported by separate legs or hooks. All the Ban Kao pieces are thought to date from around 2000 B.C. and add further evidence to new theories that in antique times, Thailand's dense jungles sheltered an immensely creative people who fashioned highly sophisticated objects of enduring beauty.

Below: Baked clay pots with corded design from Ban Kao, thought to date from 2000 B.C. (Bangkok National Museum)
Bottom: A bronze peacock and bird, the work of Don Tha Phet artisans of 1000 B.C. (Bangkok National Museum)

The Indianization of Thailand

Opposite: *Stone Vishnu from Surat Thani, 1.69 m. tall and dated between the 7th and 9th centuries, though new evidence suggests an origin as early as the 6th century. Influenced by the southern Indian Pallava style, it is recognized by the slant of its belt and the large bow in which it is tied on the right side. (Bangkok National Museum)*

It is unclear what became of the indigenous populations of prehistoric Thailand. They probably continued to clear the jungles, cultivate rice and produce utensils and art objects as before, but the artistic flame which burned so brightly at Ban Chieng and other sites seems to have dimmed for several centuries (at least until the next archeologist's shovel strikes new evidence that proves otherwise).

Throughout the first centuries A.D. following the decline of Ban Chieng, new peoples were arriving in Southeast Asia. Indian merchants seeking new products and markets began moving eastward. Unlike many gypsy merchants, they sought to set up trading posts at key ports of call, integrating themselves into the local communities. In the process, they introduced new concepts including art subjects and techniques.

The effect of these and later Indian adventurers on Thai art and life cannot be overemphasized. Indian architecture, art, government, philosophy, religion and literature had an incalculable impact on Thai (and most of Southeast Asian) art, far more than China, which is geographically and racially more akin to Thailand. In the initial stages, Indian influence was direct — artifacts and ideas — but long after trade was taken over by local merchants, India would continue to have an indirect effect through the arrival in Thailand of other people who themselves had come under the same Indian influences and created art reflecting the philosophical, religious and artistic concepts of the sub-continent.

The art of Thailand in the 1st through 6th centuries A.D. (and to the 8th century in the South), is characterized by a total Indian domination either by imports of statues or by local creation of sculptures and other objects which were copies of Indian works or whose stylistic elements can be directly traced to a particular Indian school of art. Indian concepts would continue to influence Thai art until the 16th century.

Early artists concentrated on creating images to serve the Hindu religion that most of the inhabitants of the region professed. After the 5th century, sculptors began producing Buddha images, a reflection of changing religious beliefs. Over time, the creation of Buddha images became sculptors' principal activity, though they would continue to produce Hindu images until the 19th century.

Above: *Limestone Vishnu, 67 cm. tall, found at Wat Sala Thung in Chaiya. Early-Gupta influence is evident in its modeling and costume. Originally dated to the 5th century, recent research has suggested it may have been created in the 4th century. (Bangkok National Museum)*

Below: *Found at Nakhon Si Thammarat, this 78 cm. tall stone Vishnu dates from the 5th century. (National Museum, Nakhon Si Thammarat)*

Art of the Peninsular Region

From early times, Indian sailors had been masters of the seas. Contemporary accounts say their ships were 200 feet long and capable of carrying 700 persons swiftly through stormy weather and choppy waters, a feat the Chinese ships were unable to duplicate until much later. In their trading ventures with East Asia, the Indian merchants established halfway points to serve as supply ports, sources of new products and markets for their goods. Chinese annals of the 3rd century A.D. note the existence of more than 10 coastal kingdoms hugging the shoreline of the Gulf of Thailand, usually at the mouths of rivers where they were receiving points for goods from the jungled interiors of the peninsula. Their local rulers welcomed the products these travelers from the west could bring them.

The most important of the 10 kingdoms was Dan Sun, which flourished from the 3rd to the 5th centuries. Stretching across the peninsula in the region of Surat Thani, Dan Sun was a well organized state whose artisans possessed considerable expertise in casting bronze as evidenced by bronze drums found at several sites.

The principal remains of the culture — stone statues of Vishnu — have been found north and south of the kingdom. The four-armed Hindu god stands stiffly erect with shoulders thrown back and is wasp-waisted and thick-hipped. One, from Wat Sala Thung in Chaiya, dates from the 4th century and is reminiscent of Gandhara art of northern India. Two others, from Nakhon Si Thammarat, have thick bodies and reflect local influence in the face and decoration. The images have caused problems for art historians, some of whom ascribe them to the Srivijaya school and date them as 8th-9th centuries works.

In the 5th century, Dan Sun was eclipsed by two neighboring kingdoms: Chi Tu to the north near Chaiya, which would subsequently be the stronghold of the Srivijayan culture in Thailand, and Dan Dan near Phatthalung. At Dan Dan, departments and divisions were charged with overseeing the daily affairs of the kingdom, suggesting a high level of social organization and economic development. Court functions were lavish as noted by Chinese visitors in the 7th century, who marveled at the sumptuousness of the palace and the pomp of state ceremonies held to receive them.

No examples of architecture remain from this period, and there are no contemporary descriptions of building design. If the buildings were made of brick, the construction material for later monuments, it is likely they were destroyed by nature over the centuries. What is more likely is that, as is still the case in many parts of the South and in Malaysia, the principal buildings were made of wood which eventually succumbed to the damp and insects.

By the 6th century, artists were moving into new areas of expression. Chinese annals noted that in the year 530 A.D., a Dan Dan mission to the Chinese imperial court took gifts including a hibiscus flower made of gold, two ivory images and two carved stupas, all of them dedicated to Buddha,

Left: *Vishnu from Takna Pa, 2.02 m. tall and dated as late as the 8th-9th centuries. The Takua Pa style is characterized by the loose pleats that hang down the front. (Bangkok National Museum)*

Below: *This stone Vishnu, 65 cm. tall, was carved in the 5th century and later found in Nakhon Si Thammarat province. (Wat Mahathat Museum. Nakhon Si Thammarat).*

Right and Below: *This 2.35 meter 7th-century stone Vishnu, heavily-influenced by the Pallava style of India, was the central figure of a group of three which were enclosed by two trees in the area of Takua Pa. Vandals cut off its head. Later study showed that the head had been added at a later date to replace the original head. When the statue was excavated, half of the real head was found buried near it. The head*

was reunited with the body and the restored statue is now displayed in the National Museum of Nakhon Si Thammarat.

Left: *Stone Vishnu from Dong Si Mahaphot standing 148 cm. tall on a 74 cm. pedestal shaped like a stake that could be driven into the ground to anchor the statue. (National Museum, Prachin Buri).*
Below: *Stone linga from various sites in the area of Nakhon Si Thammarat. (National Museum, Nakhon Si Thammarat)*

Above: *Boy with Monkey, this pair of red terracotta images are 8 cm. tall and date from the 4th-5th centuries. Found in U Thong (U Thong National Museum)*

reflective of a new change that had come to the people of Thailand north and south: the conversion to Buddhism.

Supreme artistry is displayed in numerous Buddha images in bronze and stone which bear more than a small resemblance to their Gupta and other south Indian predecessors. The finest examples among the standing Buddhas appear to have been imported from India. They are denoted by the very pronounced pleating of the robes which leaves the right shoulder bare, by the left hand grasping one end of the robe, and by their flat curls, all of which suggest origins in the Amaravati school.

One of the finest pieces is a Meditating Buddha carved of limestone sometime in the 6th century by an artist of Dan Dan. The seeming solidity of the piece, the curls in precise rows and ranks, the absence of a well-defined robe, the thick lips and features suggest an amalgam of several Indian schools together with local styles. It is an unpretentious piece ably reflecting the peace the meditating Buddha has achieved.

Votive tablets made of sun-baked clay and dating from the 7th century have been found in Songkhla, Krabi and elsewhere. Measuring up to 10 centimeters high, they are crudely fashioned and devoted to Buddhist subjects, portraying, for example, Buddha delivering a sermon usually to disciples or deities. Other objects from this period include terracotta figurines which show strong Amaravati influence. Artists of the 7th century also produced some fine pottery, normally with flared mouths and red bands around their necks.

The North

In the North, Indian merchants moved across the mountains of Burma on their way south to the mouth of the Chao Phya River or east to Indochina. One of the earliest archeological finds from this period is a bronze Roman lamp thought to have been cast in Alexandria, Egypt in the 3rd century A.D. It was discovered at Pong Tuk, Kanchanaburi on the route from Burma that crosses the Bilauk Mountains at Three Pagoda Pass.

Statues of Vishnu and linga carved with the face of Siva (Sivalinga or Mukkalinga) have been found at various sites but not in the numbers discovered in the South. Among the more intriguing finds are three terracotta pieces dubbed "Boy with a Monkey" which were unearthed in the Chao Phya Valley and may date from as early as the 5th century. The boys' heads are missing but their youth is captured in the bodies' poses and the vitality of the pieces is conveyed in the face of the frightened monkeys that cling to their legs. It is not certain what purpose these charming pieces served but they are a testament to a keen eye and a humane spirit. Indian presence is also evident in the pottery found in 6th century Chansen.

Art of the 1st to 6th centuries was also heavily influenced by the kingdom of Funan to the east, which seems to have exercised political control over the valley populations. Funan is another of those shadowy empires about whose origins little is known and about whose people even less is certain. It arose in Kampuchea in the 1st century A.D. and flourished

Left: A bronze 20 cm. standing Buddha in the gesture of abhaya mudra. It has been variously dated between the 5th and 6th centuries. (National Museum, Nakhon Si Thammarat)
Below: A 1.04 meter tall, 6th century stone meditating Buddha on a lotus seat from Wat Boromathat in Chaiya. (Wat Phra Mahathat Museum, Chaiya)

Below: 1.48 m. stone Vishnu from Wieng Sa district of Surat Thani province which has been dated as early as the 6th century. It is similar to the Vishnus of the southern peninsula but the body is more muscular and wider hipped. It is recognized by the sarong, which is twisted at the waist suggesting a belt, and by the roll of pleats which fall to the ground to support it. (National Museum, Bangkok)

until the 6th century when internal dissention began to weaken it. Judging from Buddha images found in Nakhon Ratchasima, Nakhon Pathom and U Thong, it was, like the South of Thailand, heavily Indianized from an early date, perhaps by the same people who crossed Thailand from west to east in the early centuries of the millennium. There have even been suggestions their progenitors were Indonesians who sailed the open seas to settle there. It is recorded in the 10th and 11th centuries, "vicious, black Indonesians" made numerous raids on Angkorian territory, looting small towns before retreating to their boats. Chinese accounts note that by the 3rd century, Funan had expanded to the shores of the Gulf of Thailand and had sent envoys bearing vassalage to the courts of China.

Stone Buddha images of the Amaravati style are among the most important finds from Thailand's Central Plains during this period. It is not certain if they were originally created in Funan or taken there from India aboard merchant ships and later transported to Thailand. Within a short while, however, craftsmen in Thailand were creating art with decidedly new, non-Indian characteristics. One of these images found its way to Songkhla. Carved late in the 6th century, it features a square head with very large hair curls, the barest hint of a robe, a small ushnisha and narrow eyes. Narrow waisted, it is well proportioned and demonstrates a pleasing solidity and serenity.

In addition to Buddha images, Valley sculptors continued to fashion statues of Hindu deities. In contrast to the earlier period when images were between 15 and 70 centimeters tall, later Hindu statues were generally life-sized or taller. Moreover, they were of superior workmanship, as if over the centuries, the carvers had gained a better grasp of their art and a firmer hand on their chisels. The most outstanding pieces were among a series of 7th century stone Vishnus found at Dong Si Mahapot. Two other creations of this period worth noting are two Chinese statues found in Phetchaburi which are in the Sui period style of the late 6th-early 7th century.

The name Funan has also been given to a particular style of pottery. Early Funan pottery (250-450 A.D.), is divided into two types. The first comprises solid gray-black wheel-thrown pots with incised decorations on the shoulders. The second group includes small jars with flared mouths as well as brightly burnished red-orange bowls.

The term "Later Funan" (450-600 A.D.) is applied to a rich variety of pottery styles. Hand-molded figurines, lamps, seals, and shallow bowls with bevelled rims and dark gray, glossy surfaces are its most important representatives.

Found at U Thong were a brick carving of three monks with alms bowls and a kinnari made of stucco. More than likely they were early works by a school that was just beginning to try its wings: the Mon, or as it is also known, the Dvaravati school, the first truly indigenous school of art to emerge in Thailand.

Left: *1.48 m. stone Vishnu from Dong Si Mahaphot. (National Museum, Prachin Buri).*
Below: *86 cm. remains of a stone trident, possibly carried by Siva. Found at Dong Si Mahaphot. (National Museum, Prachin Buri)*

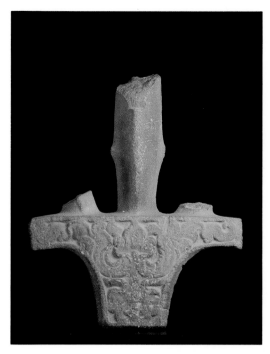

Dvaravati

Previous pages: *Bas reliefs on the wall of Phra Ngam cave near Saraburi depict Buddha, Brahma, Vishnu and flying figures. Dated from the 7th to 9th centuries.* Opposite: *Excavations at the Chedi Chula Paton site at Nakhon Pathom have revealed a wealth of stucco images, this Dvaravati Buddha head 28.8 cm. tall dating from the 8th century among them. (Bangkok National Museum)*

In the 6th century, Funan, beset by internal problems, began to retreat into itself, abandoning the outer reaches of its empire to the indigenous populations. Successors would return in force in the 10th century as the great Angkorian civilization, but for the moment, the central region of Thailand was without political overlords.

From inscriptions found at various sites in the lower Chao Phya River Valley, it is thought that the dominant population of central Thailand was Mon, an ancient race of unknown origin that had developed a very advanced culture during their subjugation by the Funanese. Left to themselves, its artists began producing the first Buddhist art in Southeast Asia that no longer looked to India for inspiration but was uniquely its own.

This new school of art spanning the 6th to 11th centuries had traditionally been called "Dvaravati", a term used by neighboring kingdoms to describe a culture centralized in the region between U Thong and Nakhon Pathom and the name subsequently discovered on several of its coins. The application of the word "Dvaravati" to the art of the entire central region of Thailand has been contested on the grounds that it describes only one of many kingdoms, all inhabited by Mons and all possessing similar high cultures capable of creating superior art. It has been suggested that the period be labeled "Mon", a proposal with considerable merit. Bowing to tradition, however, it is herein called "Dvaravati".

Dvaravati quickly expanded its borders to fill the vacuum left by the departure of the Funanese. More than 20 towns have been identified within an area bounded by the towns of Muang Fa Daed in the Northeast, Ku Bua near Ratchaburi and Si Thep and Haripunchai in the north. Haripunchai, an independent kingdom purportedly founded in the 7th century by the wife of a Mon prince, would ultimately create its own distinct school of art.

The first Dvaravati capital seems to have been at the Central Chao Phya River Valley town of U Thong, an ancient site with roots in prehistory. The chief cities of Dvaravati — U Thong and later Lop Buri and Nakhon Pathom — were centers of learning and religion to which Theravada Buddhist monks from distant lands journeyed to discourse on the Great Teacher's scriptures.

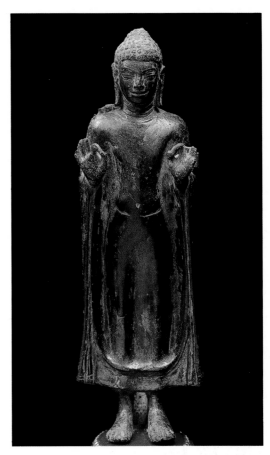

Above: *A bronze standing Buddha from the 7th-8th centuries displays the vitarka mudra and has the U-shaped robe hem typical of Dvaravati standing images. (Praku Knanumsommanajara collection)*

Below: *Buddha descending from Tavatimsa Heaven and displaying the vitarka mudra with both hands, a Dvaravati convention. This bronze 8th century image stands 1.10 meters, the largest Dvaravati bronze image yet found. Discovered at Ban Fai in Buri Ram Province. (Bangkok National Museum)*

Over the centuries, Dvaravati advanced from plateau to plateau, each more impressive than the one before. In the 9th and 10th centuries, Dvaravati fell under the political influence of Srivijaya to the south but succeeded in maintaining the integrity of its art. In the 11th century, however, it succumbed to the superior strength of the Khmers led by one of the greatest Angkorian kings, Suriyavarman I (1002-1050 A.D.). At the same time, the western portion of the Mon kingdom came under the rule of the Burmese king Aniruddha.

Architecture

Aerial surveys reveal that Dvaravati towns conformed to a general plan with early towns like Chansen characterized by oval layouts surrounded by one or two defensive moats. Later towns like Nakhon Pathom were laid out in rectangles defended by earthen ramparts broken by wooden gates. When the town grew, a new moat encompassing new territory would be dug without disturbing the original moat.

Monuments were set on square (the most common), round or octagonal foundations made of laterite. A brick platform was built upon the foundation and stucco was smoothed over its walls which were then decorated with stucco figures molded onto it. Atop the base, a chedi was erected as a reminder of Buddha's doctrine. Unfortunately, these materials have not proven durable enough to survive the centuries so there is little to study of Dvaravati architecture except foundations.

The base of the only Dvaravati building of any consequence yet discovered was unearthed in 1968 near Nakhon Pathom. A reconstructed model of the monument, the Chedi Chula Pathon, suggests it had a square base seven meters tall and 18 meters on a side and was surmounted by a chedi. Each side of the base was punctuated by five niches holding standing Buddha images. Especially noteworthy was a series of terracota and stucco reliefs illustrating the Buddhist scriptures.

The original chedi at the most famous Dvaravati monument, Phra Pathom Chedi at Nakhon Pathom, lies beneath an immense orange-tiled, bell-shaped chedi built by King Rama IV (1851-1868) which is reputed to be the largest in the world. The idea of building a new structure over the original is an old practice in Thailand stemming from a reluctance to re-build a collapsed monument or to destroy its remains, as it is still considered to be a holy structure regardless of its state of repair. Many large monuments have another or even a third encased within them. It is thought that the small chedi standing at the southeastern corner of the Phra Pathom Chedi may be a replica of the original.

The other remaining testaments to Dvaravati architectural skill, the square and octagonal chedis at Wat Chamatewi (Wat Kukut), are generally considered to be Haripunchai monuments, so are treated in the Northern Kingdoms chapter. New light may be shed on Dvaravati architectural styles when the excavations of the inner city of Si Thep are completed.

Left: *Buddha in bronze dating from the 7th-8th centuries and standing on a bell-shaped base. (U Thong National Museum)*
Below: *A 37 cm. stone Buddha head from the Dvaravati period. (Bangkok National Museum)*

68

Right: *Stone Dhammachakra or Wheel of the Law (1.05 m. tall) and a deer (27 cm. tall). Dating from the 7th-8th centuries and found at Nakhon Pathom, the wheel represents the Buddha's doctrine while the deer symbolizes Deer Park in Sarnath where Buddha delivered his first sermon. (H.R.H. Prince Bhanubhand Yugala collection, on loan to the National Museum, Bangkok)*

Above: *Buddha meditates sheltered by a naga. Bas relief on a sandstone bai sema. (National Museum, Khon Kaen)*

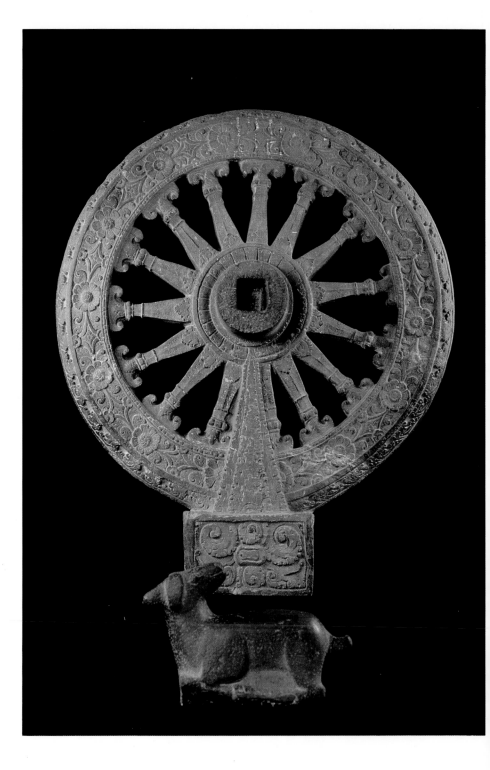

Sculpture

Though not the most accomplished sculptors the land ever produced, the Mons were innovators credited with creating some of the first truly Southeast Asian sculpture without any obvious references to Indian antecedents. More adept at shaping than at carving, they excelled at creating stucco bas reliefs and terracotta figures.

Their lack of brilliance in stone sculpting stems more from the nature of the stone they were using than from a deficiency of artistry. The limestone available to them was a brittle schistous variety riddled with internal fault lines; an errant tap with a chisel could destroy months of work. To overcome its weakness, the sculptors were forced to design figures that to the observer appear excessively heavy. Standing figures were invariably carved in full frontal positions, as wide at the top as they were at the bottom, an effect achieved in part by letting the edge of the robe fall to the ground in a straight line paralleling the upper torso. The elbows were pinned to the sides of the body with the arms held tightly against the chest and only the stubbiest of hands protruding from them. Even these precautions were in vain; in succeeding centuries, the hands tended to break at the wrist with the result that today almost every statue is handless. Sculptors attempted to get around their problems by carving hands separately and attaching them by tenon joints to the main body, but in almost every case the result is an artificiality that destroys the overall effect.

Dvaravati statues are characterized by somewhat asexual bodies covered by smooth, pleatless robes that cover one or both shoulders and include an undergarment whose bottom edge hangs lower than the rounded hem of the outer garment. The presence of a belt is suggested by a slight bulge at the waist. The back of the statue is smooth and featureless as if the image was designed to be placed next to a wall.

Perhaps more so than at any other period, the physiognomy of the creators is evident in their sculpture, especially the stucco work. Faces are somewhat corpulent with wide, flat noses and thick lips. Thickly ridged eyebrows are joined at the center to form a bow. The head is covered by thick, heavy curls and surmounted by a cone-shaped or hemispherical ushnisha often terminating in a tall cone or a large knob. The vitarka mudra sign with the right hand is the most common gesture for standing Buddhas but one Dvaravati innovation is for an image to be performing the same gesture with both hands, a convention not found in Indian art.

While standing images lack the fluidity of earlier Indian works, Dvaravati sculptors fared better with stone seated Buddhas. The seated images are carved in a greater variety of poses and manner of draping the robe than standing images. The seated images are posed in the Indian mode with the knees far apart and the soles of the feet facing upwards in the virasana position. The choice of this blocky treatment has less to do with style than with overcoming the limestone's weakness. New to the seated images is the practice of leaving several layers of the robe's hem over the top of the left shoulder and falling a short distance down the chest, a feature

Below: *Detail of a 1.45 meter tall limestone standing Buddha. The 7th-8th century image has a smooth finish, and very youthful, almost asexual face. Found in Wat Na Phramane in Ayutthaya. (Bangkok National Museum)*

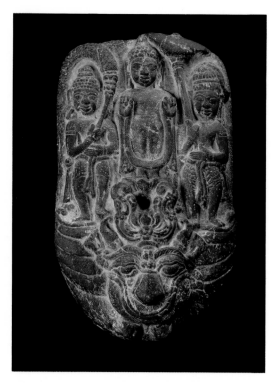

Opposite: *Stone Buddha in meditation under the Bodhi tree. Carved by Dvaravati sculptors and found at Dong Si Mahaphot it stands 1.03 meter. (National Museum, Prachin Buri)*

modified in a wealth of ways by sculptors of later periods. In general, the mudras for seated images are the same as those for standing images.

Dvaravati sculptors introduced the Indian concept of seating Buddha on a throne with his feet placed solidly on the ground, an attitude described as sitting in the "European fashion". He holds his right hand in the vitarka mudra gesture while the left hand is held slightly above the knee in the same position but with the palm facing upwards. It is an echo of some of the earliest representations of Buddha on bas relief sculptures showing him preaching to his mother and the gods in heaven. The throne may also refer to his royal upbringing or to ancient myth that when the Buddha was born as Prince Siddhartha, he had a choice between becoming the Buddha or a Chakravartin (Universal Monarch), the latter providing him another avenue to save mankind. In the end, Prince Siddhartha chose to be a Buddha. The pose is not found in Kampuchea, and appears only once in Burma but is similar to one used in Chandi Mendut, Indonesia; the pose appeared only rarely in Srivijayan and Ayutthayan sculpture. The four 4.3 meter tall quartzite Dvaravati images found to date are unusual in that they are carved of very hard quartzite. Originally occupying the porches of Nakhon Pathom's ruined Wat Pramane, they were removed by King Rama IV, who placed one each in the vihan and bot of the giant Phra Pathom Chedi he had just restored. Another was removed to Bangkok's National Museum and the fourth is now displayed in Ayutthaya's Chao Sam Phraya National Museum. A fifth enthroned image carved of limestone was removed from Wat Pramane and a vihan was built at Ayutthaya's Wat Na Pramane to hold it.

Numerous bronze statues duplicate the iconography and style of the stone images. They are generally gilded and often have eyes inlaid with copper or tin, the only period of art other than Lanna and Bangkok to treat the eyes in this manner.

One of the most intriguing groups of stone bas reliefs are the "Buddha on Panaspati" figures. In several reliefs, Buddha stands on the back of a mythical creature with the body of a bull, the wings of a swan and a hawk-like beak. He is attended by two figures tentatively identified as Indra and Brahma or as two Boddhisatvas. The beast is a composite of the vehicles ridden by the principal trinity of Hindu deities i.e. the body of Nandi the bull (Siva), the wings of a hong or swan (Brahma) and the beak of a garuda (Vishnu). His position atop the winged beast is thought to symbolize the omnipotence of Buddhism over Hinduism. In other variations of the theme, Buddha may ride on the back of a garuda with a human face who flies on broad wings and has a miter signifying his role as Vishnu's mount. In his human hands, the garuda holds two lotuses which serve as platforms for two attendants similar to those in the previously described figure. The flying beast may also resemble a winged lion with a hawk-like head.

Another creation of the stone carvers are the large Dhammachakra or Wheels of the Law. The chakra is an old Hindu device, a disk symbolizing the sun. To Buddhists, the wheels represent the Doctrine of Buddha and of

Below: Stucco heads found at Chula Pathon Chedi in Nakhon Pathom. The 8th century pieces are of Siva (on left) and other deities. (Bangkok National Museum)

his first sermon at the town of Sarnath. They were given great importance in Buddhist iconography during the reign of Asoka, the 3rd century B.C. Indian emperor reputed to have sent missionaries to introduce Buddhism to Suwannabhumi, a land to the east of India which some scholars have interpreted to mean Thailand. The stone wheels were set atop tall pillars so that even from a great distance the Buddhist faithful would have a constant reminder of their Teacher's precepts. In Thailand, it is usually accompanied by deer curled up before it listening, a stylistic device recalling Sarnath's Deer Park where the sermon was delivered.

Large free-standing terracotta statuary was attempted by some Dvaravati artists but was abandoned because it was too difficult to mold the material into large figures. The most extensive terracotta remains are from Ku Bua south of Ratchaburi.

Dvaravati stone bas reliefs, only a few of which have been found, depict religious figures but they are softer, more natural than the stone Buddha images, probably because the brittle stone was easier to work in two than in three dimensions. Bas reliefs have also been found on bai sema at Muang Fat Det near Kalasin in the Northeast, and in Ratchaburi. Several of the reliefs at the latter site have been rendered in stucco and depict mythical figures, personalities from the Tosachat and apsaras.

Dvaravati stucco reliefs on the chedi of the Chula Pathon Chedi in Nakhon Pathom are devoted to episodes from the Tosachat. Eighteen 80 cm. high panels line each side of the base, a total of 72 panels. Highly imaginative, the artists have also included Boddhisattas, elephants, lions, garudas and strange figures like elephant-headed birds and lion-headed men. Those at Kok Mai Den depict similar whimsical figures.

Two other motifs are worth noting. Dvaravati sculptors were the first in Southeast Asia to carve figures of a meditating Buddha with the protective coils of the naga king Muchalinda raising him above the floodwaters and spreading the hoods of his seven heads to shield him from the lashing rain. The pose recalls an event in the fifth of the seven weeks during which Buddha meditated after reaching Enlightenment. In this instance, he sat at the edge of Lake Muchalinda in deep meditation oblivious to a heavy rainstorm and the rapidly-rising lake. The motif was destined to become a favorite subject for carvers throughout the region, especially among Khmer sculptors during the Angkor Wat and Bayon periods. Similarly, the Buddha meditating under the Bodhi tree was a favorite subject for Dvaravati carvers of stone reliefs.

Votive tablets are among the finest productions of this very prolific school. They are divided into two groups: early and late. The earliest, dating from the 4th to 7th centuries, depict the miracle at Savatthi when Buddha confounded the heretics. A few words in Pali written in the Khmer script identify the scene. The images, of high quality and durability, were found in the Phra Pathom Chedi. Votive tablets from later in the period were oval, square or in the shape of a lotus bud.

Left: *Stucco relief of deities from Chula Pathon Chedi Pathom and dating from the mid-7th century. (U Thong National Museum)*
Below: *Lion bracket of terracotta 35 cm. tall dating from the 8th century and found at Ku Bua. (Bangkok National Museum)*
Bottom: *Stucco Yaksa, 31.5 cm. tall dating from the 9th century and found in Nakhou Pathom. (Bangkok National Museum)*

Srivijaya

Previous pages: *Sun-dried clay votive tablets, 9 cm. tall depicting Avalokitesvaras with four and ten arms and a Standing Buddha. They date from the 8th-9th centuries and were found in Trang Province in Thailand's south. (Bangkok National Museum)*

Opposite: *The Buddha of Grahi is one of the Srivijayan period's most notable images. Found at Wat Wieng, Chaiya. (Bangkok National Museum)*
Above: *A sandstone Avalokitesvara, 1.15 m. tall found at Chaiya and dating from the 8th century. Many early stone pieces were decorated with real jewelry. (Bangkok National Museum)*

In the 7th century, the southern peninsula of Thailand was overrun by a new set of invaders, these less benign than the Indians of previous centuries. The drive for hegemony over the southern seas came from powerful new kingdoms emerging in Central Java. Though thoroughly Hinduized like the rest of Southeast Asia, these new people had created a culture distinct from that of their Indian predecessors. Their energy soon bubbled over and, gripped by a zeal for expansion, they fanned out north and south of the equator, establishing a new realm named Srivijaya.

Srivijaya was the dominant force in the region between the 8th and 13th centuries. While historians know the type of culture the term "Srivijaya" describes, they are in disagreement over the nature and compass of the Srivijayan empire. The T'ang annals of China note that in Srivijaya, a man cast no shadow at noon on the vernal and autumnal equinoxes. Various locations for this shadowless spot have been posited ranging from Maura Takus on the west coast of Kalimantan (Borneo) to Palembang in southeast Sumatra to Chaiya in southern Thailand, the latter being the cultural center of Thailand's South from the 5th to the 12th centuries. Other theories suggest that over the five centuries of its existence, its capital may have been shifted several times for economic or strategic reasons.

Srivijaya's monarchs were related by marriage to the Sailendra ruling house of central Java. Long before the island's conversion to Islam, a process completed by the 14th century, Java practiced Hinduism and Mahayana Buddhism, and it was the latter school they brought to Thailand. A number of Srivijayan kings were patrons of the Mahayana Buddhist University at Nalanda in northeast India, adding yet another dimension to Srivijayan art.

In the 10th century, Srivijaya became embroiled in a series of ruinous wars with the Cholas of southern India that drained it of much of its energy and drive. It continued to hold sway in the Peninsula, due primarily to the lack of any strong rival to challenge it, but by the 13th century had effectively faded from the political scene.

Srivijaya marks a high point in Thailand's artistic development. The period's artists are responsible for some of the finest stone sculpture ever produced in the country and for reaching new heights in bronze casting,

78

Below: *Perhaps the most famous of Srivijayan images is this bronze Avalokitesvara. Found at Wat Phra Mahathat, Chaiya, the 70 cm. tall image dates from the 8th-9th centuries. (Bangkok National Museum)*
Right: *A bronze Avalokitesvara, 65 cm. tall found at Chaiya and dating from the 9th-10th centuries. (Bangkok National Museum)*

especially in creating large pieces. Srivijayan was an enduring art as well; though the empire disappeared as a political entity in the 13th century, its schools of art and their highly evolved styles continued to thrive until the beginning of the present century.

It is a period that defies easy categorization. Art historians have been stymied in their efforts to formulate crisp definitions that cover the entire body of work. Srivijaya's geographical position as a trade crossroads meant that those new styles, which hadn't passed through the filter of Javan or peninsular aesthetics, were constantly being introduced from outside. Moreover, the Peninsula's many schools flourished independently and in widely separated locations having little contact with each other.

In the 6th and 7th centuries, before Srivijayan monarchs had consolidated their hold on the region, the art is characterized by close contact with northern and southern schools of Indian art with their own distinct and often varying iconography. Concomitant with it was the deepest penetration Dvaravati styles ever made in the South. The Dvaravati presence can be seen in several images bearing its particular iconography and in a number of stone Wheels of Law, items the Srivijayan culture never produced and which were probably imported.

In the 8th and 9th centuries, the major Indian influence came from the Pala school of northern India, a style which would also be evident in Early Chiengsaen (13th century) art of the Lanna kingdoms of the far north of Thailand though having arrived there via Burma. During the same period, the few Buddha and Boddhisatva images the Srivijayan artists produced were inspired by the art of central Java. In the 9th and 10th centuries, traces of Cham styles from southern Vietnam and eastern Kampuchea can be discerned. With this multiplicity of infusions it is difficult to define precisely what the term "Srivijayan" denotes and whether the term can be applied with accuracy to the creative productions of Thailand's South. It has even been suggested that the period be called "The Arts of Southern Thailand between the 7th and 13th Centuries".

Architecture

Little survives from this period, and what does has been restored numerous times over the centuries. The best-known structure is the Phra Mahathat stupa at Chaiya. Built in central Javanese style with brick and vegetable mortar, it dates from the 9th and 10th centuries but has been restored several times, most recently in 1901 and 1930. The monument stands on a square foundation and has a wide porch rimmed by small stupas. Four square tiers ascend in decreasing size with small stupas on the corners and plaques in the middle of each tier which give the effect of a gentle tapering to the spire finial. Badly ruined but still providing hints of its former grandeur is Wat Kaew, also at Chaiya. Built in Javanese cruciform shape, its upper portions suggest a Cham tower.

The original stupa of Wat Mahathat in Nakhon Si Thammarat, one of the most important Srivijayan cities, has, like the Dvaravati stupa at

Below: *Wat Kaew in Chaiya is one of the few known Srivijayan buildings. The brick structure is built in cruciform Javanese shape but its upper section resembles a Cham tower.*
Bottom: *The Sri Lankan-style stupa of Wat Mahathat in Nakhon Si Thammarat is thought to encase an earlier Srivijayan stupa. The large stupa dates from the 12th century.*

Below: A 21.5 cm. four-armed bronze Avalokitesvara created in the 9th century. (Wat Phra Mahathat Museum, Chaiya)

Nakhon Pathom, been encased in a later, larger Sri Lankan style structure. A small stupa at one corner is thought to be a model of the original. The stupa dates from about the 12th century, just before the peninsular people converted from Mahayana to Theravada Buddhism.

Sculpture

Carvers of stone Hindu and Buddhist images reached heights of perfection not since equaled except in Si Thep. Bronze craftsmen produced Buddhist images, principally Boddhisatva Avalokitesvaras of flawless beauty that stand as the finest examples of the art in Southeast Asia.

The main activity was concentrated between the 8th and 10th centuries. Between the 10th and 12th centuries there was a hiatus brought about by the necessity to devote resources to the wars with the Cholas. Activity resumes in the 12th and 13th centuries but with less intensity and in more widely separated locations. It is then that the outlying areas take up the Srivijayan mantle, carrying on the tradition long after the impetus that had inspired its original artists had been exhausted.

Srivijayan sculpture can generally be characterized by its lightness and grace, its full-bodied execution, sinuosity and the smoothness of its finish. One can feel confident strength flowing from its figures, especially its stone depictions of the Hindu deity Vishnu, whose portrayal occupied the attention of early Srivijayan sculptors.

The deities are depicted in three dimensions with all surfaces carved. While sandstone permitted the sculptors greater latitude than the brittle limestone used by Dvaravati carvers, compensations had to be made for its weakness. Vishnus were carved with very sturdy legs and solid feet, with a gathering of pleats falling from the waist to the statue's base to anchor it and with a club and a globe on a stand on either side to form a fourth and fifth support. Their fears about the stone's ability to support itself were, alas, justified. Despite the elaborate propping, most statues have been found snapped off at the ankles.

The Vishnus have narrow waists and broad shoulders with their four arms separated where they enter the shoulders. The hands hold various objects associated with Vishnu (vajra, lotus, conch, rosary and others) and have been carved without any props, again an act of rashness by Srivijayan carvers as time has robbed the statues of all their arms. The images wear tranquil expressions with full cheeks, gently curving eyebrows and finely sculpted lips. The miter, which is the principal identifying mark of a Vishnu, is generally cylindrical and smooth, lacking decoration of any sort. The neck is natural-looking and often displays an Adam's apple.

No images of Brahma have been found and Siva images are only slightly less rare. Depictions of Siva are confined to faces carved on linga, a symbol of potency in Brahmanic iconography. Almost all Hindu images are carved from stone. Bronze was reserved for Buddhist figures.

The Boddhisatva Avalokitesvara was the most popular Buddhist subject among peninsular sculptors during Thailand's Mahayana Buddhist

Left: *Standing bronze Avalokitesvara, 34 cm. tall and dating from the 8th-9th centuries. Found at Betong in Yala. (Wat Matchimawat Museum, Songkhla)*
Below: *Stone Buddha head, 29 cm. tall, a superb piece carved in the 8th-9th centuries. (National Museum Nakhon Si Thammarat).*

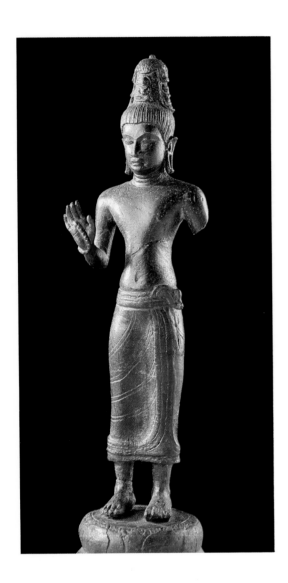

Below: *Standing bronze Siva, 35 cm. from Sating Phra. (Wat Matchimawat Museum, Songkhla)*

phase. In the Srivijaya period, they far outnumbered images of other Boddhisatvas and of the Buddha himself. A sandstone Avalokitesvara found at Wieng Sa south of Chaiya and dated in the mid-7th century is the earliest known in Southeast Asia. It is in the Gupta tradition of the Sarnath school of northern India and was probably imported. A triple-flexioned body common to all Srivijayan Vishnus and Avalokitesvaras is covered by a sarong tied at the waist by a cord. Such images were variously depicted with an antelope skin draped over the left shoulder or a tiger skin tied at the waist, the latter affectation a symbol of Avalokitesvara found only in peninsular Thailand and Indonesia.

It is in the bronze images, notably two famous statues from Chaiya, that the Avalokitesvara is portrayed in its supreme beauty. The Buddha-to-be stands either upright or in the hipshot triple-flexion stance. The upper torso is highly decorated with strands of jewelry and with the antelope and/or tiger skin noted above. His hair is tied in a chignon (Jatamukuta) and is heavily ornamented. The face is distinguished by full cheeks and finely-crafted eyes in which deepset pupils remain dark regardless of how the statue is lit, giving the image a very natural look. The full molding of the torso and the sheen given the slightly pitted skin by the use of bronze makes these statues some of Asia's most compellingly beautiful art.

While nearly all stone Hindu and bronze Boddhisatva Avalokitesvara figures are in a standing position, there are only a few stone standing Buddha images until very late in the period. The Buddhas sit in the vajrasena position, a trait they share with Lanna and other period images. The torso is often tilted back, a stylistic innovation not found elsewhere and one for which there is no explanation. Whereas the most common hand gesture in Dvaravati Buddhist sculpture is the vitarka mudra (teaching), the most frequently favored by Srivijayan artists is the bhumisparsa mudra to depict the Buddha in Maravijaya. The Buddha heads display unique stylistic features as well. The ushnisha is more pronounced than in Dvaravati art.

The latter part of the Srivijayan period following the lull in artistic creativity saw less activity, and its representative examples are easier to classify because there is more homogeneity in their features. Several new elements, perhaps inspired by Khmer art, are evident. The ushnisha of many images is more spherical. Moreover, it is smooth, lacking the tight curls normally found on Buddha heads. The robe end is not held in the left hand but falls over the left shoulder in a flat pleated mat that terminates at the chest. The robe is fastened at the waist by a buckle cinching pleats that fall down the front of the statue to the feet like those of the Vishnu images.

One of the best-known and certainly most endearing Buddha images is a bronze Buddha in the posture of Maravijaya or "Victory over Mara". Its inscription reads "1183", a date which experts dispute, feeling it was probably cast a century later in 1291. The Buddha is protected by a canopy formed by the naga king Muchalinda. The naga motif, a Dvaravati pose, was copied by Khmer artists but the Maravijaya attitude rare in

Thailand's art was never used by the Khmers.

An interesting convention found in Mahayana but not Theravada Buddhism was the portrayal of Buddhist goddesses, a Pala influence from northeastern India. The goddess Chunda, an emanation of Vajrasattva (Buddha with the Thunderbolt), a late Mahayana Buddhist concept, sits on a base backed by an aureole. The lower pair of her four arms are in her lap in the position of meditation. The upper two hold what might be a beaded rosary and a book. She is dressed in a long dress with floral patterns and wears a coronet on her brow. The goddess Tara is depicted with the same style of dress and ornamentation as the Chunda but her hands display different gestures. The lower left rests in her lap while the lower right signs the varada mudra (charity). The upper pair of arms hold objects whose identity has been obscured by deterioration.

While Srivijaya undoubtedly produced ceramic objects, few have been turned up by excavator's picks and these have not yet been thoroughly studied by art historians.

Votive tablets have been found in abundance. Made of unbaked clay and depicting Mahayana Buddhist themes, they are round or oval and bear inscriptions in Sanskrit. They show Buddha or the Boddhisatvas (especially the Avalokitesvara) in various attitudes.

The School of Nakhon Si Thammarat

There is some question of whether a separate school should be designated for the wealth of art from Nakhon Si Thammarat or whether it belongs to the main body of Srivijayan work. The objects date from the latter part of the period and share certain stylistic elements not found in other Srivijayan art objects.

The school is responsible for producing the region's first Vishnu image, a 5th century statue depicting the deity holding a conch shell on his hip. Its main importance, however, is that it is tied to the rise of Nakhon Si Thammarat as a major political center.

The most famous image claimed by this school is a Phra Buddha Sihing, a 16th century creation that was the most revered image in Nakhon Si Thammarat and peninsular Thailand. Not to be confused with the Phra Buddha Sihing made in Kamphaeng Phet in the 15th century and now in the Buddhaisawan Chapel of Bangkok's National Museum, it bears a resemblance to images of the Lanna period with its broad face, parrot's beak-like nose, and a curl-covered ushnisha topped by a smooth, conical ornament. The image sits in the Maravijaya attitude with the legs in the vajrasena or soles upward position. The right shoulder is bare and the left is graced by a heavily-pleated flap, so unusual that the Thais have given this genre of images a special name: Khanom Thom.

Below: *The Phra Buddha Sihing of Nakhon Si Thammarat. The 16th-century statue is the supreme example of the genre of images called "Khanom Thom". (Chapel of the City Hall in Nakhon Si Thammarat)*

Lop Buri

The term "Lop Buri" describes a school of art that was active in the central and northeastern regions of Thailand between the 10th and 14th centuries A.D. Named for the central Chao Phya River Valley town where its sculptures were first discovered, it coincides with the brilliant schools of Kampuchean art that created the architectural wonders of the Baphuon, Angkor Wat, Angkor Thom and the Bayon and countless superb stone statues and bas reliefs. As the Khmer empire expanded westward, its art styles would have such a profound impact on Thailand's art that in many instances it is difficult to know which works were executed by Khmers and which were created by Central Valley artists hewing to Khmer-defined modes.

To understand the Lop Buri period, it is necessary to consider its antecedents: the period of Khmer art known as pre-Angkorian (7th-10th centuries A.D.) when many Khmer temples and monuments were erected in Thailand's northeastern region. The Chao Phya Valley, under the cultural domination of Dvaravati, did not feel the impact of Khmer art styles until the 11th century. One exception is the town of Si Thep, which seems to have absorbed (or in its own development closely paralleled) Khmer concepts from an early date.

While architecture of the Northeast and the Central Valley were clearly constructed according to Khmer concepts, by the 13th century when the Khmer empire was on the wane, Central Valley sculptors were beginning to create their own aesthetics. Except for this late period, however, the term "Lop Buri" must include art (a) brought into Thailand from Kampuchea, (b) created in Thailand by Khmer artists, and (c) created in Thailand by local artists either as original works or as copies of Khmer pieces.

Si Thep

Si Thep, an early kingdom near Phetchabun, pre dates the Lop Buri period and, in its later efforts, is an adjunct to Khmer art. Though located at the farthest extremities of the Khmer empire, it produced art as early as the 7th century which bears more resemblance to pre-Angkorian art than to contemporary Dvaravati art.

The town of Si Thep appears to have had a two-part history, having

Previous Pages: *Courtyard of Prasat Hin Phimai, with the barred windows typical of later Khmer architecture.*
Opposite: *The stone prang of Prasat Hin Phimai dating from the period of the Baphuon style in Khmer art. It was converted to a Buddhist sanctuary in the 13th century.*
Below: *Brick chedi on a laterite base recently cleared of jungle vegetation at Si Thep.*

Below: *Stone standing Vishnu from Si Thep, 96 cm. tall dating from the 8th century. The deity wears a tall, smooth miter and stands in the triple-flexion stance. (Bangkok National Museum)*

been ruled by Mon princes between the 6th and 7th centuries and then having fallen to the Khmers from the 10th to the 12th centuries. Its principal art dates from the early period; in the latter centuries, it lost much of its vigor and came to parallel closely the aesthetic ideals propounded by the Khmers.

Its history is reflected in its architecture. An inner city constructed by Dvaravati architects contained numerous temples, most of which have fallen into ruin. An outer city surrounded the inner city on all four sides and was the work of Khmer planners. It measured four kilometers by 1.5 kilometers making it one of the largest ancient cities in Thailand. Like all Khmer cities, it was encircled by a wall and a moat and contained temples built in the mode of Mount Meru ringed by the primordial ocean. Excavation still underway has revealed more than 25 monuments, including three in the inner city and a colossal structure in the outer city which may have been 150 meters long, 80 meters wide and 50 meters high.

Despite its short history, Si Thep produced superb art. The most striking images are those of Vishnu which date from the 8th century. Rendered life-sized, they display a fluidity and boldness that make them some of the finest sculptures ever created in Southeast Asia. Carved of sandstone, the lithe, boy-like figures covered by the briefest of loincloths seem to lounge as they stand in the triple-flexion stance. This ability to give life to hard stone is most evident in the treatment of the heads. The face is slightly effeminate, almost pouting. Beneath a smooth miter, the hair often falls in soft ringlets over the nape of the neck, a stylistic idea shared with similar pre-Angkorian works from other areas in the region.

What is most remarkable is the sculptors' supreme confidence (misplaced as it turned out) in the strength of the stone. They seem to have ignored the stone's intrinsic weaknesses, determining that it would have to follow their inspiration rather than the other way around. This overweening confidence is seen in the carving of the god's two pairs of arms which, unlike Srivijayan statues, were joined before entering the shoulder. In a moment of rashness, one sculptor has even carved an uplifted arm, trusting implicity in the stone's ability to support itself. As a result, of course, none of the statues today has arms, all having long ago broken off under their own weight. The loss, however, in no way detracts from one's appreciation of their creators' brilliance.

Si Thep sculptors are also credited with carving Buddha images, but not in the numbers of the Hindu images. Only one has been found. It sits in the position of samadhi (meditation) but is headless and its body is broken into two parts. Similarly, the lower half of a stone Wheel of the Law in the Dvaravati fashion has been discovered in the inner city of Si Thep, another tribute to the wealth of artistic activity of a high level that flowered in a remote area far from the centers of learning but which was their equal in imagination and skill.

Lop Buri

To understand the design and symbolism of Khmer monuments in Thailand, of Lop Buri (and early Sukhothai and much of Ayutthaya) architecture and, in part, Lop Buri sculpture, one must study their Khmer antecedents. Pre-Angkorian history begins some time in the 8th century after dissension between the northern and southern peoples of Funan in western Kampuchea led to civil war. The highlanders from the Dongrek Mountains prevailed over the plains people, establishing the Khmer empire and laying the foundation stone of what was to become a grand network of buildings that lay between the Mekong River and the Tonle Sap and would eventually reach beyond the Chao Phya River.

The growth from a kingdom to an empire begins with Jayavarman II (802-850 A.D.). During his reign, the principal religion was Hinduism and its major deity was a fusion of two gods, Vishnu and Siva, the so-called Harihara. The period of monument building begins with Suriyavarman I (1002-1050 A.D.), the prime mover behind the Baphuon. This period corresponds with the construction of the main Khmer monuments in Thailand, notably Prasat Hin Non Ku and Prasat Phanom Wan in Nakhon Ratchasima province, Prasat Thamuen Thom (Surin), Prasat Muang Tham (Buri Ram) and the beginnings of Prasat Phanom Rung (Buri Ram).

Suriyavarman II (1113-1150 A.D.) was the builder of Angkor Wat. In his reign, the major temples were dedicated to Siva but in the 12th century Siva was replaced by Vishnu. For some time missionaries had been propagating Mahayana Buddhism in Kampuchea. So successful were they that by the late 12th century, Hinduism had been supplanted by the religion of the Great Teacher. It is during this period that the last and greatest of the Khmer monument builders, Jayavarman VII (1181-1218 A.D.) ruled. He built Angkor Thom with its incomparable Bayon and dozens of other buildings, and adapted many older Hindu structures, including Phimai, to accord with the tenets of Buddhism.

The architects of Khmer temples conceived of Angkor and others as complexes of earthly abodes for the deities. These magnificent edifices were built of stone, laterite or brick in the belief that only the deities were entitled to permanent homes; kings and ordinary mortals lived in wooden palaces and houses, a practice followed in Thailand until the 17th century.

The principal concept which found its way into Thailand's architecture was the central tower or prang representing Mount Meru, the realm of the Hindu deities. Buddhists adopted this structure to symbolize the 33 stages of perfection, the topmost being Nibhan (Nirvana). The prang gained paramount importance as the center of Buddhist wats during most of the Ayutthaya period.

Architecture

Thailand's northeastern region is dotted with dozens of prangs or piles of laterite which are mute testimony to the extent that Khmer

Below: *A female deity thought to be Uma. The 69 cm. tall sandstone image is in the Baphuon style of the 11th century. Found at Prasat Phanom Rung, Buri Ram. (Bangkok National Museum)*

Below: *Phra Prang Sam Yot in Lop Buri town likely sheltered images of Avalokitesvara, Buddha and Prajnaparamita. Built in the late Bayon style, it has been attributed to Jayavarman VII, the last great king of Angkor.*
Bottom: *The antechamber of the central prang of the 11th century Prasat Hin Phimai, the most famous of the Khmer temples in Thailand.*

Opposite: *The sanctuary of Prasat Phanom Wan, a 10th century Khmer Hindu temple later converted to a Buddhist structure. The Buddha images are from a later date.*

concepts dominated the cultural life of Thailand at the height of its influence. In truth, it would not be remiss to call all architecture of the period "Khmer" and leave the term "Lop Buri" to describe the sculpture of the Central Valley between the 11th and 13th centuries.

Many of the earliest monuments pre date Angkor but are little more than shells, their main structures having collapsed or having been augmented by later additions. The most enduring elements of the pre-Angkorian period temples are the stone lintels which once decorated them. One of the earliest is a low-relief stone lintel from Wat Tongtua in the southeastern Thailand town of Chanthaburi. Similar in style to the Thala Borivat lintels of the early 7th century Khmer kingdom of Chenla, it depicts a makara disgorging an arch decorated with a creature that is half-bird, half-dwarf; an early form of the garuda. Two late 7th century lintels provide similar indications of the high sophistication of pre-Angkorian carving and temple construction. From Prasat Phumpon in Surin province and Prasat Ban Noi in Prachin Buri province, they include finely carved floral patterns surrounding mythical animals like the hong.

One of the most complete pre-Angkorian structures is the late 8th century Hindu temple, the Phra Prang Khaek in Lop Buri itself. In the pure Lopburi Phra Prang Sam Yot, three brick prangs thrust skyward with stone door frames carved to replicate wooden frames. The prangs are beautified by stucco decorations and numerous redents which are somewhat of a departure from the pure Khmer style.

Corresponding to the Baphuon style of the late 10th and 11th centuries are five Khmer temple complexes located in the Northeast of Thailand. One of the most important is Prasat Phanom Wan, a 10th century Hindu temple later converted to serve as a Buddhist wat. Four symmetrical entrances lead to a rectangular courtyard dominated by a central prang and ringed by four older prangs. The central prang has four doorways, one of which is connected to an antechamber. The windows of the latter structure have the turned bars typical of Khmer structures as well as several false windows. Most of the beautifully-carved stone lintels have been removed to Phimai or to museums elsewhere, but one remains: that above the northern entrance to the main sanctuary. The wat also contains a number of fine Buddha images added at a later date. Two other fine examples of Baphuon-style temples from this era are Prasat Hin Non Ku (Nakhon Ratchasima province) with fine lintels dating from the mid-10th century, and Prasat Thamuen Thom in Surin province.

Prasat Muang Tham in Buri Ram province is perhaps the best complete example of Hindu architectural symbolism. At its center is a brick prang (now collapsed) surrounded by four smaller brick prangs and bounded by a sandstone wall with elaborately carved doorways. Beyond them at the four corners are four L-shaped ponds surrounded by a beautiful stone balustrade which terminates at their corners in a cluster of carved nagas. The Prasat Muang Tham is especially rich in stonework, the beautifully carved stone mullions on the four windows flanking the

Below: *The central sanctuary of Prasat Phamon Rung, begun in the 10th century and never completed. The stone sanctuary was complemented by the mondop to the right facing the main entrance.*

northern and southern entrances, the stone reliefs on the minor prangs, the various door lintels and entranceway carvings being the most noteworthy.

Contemporary with Prasat Muang Tham, is Prasat Phanom Rung (Phanom or Phnom means "hill" as in "Phnom Penh") which sits on the southern flank of a picturesque little hill in Buri Ram province along the road that once led from Angkor to Phimai. The complex, never completed, was built in several stages beginning with three brick prangs dating from early in the 10th century and a small square prang with offsets built late in the 10th century. The final building, the main sanctuary, was added in the 11th century.

A broad esplanade built by Jayavarman VII is 200 meters long and 12 meters wide. Its outer edges are marked at four-meter intervals by sandstone posts tied together by low walls. It climbs to a cruciform terrace whose balustrade is comprised of nagas. This naga motif continues up a series of short stairways broken by landings and arrives at an antechamber which forms the entrance to a central courtyard holding the main sanctuary. A phra rabieng surrounds the courtyard.

Like the stairway and terraces, the main sanctuary is set along an east-west axis. It comprises a small mondop which faces the courtyard doorway and is connected by a short passageway to the main structure, a tall prang set on a square base just behind it to the west. Antechambers on each side lead to a vaulted interior which holds the principal image. Recently restored, the Prasat Phanom Rung is a fine example of the Khmer genius for utilizing a hill location to its fullest potential.

One of the finest examples of early Angkorian art is Prasat Hin Phimai. Dating from early in the 12th century, it was built of sandstone in the style of Angkor Wat but was later modified to serve as a Mahayana Buddhist sanctuary. The complex sits in a large rectangle that once contained a small town and was surrounded on four sides by the Mun River, two natural canals and one man-made canal, making it an island. The complex itself comprises an outer wall encompassing a wide courtyard containing four ponds. Within this is an inner wall enclosing the central prang which once held the main Buddha image.

The outer wall is broken on the south by the Pratu Chai (Victory Gate) which faces Angkor Wat. Just before the gateway is the Khlang Ngoen (Treasury) which probably served as the resthouse for important pilgrims. Once through the Pratu Chai, one encounters a raised pathway that leads past the now dry ponds and a pair of pavilions added by Jayavarman VII to serve as royal resthouses. Inside the inner courtyard is the Prang Bhromathat which formerly held a statue of Jayavarman VII, who converted Phimai to a Buddhist structure in the 12th or 13th century. The statue, one of several that Jayavarman VII placed in important cities in the far corners of his empire, marks the first time in Southeast Asia that a portrait of a human being was sculpted. Only four remain, one of them in Bangkok's National Museum.

The central sanctuary pre dates the construction of Angkor. It is cruciform and despite its small size gives the impression of majesty. Its entrance door is one of four and, like them, features five-headed nagas on the pediments. The lintels on the interior of the building are beautifully carved depictions of events in Buddha's life and of Tantric deities. On the exterior walls are scenes from the Ramakien. The main chamber which once contained the principal Buddha image rises in a cone and is capped by a stone lotus bud. Contemporary with the conversion of Phimai were Ta Pha Daeng in Sukhothai and Prasat Ban Ra-ngaeng in Surin province.

The final era of Khmer architecture, the Bayon period, corresponds to the reign of Jayavarman VII, who is credited with converting a number of other Hindu structures for use by Mahayana Buddhists.

Inscriptions at Angkor note that in 1191, Jayavarman VII consecrated a temple at Phra Khan in the vicinity of Angkor and caused 23 statues of Buddha to be carved and placed in various temples in the realm. Two were taken to Sukhothai and Phimai and a third was put in Lop Buri. It is thought that the Phra Prang Sam Yot was built to house it.

Late Bayon period votive tablets suggest that Jayavarman VII may also have built the Mahayana Buddhist Phra Prang Sam Yot to honor his dead parents or a deceased teacher. As such, it would have held three images. The south tower would have held Avalokitesvara, the middle Buddha/Jayavarman VII and the north tower the statue of Prajnaparamita. The structure is unusual in that the walls are not highly decorated, and of the decorations, two of the motifs cannot be identified as Khmer, further evidence that its designers were local residents who were incorporating the best of Khmer and Burmese Mon traditions.

Even more puzzling is Wat Phra Si Ratana Mahathat in Lop Buri. The wat is usually identified as a Khmer structure because of its basic shape but there have been suggestions that it dates from the 13th century and by its Thai structural and decorative elements, especially in the prang, might better be classed as the first authentic Thai prang. The plan for the prang is duplicated by Ayutthaya's oldest prang, that of Wat Buddha-isawan built in 1353.

On Wat Phra Si Ratana Mahathat's southern terrace is an ancient lintel which might have come from an older shrine, the ruins of which can be seen to the west of the wat. As for the rest of the stucco decoration, the one of the basement appears to be original but that on the pediments appears to date from the late 15th century. Again, there are Burmese Mon elements in the floral decoration on the northwest corner. The north and south wings are built of brick and may be later additions. Other interesting features are the mondops on the north and south wings which contain images of Buddha sitting in the attitude of victory over Mara. Notable Lop Buri structures are the prang at Wat Kampaeng Laeng in Phetchaburi, the wall which surrounds Ratchaburi's Wat Phra Si Ratana Mahathat, Wat Phra Phai Luang in Sukhothai and, the westernmost evidence of Khmer expansion, the Prasat Muang Singh in Kanchanaburi province which contains many statues made by local artists.

Below: *The Prasat Muang Tham, a Khmer edifice, dates from the Angkorian period of Khmer art in the 10th and 11th centuries. A cluster of nagas ring the inner ponds that form the primordial ocean.*
Bottom: *Wat Kamphaeng Laeng in Phetchaburi, built of laterite in the early 13th century, marks the southernmost expansion of the Khmer empire.*

Sculpture

While the architecture of the Northeast from the 7th to the 13th centuries is virtually indistinguishable from the monuments built by Khmer architects, the sculpture of the Lop Buri school has a flavor all its own. Lop Buri's location on the outer rim of the Khmer empire contributed to its artists' sense of independence while the pervasive influences of Mon sculpture, with which much of the period was contemporaneous, gave a unique stamp to its art. Another important factor was Lop Buri's long-standing reputation as a thriving religious center, at first professing Mahayana Buddhism and later Theravada Buddhism. Thus, while Hindu deities provided the key subjects for early Angkorian sculptors, it was the Buddha and Boddhisatvas which were the principal subjects of Lop Buri art.

Some Khmer influences found their way into Lop Buri sculpture. The solidity and gravity of Angkorian architecture can be seen in its sculpture as well. Even when the figures are slender, they have a weight quite distinct from the Srivijayan lightness and more closely akin to the Mon sculptures. The most pronounced features are the diadems and the cones of the ushnishas. The forehead of the Buddha image is generally separated from the tight curls of the head by a thin band. The Khmer fondness for incorporating tiny flames into the diadems, necklaces and screens that back the images is another distinguishing characteristic. The flames in the diadems of some 13th and 14th century Buddhas are even more prominent, resembling a fire licking at the hair. On Hindu sculpture, Khmer artists were wont to place pockets on the left sides of the sarongs and folds which resemble curved knives on the right sides. Yet another characteristic feature are the sarong hems which have been likened to the tail of a fish. Often, several of these are placed one above the other, a stylistic convention which prevailed into Ayutthayan times notably in the studios of Kamphaeng Phet.

The Khmer influences in sculpture proved to be ephemeral. With the waning of Khmer power in the 13th century, many of these distinguishing characteristics of Khmer sculpture died due perhaps to a rejection of Khmer values forcefully imposed during the 10th to 12th centuries when Angkorian civilization was at its height.

Lop Buri sculpture is generally divided into two periods:

10th-12th centuries:

Angkorian: Coerced by the Khmers to produce in an officially recognized style, Dvaravati-trained artists created works that lack the vitality of the Dvaravati sculptures themselves.

13th-14th centuries:

Late Lop Buri: Having regained their independence, Lop Buri artisans moved sharply away from the Khmer modes to create an individual art that recalls the Angkorian period but is unique.

Opposite: *Detail of a meditating Buddha seated under Muchalinda. The 1.85 meter stone image dates from the 12th century and was found at Wat Na Phramane in Ayutthaya. (Bangkok National Museum)*
Below: *A crowned Buddha in bronze, dating from the late Lop Buri period of the 13th century. (Chao Sam Phraya National Museum, Ayutthaya)*

Above: *The earliest known stone Khmer lintel dates from the early 7th century and was found at Wat Tongtua in Chanthaburi. The 84-cm. x 63-cm. slab depicts a makara from whose mouth issues an arch decorated with a plaque of a garuda clasping two nagas. (Bangkok National Museum)*

96

Below: *A stone lintel at Prasat Muang Tham dating from the 10th-11th centuries depicts Siva seated on the bull, Nandi.*
Bottom: *A stone lintel from Prasat Hin Phimai depicts a scene from the Ramakien with monkeys bearing a deity in a palanquin.*

During the pre-Angkorian period (7th-9th centuries), artists of the Central Valley were relatively far removed from the center of Khmer power and thus were able to pursue their own course, as is evidenced by the numerous Buddha images they produced while Khmer artists were still depicting Hindu deities. Most of the stone sculpture of the period has been found in the eastern regions of Thailand and is undoubtedly of Khmer origin. Among the best known pieces is a statue of the Hindu goddess Uma. Found in the area of Aranyaprathet near the present border with Kampuchea, it dates from the 7th century and is of extremely fine workmanship. The oldest Khmer lintel, already noted, dates from the same century and was found in the southeastern Thailand town of Chanthaburi.

In the Valley, Lop Buri artists preferred to work in bronze, often going to great lengths to cast monumental pieces up to 3.3 meters tall and to experiment with unusual alloys. Among the latter is a Buddha image which has been cast of a bronze with a high silver content giving it the look of oiled iron or polished tektite.

The early Lop Buri sculptors concentrated their energies on creating Mahayana Buddha images including Boddhisatva Avalokitesvaras and Maitreya Boddhisatvas. The standing Avalokitesvaras display the vitarka mudra like Mon statues. The Maitreya Boddhisatvas are also standing, some with slight flexion of their very slender bodies. Identifying marks include thin mustaches, no ornaments and very short robes bordering on skirts. The chignon is high and full and often set with strands of braided hair.

The period between the 10th and 12th centuries saw the rise to pre-eminence of the Angkorian empire and of the obdurate will that created its architectural wonders. Few decorative carvings survive from the 10th century and the 11th century is marked by absence of originality probably because the Lop Buri school's Khmer masters were dictating the proportions to be used and the subjects to be depicted. The 12th century, however, was a period of flowering when decorative sculpture attained new heights, in sharp contrast to its somewhat lackluster statuary. The lintels of the 12th century are carved in high relief, those created for Phimai being among its finest examples. These lintels are rich in detail and display a pleasing harmony in their treatment of scenes from the Ramayana and of Mahayana Buddhist themes.

A similar phenomenon is missing in the statuary of the 12th century. The proximity to Angkor dictated a style of sculpture with which the Lop Buri sculptors do not seem to have been at ease with the result that the images lack vitality. The major design idea which passed between the two cultures went from subject to master. The Buddha meditating beneath the protective hood of the seven-headed naga, which was a creation of Mon sculptors, found great popularity among Angkorian carvers, an enthusiasm that was transmitted to the Lop Buri artists who turned it into some of the period's finest sculptures.

Opposite: A crowned late-12th century bronze Buddha. The 25 cm. tall image was found at Ban Dok Rak, Kanchanaburi. (Chao Sam Phraya National Museum, Ayutthaya)
Below: A stone Buddha head from Wat Mahathat in Lop Buri dating from the 13th-14th centuries. (National Museum, Nakhon Si Thammarat)

Below: *Head of a 100 cm. tall sandstone Buddha of the late Lop Buri school, 13th-14th centuries, now rests at Wat Mahathat, Lop Buri. Right: A sandstone portrait of Jayavarman VII, 1.32 m. tall dating from the late 12th-early 13th centuries and placed around that date in Prasat Hin Phimai. (Bangkok National Museum)*

The period saw the creation of the first of the standing images of the Buddha clad in royal clothes and displaying the abhaya mudra (dispelling fear) gesture. The images are recognized by their ornate decoration, conical ushnisha and the diadem which distinguishes all works influenced by Khmer ideals of beauty.

The rise to power of Jayavarman VII marked a paradoxical nadir in the quality of art. In his zeal to build for the greater glory of Mahayana Buddhism, he decreed the construction of more buildings than there were artisans to supply them with sculptures. In the drive to complete the requisite number in the shortest possible time, quality suffered. Yet surprisingly, the stucco yaksa masks at Phra Prang Sam Yot in Lop Buri town are original, lively and of high quality. The workshops of the Northeast, far from the center of power, notably those at Phimai, produced some superb bronze works. Mounted on tall poles, the garudas are but one example of the vibrant spirit that ruled the bronze casting studios.

As Angkor declined in the 13th and 14th centuries, Lop Buri regained much of its vigor, demonstrated superbly in its creation of sandstone Buddha images. Buddha protected by a naga parasol and an innovation — Buddha without any ornamentation whatsoever and a head topped by several tiers of lotus petals — were the primary subjects of sandstone sculpture. The realms of decorative sculpture saw the development of more intricate, crisper designs, notably plant foliage.

While stone sculpture thrived, bronze statuary became more conservative. Among the creations of the period were the Buddha with naga umbrellas and screens with the flame borders and the standing Buddhas with their hands in the abhaya mudra or often the vitarka mudra gesture and with detailed belts and frontal flaps on their robes. The faces, however, are highly stylized with insipid smiles and dull eyes. Among the more successful images were the Bayon-patterned Buddhas which wear crowns with high points like American Indian feathered headdresses. They are usually backed by elaborately-decorated screens bearing Boddhisatvas and leogryphs. Other fine creations of the period are a number of votive stupas and bronze pedestals designed to support seated Buddha images.

Votive tablets were created throughout the period, but only those from later centuries are noteworthy. After the 12th century, perhaps concurrent with Jayavarman VII's new-found interest in Buddhism, they came into vogue and developed into some of the Lop Buri period's finest art. The tablets, some of them with very complex designs, reveal an excellent eye for design and symmetry and have been executed by very sure hands. Produced from metal or baked clay, they were devoted to Mahayana Buddhist themes including Buddhas of the Past and Buddha in the Maravijaya attitude with an arch and often with the Boddhisatva Avalokitesvara (symbolizing compassion) on Buddha's right and Prajnaparamita (symbolizing wisdom) on his left.

Below: *The eight-armed Boddhisatva, the so-called "Radiating Avalokitesvara" for the multitude of small images that cover its body. The 1.61 m sandstone image is in the Bayon style of the late 12th-early 13th century. Found at Prasat Muang Singh in Kanchanaburi. (Bangkok National Museum)*

Sukhothai

Previous pages: *A Buddha at Sukhothai's Wat Mahathat is reflected in a lotus pond.* Opposite: *A brick and stucco standing Buddha image at Wat Saphan Hin, Sukhothai.* Below: *The 8.00 m. tall Buddha Sri Sakyamuni bronze image was cast in the 14th century and placed in Wat Mahathat, Sukhothai. King Rama I moved it to Bangkok's Wat Suthat where it now rests.*

Since ancient times, Thailand has been a meeting point for diverse cultural traditions from the west, south, and east. Until the 10th century, however, the mountain barriers of the north discouraged all but a trickle of immigrants. In the latter part of the first millennium, the walls were breached and a new people, the Thais, a vigorous race restless with untapped energy, quietly filtered in from the area along the border with China to farm the northern valleys.

Traditional history holds that in the 13th century the Thais were driven south before the onslaught of the Mongols led by Kublai Khan, who was bent on building an empire. Judging by the number of kingdoms and principalities which held sway in the myriad valleys of the northern hills, it is more likely that the Mongol hordes merely accelerated rather than precipitated the flow. From an early date, there were two groups of kingdoms: those in the proximity of the Mekong River and those clustered at the headwaters of the Chao Phya River. Those in the northernmost sector — Chiengsaen, Chiang Rai, Chiang Mai, Phayao and, to a lesser extent, Haripunchai (Lamphun) and Lampang — are associated with what came to be called the Lanna school, though Haripunchai continued to thrive as an outpost of the Dvaravati school.

Those principalities near the headwaters of the Chao Phya River — Sukhothai and its satellite cities of Si Satchanalai, Kamphaeng Phet and Phitsanulok — grew up in the waning shadow of Angkorian greatness, biding their time until they could at last throw off the Khmer yoke and seek their own destinies. That moment came in 1238 when the ruler of Sukhothai, King Intradit, created a federation of neighboring kingdoms under one banner and founded the brief but brilliant culture named for his city-state.

History has given far more attention to the exploits of Intradit's second son, Ramkamhaeng. The young king began the grand building scheme completed by his successors which carpeted the Sukhothai plain with a wealth of beautiful architecture and created a style of Buddha image unique in the annals of art history. Ramkamhaeng came to prominence quite young after soundly defeating a rival prince of Mae Sot on the border with Burma, a land which would in the following centuries provide more than ample numbers of enemies determined to grind the Thais to dust. An

Below: *Buddha descending from Tavatimsa Heaven, the most famous of Sukhothai's stucco images, decorates the wall of Wat Trapang Thong Lang. The Buddha is accompanied by Indra and Brahma and bears traces of color suggesting it was once painted.*

inscription left by Ramkamhaeng says that in his reign, the borders of Sukhothai encompassed Luang Prabang on the Mekong River in present-day Laos, lower Burma and Malacca in Malaysia, though the hold on the outermost regions was probably tenuous at best.

It is recorded that in 1294 and 1299, Ramkamhaeng sent missions to Chinese imperial courts. About the same time, Chinese potters established the famous kilns of Sukhothai and of Sawankhalok in which Si Satchanalai is centered. Despite these close contacts with the Chinese, Sukhothai art bears no trace of Chinese styles, nor do its Buddhist images carry any of the Mahayana Buddhist iconography of the Middle Kingdom. Instead, it drew on the same wellsprings as its predecessors to the south: Sri Lanka, India and, to a lesser extent, the Khmer and Southeast Asian cultures that India had influenced.

Sukhothai faded from existence in the 15th century. Various theories have been advanced for its demise. One suggests that the river that watered it changed course, rendering it difficult to maintain a large population. Others suggest it simply lost its vigor. Its later kings were ardent Buddhists who may have devoted more time to religion and monument building than to statecraft. By 1350 Ayutthaya, a new kingdom to the south, had grown powerful. It conquered all the territories formerly ruled by Sukhothai and in 1378 reduced the city to the status of a vassal state. Finally, in 1438, it formally annexed Sukhothai, sending its own governor to rule it.

Architecture

Sukhothai is a ruined city of spires and blocks of masonry, but like many ancient monuments still fills one with a sense of awe at the grandeur and audacity of its creators in pursuing such a mammoth endeavor. At dawn, the Buddha images looming in the dark and the moats catching the silent spires etched in black against the purples and salmons of the morning sky suffuse one with a sense of wonder at how perfectly the city's creators succeeded in conveying the mystery of religion through laterite, brick and stucco. Here is the beginning of the Thai pre occupation with size in the seeming belief that large means impressive. It is all within scale, however, so that even when one turns a corner and is surprised by an enormous Buddha image smiling down, one is aware of majesty and awesome, overpowering presence, not of crushing immensity.

Sukhothai's axial alignment and the presence of several Khmer-style buildings has led many to suggest it may have originated as a Khmer city. Three earthen walls encompass a 1,400 meters by 1,600 meters rectangle that is a seeming replica of an Angkorian city with its complex cosmological symbolism. It is thought that the city's original rulers intended that Sukhothai be modeled on an Angkorian monumental city but that history caught up with them and they were expelled before they could complete the work they had begun.

Only three buildings bear the imprint of a Khmer or Lop Buri

Below and left: *Wat Si Sawai, Sukhothai, was originally a Khmer structure with three prangs, later converted into a Buddhist temple.*

architect: Wat Si Sawai and the Ta Pha Daeng Shrine in the city proper and Wat Phra Phai Luang surrounded by its own primordial ocean to the north of the city walls. The Thai architects seem to have abandoned the Khmer grand scheme and laid out their 106 buildings and monuments in a somewhat haphazard pattern, but individually the structures accord to the symbolism of the Traiphum. Though they dug the double moat which encompasses the city, the Thais eschewed the intricate Khmer system of canals and hydraulic devices, preferring to dig deep wells for their water. The spaces between the monumental buildings were filled with wooden palaces and houses as evidenced by numerous post holes found in the laterite foundations.

What is most astounding about the city is its wealth of architectural styles. Indeed, Sukhothai serves as a study in the art styles of the region. The reason can be found in the determined attempt by the builders to replicate particular buildings in other holy cities as if to enhance the sanctity of Sukhothai by concentrating the powers of many diverse sites within one precinct. Thus, one can find octagonal-based Mon monuments; chedis whose bases are supported by elephants, reminiscent of Sri Lankan chedis; and thick Khmer prangs in brick and stucco rather than stone. Sukhothai's own architects, however, were responsible for the lotus bud finials on the slender chedis which are the hallmark of Sukhothai architecture.

Sukhothai's most famous buildings were renovated in succeeding centuries altering their original design somewhat. Wat Mahathat, for example, is thought to have been restored by Sri Lankan architects in the 14th century. Others were built and rebuilt by Ayutthayan architects who respected the city's special religious significance if not its political sovereignty. The buildings which can be seen today in Sukhothai, Si Satchanalai, Kamphaeng Phet and Phitsanulok, are religious structures, Sukhothai kings having held the Khmer credo that only sacred buildings should be constructed of durable materials. None of the wooden palaces has survived but one can gain some idea of how they might have looked, by studying the palaces depicted in the stone engravings of Wat Si Chum which tell the tales of the Tosachat.

The oldest religious structure is the Ta Pha Daeng, a small Hindu shrine inside the northern wall of the city. It resembles Angkorian monuments from the reign of Suriyavarman II (1110-1175) which suggests that Sukhothai may have been a thriving town by the beginning of the 12th century. Wat Si Sawai just inside the southern wall is made up of three prangs begun in laterite by the Khmers and finished in brick and stucco by Thai architects. The vihan in front of the three prangs was probably added in the 15th century.

The most typically Khmer monument is Wat Phra Pai Luang to the north of the city. Surrounded by a large moat, it is composed of three prangs which face the rising sun. Built in the reign of Jayavarman VII (1181-1218), it held a Buddha image with the Khmer king's face and

Opposite: *A stuccoed laterite stele frames a walking Buddha at Wat Phra Si Ratana Mahathat, in Chalieng.*
Below: *Wat Phra Si Ratana Mahathat in Chalieng has a 15th century prang that may have been built over an earlier Khmer structure. Also evident are the slit Khmer-type windows of the vihan.*

Below: *Wat Suan Kaew Utayan Noi at Si Satchanalai with its lotus bud stupa and a vihan with a tall arched door.*
Bottom: *The only standing prang of the three which formerly dominated Wat Phra Pai Luang in Sukhothai. Built of laterite with traces of stucco decoration, it was erected by Khmer architects prior to the ascension to power of the Thai people.*

body, one of several carved in important towns around the Khmer empire. The bases of the small chedis in the courtyard resemble that of the chedi in Chaiya and may have been modeled on it to commemorate the extension of Ramkamhaeng's domain to include the former Srivijayan kingdoms of the far south. The most noteworthy feature of the wat is a mondop with two huge standing Buddha images which, while Khmer, have been seen as forerunners of the Sukhothai style of standing Buddhas.

The first truly Sukhothai monument is Wat Mahathat (Great Relic Wat), the city's most important religious complex. It was begun by King Intradit, Sukhothai's founder, continued by Ramkamhaeng and completed by King Lu Thai around 1345. Comprising nearly 200 chedis and the bases of 10 vihans plus numerous other structures, it is an amalgam of several styles including Srivijayan and Sri Lankan. The Sri Lankan elements are attributable to Sri Lankan architects invited by King Lu Thai to restore it.

The lotus bud finial on a tall chedi at the core of Wat Mahathat may cover an older Khmer tower. The lotus flower has powerful connotations in Buddhism, symbolizing the purity of Buddha's doctrine, but Sukhothai is the only school that employed it as a finial on a spire. The lotus bud chedi was used in several other monuments, especially those built by King Li Thai, Ramkamhaeng's grandson. It appears on towers in neighboring kingdoms and may have signified Sukhothai's suzerainty over its vassal cities. Other important wats with lotus bud chedis are Wat Trapang Ngoen (Silver Pond Wat) and Wat Om Rob in Sukhothai; Wat Chedi Chet Thaew and Wat Suan Kaew Utayan Noi in Si Satchanalai; and Wat Wang Phra That near Kamphaeng Phet. It even found its way into the Lanna kingdoms, notably at Chiang Mai's Wat Suan Dok built by King Ku Na.

The fine stucco Buddhist disciples that line the base of Wat Mahathat's central chedi and the scenes from Buddha's life on the pediments, appear to have been executed at a later date. Among the many Buddha images of Wat Mahathat is an eight meter tall brick and stucco standing image. A large bronze seated Buddha was taken to Bangkok and placed in Wat Suthat by King Rama I (1782-1809).

Across the street to the east was the royal palace which now lies in ruins. Only one artifact was salvaged from it: a stone throne known as the Manangasila on which Ramkamhaeng sat to discuss affairs of state with his counselors and on which revered monks were invited to sit when discoursing on Buddha's teachings. It was discovered by King Rama IV (1851-1868) when he visited Sukhothai in the 1840s while still a monk. He removed it to Bangkok where it served as the throne on which King Rama VI was crowned.

The elephant, another powerful Buddhist symbol, became an integral part of many Sukhothai's wats. Rendered in brick and stucco, ranks of elephants ring the bases of Wat Chedi Si Hong, Wat Chang Rob and Wat Chang Lom in Sukhothai; Wat Chedi Chang Lom in Si Satchanalai; and

Below: *Sukhothai's Wat Mahathat (lower center) demonstrates both the prang-centered concept and the axial alignment along a line connecting the rising and setting sun. Smaller chedis and other monuments holding relics are aligned according to the same axis.*

Wat Chang Rob and Wat Chang in Kamphaeng Phet. Only at Wat Chedi Chang Lom in Satchanalai are the elephants' entire bodies shown; in the rest, only the front portion appears. Lions ride the backs of elephants at Wat Chedi Si Hong, a symbol of unknown meaning.

Wat Trapang Tong Lang (Coral Tree Pond Wat) is famed for its stucco bas relief of Buddha descending from Tavatimsa Heaven after preaching to his mother. This Buddha has the broad shoulders and easy gait associated with Sukhothai statuary and is considered the finest example of the period's stucco work.

Wat Si Chum is one of the most impressive wats in Sukhothai. Its chief attraction is a 15 meter high mondop containing a brick and stucco seated Buddha of nearly equal height whose serene mien gazes through a tall slit-like door at the world outside. The walls contain a fully enclosed stairway which leads to the top of the mondop and which may be the explanation for tales of the image's having spoken with worshipers, a feat easily accomplished by someone hiding at the top of the stairs and speaking through the narrow air vents to a supplicant below. Wat Si Chum also contains the only extant examples of Sukhothai engraving. Slate slabs etched with scenes from the Chadoks line the ceiling of the stairway. It is thought they were once part of Wat Mahathat but were removed to Wat Si Chum. In the 14th century they would have been brightened by paint brushed within the etched outlines, but today nothing remains to indicate which hues were used.

Other important wats and monuments of Sukhothai are Wat Trakuan with its round, Sri Lankan-style chedi; Wat Chetupon with its tall stucco bas relief of a standing Buddha; Wat Si Pichit Kiti Kalayaram dating from the 15th century and one of the last structures built in Sukhothai; Wat Mangkon with its beautiful ceramics; Wat Chedi Sung, Phra Bhat Yai and Wat Chanasongkram.

Si Satchanalai sits at the base of a range of hill 65 kilometers north along the road that leads from the center of Sukhothai. Built by Sukhothai kings, it served as the seat of government for the Deputy King who presided over the northern section of the realm. The city's architecture was identical in style to that of Sukhothai and included some of the finest examples of the genre. Its principal monuments are on the hill itself and strung out in a line at right angles to the hill paralleling the Yom River to the east. The most important building is Wat Chedi Chet Taew. Built by King Ramkamhaeng or King Lu Thai, it is similar to Wat Mahathat with its central lotus bud spire but is surrounded by other chedis in a variety of styles and shapes. The chedis are thought to contain the ashes of the Sukhothai princes who ruled Si Satchanalai. One of the chedis displays unmistakable contours of a Srivijayan monument while others are Sri Lankan in appearance and may have been built or rebuilt by the Sri Lankan architects imported by King Lu Thai to reconstruct Sukhothai's Wat Mahathat.

Wat Chedi Chang Lom is another of a series of monuments which seem to rest on the backs of brick and stucco elephants. An early Sukhothai inscription notes that King Ramkamhaeng performed an unparalleled act by digging up a number of relics at a wat in Chalieng to the southeast. That he, an ordinary mortal, was not struck dead by the gods for his audacity was considered a sign that he was a great man with wondrous spiritual powers. After displaying the relics for one year, he encased them in a new monument, Chedi Chang Lom, in the center of Si Satchanalai, an endeavor which took six years to complete.

Wat Nang Pya to the southeast of Wat Chedi Chang Lom contains a vihan whose walls are broken by slit windows and whose entire surface is covered in superb stucco floral designs. Many scholars contend that while the wat is in Sukhothai style, the stucco decorations were added in the Ayutthayan period after Sawankhalok's name had been changed to Si Satchanalai.

Three miles southeast of Si Satchanalai is Chalieng, a town whose fortunes were closely allied with those of Si Satchanalai and which contains one of the most interesting Sukhothai-style wats: the Wat Phra Si Ratana Mahathat. Chalieng is thought to have been the principal center for administering the region during the Angkorian period under Jayavarman VII. The original structure was built atop the ruins of an old Khmer temple and was enlarged after 1474 when the rulers of Swankhalok recovered the town from the Lanna kings who had occupied it briefly.

The wat's prang is Ayutthayan in style but like Li Thai's lotus bud chedis, may have been intended as a mark of Ayutthayan rule over the city and have been an alteration of an earlier Sukhothai-style chedi. The vihan contains a tall seated Buddha in brick and stucco which has been reworked several times, restorations which have coarsened its features. The vihan is covered in some of the finest stucco reliefs of the Sukhothai period including a superbly-executed walking Buddha. In the front courtyard is a covered image of Buddha meditating beneath a hood of naga heads, one of the finest examples of this pose. The wat is enclosed by a fence of large laterite blocks. The gate is surmounted by a tall thick spire on which are carved the four faces of Brahma in a style reminiscent of the Khmer Bayon period. The fence and gate are all that survive of what once may have been a Khmer temple.

Kamphaeng Phet (Diamond Wall), 80 km. south of Sukhothai, is an old town but only gained prominence as an outpost of Sukhothai during the latter part of the 14th century. Hugging the banks of the Ping River, it covers an area of 500 meters by 2.5 km. in the shape of a slight dogleg. Later it appears to have served as a defense point for Ayutthaya's northern frontier, as attested to by its many 15th and 16th century fortresses and its name which suggests impenetrability.

Wat Phra Kaew, the city's most famous wat, is situated in the center of the town. Built in the Sukhothai period and restored by Ayutthayan architects, its most noteworthy feature is the large chedi at its center. Built of laterite on a high square base, it is ringed by 32 niches that once held

Below: *The lotus bud chedi of Sukhothai's Wat Mahathat during the Loy Krathong festival.*

statues of lions. Wat Phra That, a large chedi, sits just to the east.

Sculpture

The glory of Sukhothai's creative genius are its sculptures, which are considered by most art historians to mark the apogee of Thai artistic endeavor. Sukhothai sculptors preferred bronze as their medium, to the near virtual exclusion of stone. Like Dvaravati sculptors, they probably lacked a superior stone but there may be another, more subtle explanation. Perhaps they were repelled by the violence of mallet against chisel that marked the progress of a carved piece. Essentially a gentle people, the Thais may have preferred a material which starts from nothing and evolves into something in contrast to carving, which begins with a massive block and chips away at its bulk to reduce it to the desired form. Shaping the wax and clay of a bronze mold by hand is a sensuous experience which allows the subtle feelings to flow into the lifeless clay. It also imparts the smoothness and fluidity which are the prime characteristics of Sukhothai sculpture and which cannot be achieved with stone.

The Thais learned the art of bronze casting from the Mons, southern Indians, whatever technology remained after the disappearance of Ban Chieng and the Khmers. Their techniques were perfected by Sri Lankan monks visiting Sukhothai. The latter, however, imparted their knowledge long after the Sukhothai style was well established, so were able to exert little influence on the artistic sensibilities of the sculptors.

Early Sukhothai statuary begins with the reign of King Ramkamhaeng late in the 13th century. Though few examples remain, his inscriptions refer to a city filled with images, many of gold and some 18 cubits (8 meters) tall, but give no indication of their shapes. The earliest Sukhothai images have been found at Wat Chang Lom in Si Satchanalai. They are in the Maravijaya attitude and have the broad shoulders of later Sukhothai statuary but not the facial features. Neither do they convey the ethereal quality of 14th century Buddha images.

Classical Sukhothai Buddha images date from the early 14th century. The Buddha of these images is an otherworldly, almost surrealistic figure.

While statuary of other cultures depicts a peaceful, meditating Buddha not yet successful in his quest to gain release from the material world, Sukhothai sculpture suggests a figure in the process of dematerializing, halfway between solid and vapor. He doesn't walk so much as float. He doesn't sit, he levitates, and belies his metallic nature which should be hard and inflexible. Even his diaphanous robes, which are hinted at by a single thickened line, portray a Buddha which has already shed the trappings of this world.

Sukhothai sculptors were the first to portray Buddha in all four positions outlined in ancient texts: standing, walking, seated and reclining. Many stucco standing images were rendered in high relief on wat walls. In later bronze statues, the standing Buddha wears a crown.

Most of the Sukhothai images are seated and almost always the right

Opposite: *A seated Buddha cast in bronze but covered with red lacquer and gilt. The 14th century image is 70 cm. tall and displays the bhumisparsa mudra. (Bangkok National Museum)*
Below: *Displaying the vitarka mudra, the 14th century bronze image stands 2.20 meters tall and ably demonstrates Sukhothai mastery of bronze casting.*

Below: A 77 cm. tall Buddha head cast in the 14th century from Kamphaeng Phet. (Bangkok National Museum)
Opposite: A 76 cm. tall bronze Buddha head in the style of the Kamphaeng Phet School of the late 14th century. (Bangkok National Museum)

hand is in the bhumisparsa mudra ("Calling the Earth to Witness") gesture. Sukhothai sculptors also created a few Reclining Buddhas, the best example of which is now in Wat Bovornivet in Bangkok.

The outstanding achievement of the period, however, is the Walking Buddha. The figure, in the act of moving his right foot forward, displays the vitarka mudra gesture with his left hand while the right arm dangles loosely at his side, its great length very apparent.

Some observers have found the Sukhothai Buddha a little too effeminate for their tastes. He seems almost asexual and, with his distorted body, almost grotesque. What the Sukhothai sculptors were attempting to do was to bring the image closer to its original purpose: to serve as a reminder, not as a depiction of a real person. They scoured the ancient lakshanas (see Sculpture chapter) and Sanskrit poetry for hints and interpreted them literally. So skillful were they, one almost overlooks the odd proportions, a remarkable accomplishment indeed.

That the image with its prominent chest and broad hips seems effeminate, even asexual, was meant to symbolize the Buddha's success in purging himself of desire. He is almost always portrayed lifesized. The arms "like an elephant's trunk" and "long enough to scratch either knee without bending" taper to hands with long fingers usually displaying the abhaya mudra or vitarka mudra position. His gossamer robe covering only the left shoulder is indicated by a thickened line. A robe end, looking like a strap, falls over the left shoulder and terminates at the navel in a gathered bunch with scalloped edges. He wears no visible belt, just a ridge indicating he might be wearing one. The robe of a standing Buddha curves forward, serving almost as a screen on which the Buddha has been placed. One distinguishing feature is that the bottom corners of the robe curve forward like small hooks.

The somewhat elongated head bears an ovoid face. The bow of the prominent eyes is repeated in the mouth. Brows become eyebrows that arch over the eyes and plunge down the sides of the nose in two unbroken lines. The sharply outlined curls of the head dip into the middle of the forehead to form a point and give the face a heart shape. The ushnisha ends in a flame to suggest fiery energy, a mark which would be found in all subsequent schools of sculpture.

By the 15th century, the lakshanas were being replicated without alteration in Sukhothai images. Here one finds the fingers of equal length and the wedge-shaped heels, the Phra Buddha Sihing and the Phra Buddha Jinnarat being prime examples of this predilection. The best images were cast just before Sukhothai was conquered by Ayutthaya in 1438. After that Sukhothai images became more regal, less ethereal, and as a result less attractive. They continued to be produced into the 17th century in various parts of the Ayutthayan empire, and one is compelled to ponder what heights they might have reached if the school's evolution had not been interrupted by outside forces.

Though Sukhothai practiced Theravada Buddhism, its courts were

Below: *Cast in the 14th century,
this bronze Uma stands 150 m. tall.
(Bangkok National Museum)*

inhabited by Brahman priests who dictated proper procedure for state ceremonies and the royal families' rites of passage, such as topknot cutting on a child's attaining puberty. For their use, bronze Brahmanic gods were cast, some of them up to three meters tall. Their audience was within a very small segment of the population, however, so their production was meager by comparison with the output of Buddha images. The principal Hindu subject is the god Siva, who is nearly always portrayed symmetrically and highly ornamented with diadems and a much reduced mukuta. He shares the fluidity of the Buddha images and wears very beautiful robes that hang in multiple folds along the outer edges of the legs.

Sukhothai architects clad their monuments with a wealth of beautifully executed stucco reliefs that display a vivid imagination and a willingness to experiment with new forms and subjects. The best known are the Descent of the Buddha from the Tavatimsa Heaven which decorate huge niches at Wat Tuk, and the most famous is at Wat Trapang Tong Lang. Other superb examples of stucco artistry are the Buddhas meditating during a flood, lifted above the rising waters by the coils of a naga and protected from the rain by his seven heads. The best examples are at Wat Mahathat at Chalieng and at Wat Chedi Jet Thaew in Si Satchanalai.

Elsewhere, scenes from the Tosachat decorate the pediments on wat towers as at Wat Phra Pai Luang and reliquary shrines such as those at Sukhothai's Wat Mahathat. The bases of the chedis surrounding the central chedi in Wat Mahathat feature processions of monks with hands clasped in prayer. Perhaps the most outstanding however are the complex, intricately-crafted stucco designs on the walls and windows of Si Satchanalai's Wat Nang Pya. On a larger scale are the many stucco seated and standing Buddha images. The 12 meter tall seated Buddha at Wat Si Chum is, though restored at a later date, a representative example.

Buddhist tradition notes that during his life Buddha traveled to far realms, leaving behind his footprint as a reminder of his presence and his teachings. The footprint on Adam's Peak in Sri Lanka is the most famous example, but other countries claim equally impressive footprints.

Sometime late in the 14th century, Sukhothai stucco artists began modeling footprints whose soles bore the 108 auspicious signs and the Dhammachakra (Wheel of the Law). Little did they know what they had begun because today, nearly every hill of any size is topped by a small shrine whose object of veneration is a Buddha Footprint, usually of gargantuan dimensions. The most famous is the Bangkok period shrine at Phra Buddhabhat.

As with the bronzes, Hindu stucco objects were created in rather small numbers. Superbly crafted, they include Vishnus, garudas and yaksas, plus myriad mythical figures.

Votive tablets were devoted to portraits of Buddha, usually walking but often seated. Triangular or rectangular with their upper portions terminating in pointed arches, they were crafted in metal or clay.

Ceramics

Sukhothai ceramics, among the finest ever produced by Thailand's artists, fall into two main groups: sculptural ceramics and ceramic plateware and figures. Sculptural ceramics include those created as integral parts of monumental architecture. Among the most intriguing are the dragon-like makaras with naga faces, horns and goatees on naga bodies who guard the roof peaks, rafters, and some walls of Sukhothai wats. They are likely derived from China via the courts of Champa or Kampuchea. Praying deities rendered in bas reliefs decorate the edges of the roofs while men with yaksa or demon faces guard the portals of several sanctuaries.

Ceramic plateware was produced in kilns at Sukhothai, but by far the most innovative school was at Sawankhalok in Si Satchanalai which produced a wide variety of wares for sale in Southeast Asia. The industry was begun by potters who migrated south from China and congregated at Sawankhalok to pursue their craft, imparting their expertise to local potters in the process. The period saw a flowering of ceramic art with a number of experiments in shaping and glazing not seen before in Thailand.

The principal product of Sukhothai potters is a stoneware composed of clay, silica and feldspar and fired in kilns whose design is without counterpart elsewhere. The most numerous of the pieces are the buff-colored plates with designs of chakras or of single or paired fish in brown and covered with a transparent glaze. They seem to be early examples of mass production for a broad market with little concern for quality because the upper surface of each plate is marred by five circular gouges. These were caused by the five-pronged disks used to separate each plate from its neighbor above and below in the tall stacks placed in the kilns for firing.

Sawankhalok potters, by contrast, were innovators intent on raising their craft to higher levels. As a result, they were continually trying out new shapes, designs and glazes. At the bottom end of their output were plates with a black underglaze similar to those of Sukhothai but portraying a somewhat lifeless fish. They produced covered jars with bands of brown glaze around the lower portion, on the foot and in the center of the lid.

Sawankhalok potters are also credited with a celadon ware, a term which describes a glaze which contains 3 percent of iron and which fires to a lustrous green. Celadon technology may have come from the Khmers as numerous Lopburi celadon pieces have been recovered from excavation sites in Ban Kruat district in Buriram province. That the Sawankhalok potters were not entirely successful is evident in the crackly or bubbly effect of many of the wares and in the glaze's unwillingess to adhere to the sides of the bowls but to slip down and pool in the bottom of the bowl or on the feet. They fared better with a white glaze, producing a wide range of shapes and styles. Brown and black glazed ware suffered from a similar tendency to run but the potters turned it to their advantage by applying pigment only to the upper three-fourths of a jar and letting it run down to create an attractive abstract pattern.

Among the most attractive wares are those decorated with whimsical

Below: *Thepanom, Sukhothai glazed stoneware, 14th-15th centuries. (Surat Osathanugrah Collection)*
Bottom: *Two Sukhothai fish plates, crafted in the 14th-15th centuries. (Surat Osathanugrah Collection)*

Below: *Terracotta praying figures approximately 50 cm. tall from Sukhothai. (Bangkok National Museum)*

Bottom: *An engraved stone panel 28 cm. high by 48 cm. wide, one of 100 lining the ceiling of Wat Si Chum and depicting the Chadok Tales. This, the "Bhojajania Chadok", is the 23rd when the Buddha-to-be was incarnated as a horse to serve the King of Benares.*

designs. The small buff jars accented by brown spots and the pearl and brown-colored wares, mostly jars with lids, are among the best examples of Sawankhalok creativity.

The potters also created a number of figurines. Maternity figures, whose heads would be broken off to protect a pregnant woman, were among the most popular. Others include a hunchbacked figure and a woman with a topknot. All these figurines are depicted with puffed cheeks as if containing tobacco or balls of fermented tea, refreshment common in the north.

Kilns at Phan and Wang Nua produced stoneware in large quantities. While those of Wang Nua are unexceptional, those from Phan are superb. The Phan potters seem to have been more successful in formulating their glazes thereby eliminating the problem of running. As a result, their wares have a smooth, even glaze. Among the more imaginative items they produced were oil lamps and weights for fishermen's nets.

Painting

Flecks of paint on ruined walls are all that remain of what was once a flourishing school of painting in Sukhothai. It is evident from these small traces that Sukhothai painters employed a full palette of colors and applied them liberally, preferring bright to subtle tones. Small fragments at Wat Chedi Chet Tao shed a glimmer of light on the subjects of Sukhothai paintings but say little about the overall composition. The scenes appear to have been executed in horizontal bands and in a rust-colored monochrome. The subject is Buddha, who meditates while deities and angels attend him.

The primary clues to the level of artistry come from a series of 100 etched stone panels built into the stairway of Wat Si Chum. Their execution suggests a very practiced hand, a good eye for composition, and a keen comprehension of decorative and secondary elements which give life to a painting. The panels are devoted to episodes from the Chadoks and offer a very spirited rendition of the age-old stories. If the quality of the engraving is an indication of the degree of command of color then the Sukhothai painters rank as supreme artists.

Opposite: *Bronze votive tablet of a walking Buddha, 35 cm. tall and dating from the 14th-15th centuries. (Bangkok National Museum)*
Below: *Horseman, Sawankhalok glazed stoneware, 14th-15th centuries. (Surat Osathanugrah Collection)*

Lanna

The Northern Kingdoms

Coeval with the rise of the Sukhothai school of art was the final burst of creativity in what is generally regarded as the last bastion of Mon influence at Haripunchai, or Lamphun as it is known today. Contemporary with it was the emergence of a unique school of northern art dubbed "Lanna". While Haripunchai styles would influence Lanna artists to a minor extent, the Lanna style remained a self-contained entity which reached beyond the valleys of the north only as far as Sukhothai despite producing some distinctive elements unique to the area.

Haripunchai

Haripunchai, a kingdom with a colorful history, was the northernmost outpost of Mon creativity. Both Haripunchai and the Dvaravati cities of the central Chao Phya Valley came under the domination of the Angkorian kings in the 11th century. Though the Dvaravati artists were forced to adopt the styles of their Khmer conquerers, the Haripunchai artists borrowed only what they wanted but continued to pursue their own styles as they would even after being wrested from Khmer control by Lanna kings late in the 13th century.

Fact is mingled with fancy in the telling of Haripunchai's history. The kingdom is said to have been founded in the 7th century by a daughter of the King of Lavo (Lop Buri), Princess Chamatewi, who had married the ruler of a Mon kingdom in southern Burma. For unknown reasons the princess left her husband, and though several months pregnant, journeyed on a religious pilgrimage to the north. On arriving at the banks of the Ping River, she gave birth to twin sons. Enchanted by the area's natural beauty, she decreed the construction of a city called Haripunchai, recalling an ancient legend that the Buddha had once flown from India to northern Thailand where he left a relic and proclaimed that in 1,008 years a wondrous city would be built. Around her city, Chamatewi erected a wall and dug a moat; today only the moat remains. When he grew to manhood, one of Chamatewi's sons ruled Haripunchai; the other son ruled Lampang Luang, a second city Chamatewi built to the north. Early in its history, Haripunchai established a reputation as a religious center and a thriving artists' community.

Below: *A terracotta head from Wat Phra That, Haripunchai. (Wat Phra That Haripunchai Museum, Lamphun)*
Right: *Praying disciple in terracotta, 24 cm. tall and dating from the 13th century. (Wat Phra That Haripunchai Museum, Lamphun)*

Architecture

As befits a Buddhist center, Haripunchai was dotted with wats, two of which are worthy of special mention. Princess Chamatewi is said to have determined the site of the wat named for her by ordering one of her archers to shoot an arrow to the north. The archer must have had a very strong arm because Wat Chamatewi (also known as Wat Kukut) lies some three-quarters of a kilometer to the northwest of the western gate to Lamphun. It has been rebuilt numerous times over the centuries, one of the best-known reconstructions being that undertaken by Haripunchai King Athitaraja (1120-1150) to commemorate his victory over Lop Buri.

The wat's earliest remaining structures are two chedis, one octagonal and one square dating from the 12th-13th centuries. The octagonal chedi tapers gently to a rounded peak giving it the appearance of a bottle. Several meters above the ground is a single tier of niches, one on each of the eight sides and each framing a standing Buddha image of outstanding beauty.

The square chedi rises from a high base in a pyramid comprising five tiers. Each tier has 12 niches containing standing Buddha images which decrease in size tier by tier giving the illusion of great height. Aside from Chiang Mai's Wat Chedi Chet Yot, Wat Chamatewi's square chedi is perhaps the most famous in the North. It is one of several of similar design which bear a striking resemblance to the Satmahal at Polannaruva in Sri Lanka. Other Lanna examples of this type include Wat Chedi Si Liem, the Phya Chedi in Nan and the Suwanan Chedi at Wat Phra That Haripunchai in Lamphun. The fine stucco figures which decorate the latter's brick and stucco walls are likely later additions. Wat Phra That Haripunchai itself sits within the city confines and dates from the 9th century. Its centerpiece is a large gold-clad stupa that originally stood 10 meters tall but has been augmented and restored many times over the years altering its initial shape as it has risen to its present height of 51 meters.

Sculpture

Despite their Mon antecedents, Haripunchai artists created an art unique to the kingdom. Their approach owes much to contemporary arts of other cities in the region but its artists blended these influences into an art as individualistic as the sculptors themselves. While the style they created was to have little impact on Lanna art, it may have exerted some influence on early U Thong art, which was the immediate predecessor of the Ayutthayan school of later centuries.

Haripunchai's single-minded adherence to Buddhism can be seen in the fact that for the first time in Thailand's art, no images of Hindu deities were produced. Buddha images consist primarily of stone figures, the heads of several of which have been found at Wat Phra That Haripunchai, but more frequently they were cast in bronze. Dating from the 8th century, they display the characteristics associated with

Below: *The gilded brick and stucco chedi of Wat Phra That Haripunchai dates from the 15th century.*

Below: *The chedi of Wat Chedi Si Liem, built in Chiang Mai in the year 1300, is a replica of that at Wat Chamatewi.*

Haripunchai sculpture throughout its history: large hair curls which end in points and which are proportionally the largest of any period of Thai art, wide nose, thick lips and the Dvaravati triple-curve eyebrows rendered as a ridge. As the centuries passed, the features became more stylized and the quality declined.

Haripunchai sculptors preferred standing to seated Buddha images and most often chose to work in stucco and terracotta rather than less malleable materials. Three statues at Wat Phra That Haripunchai are typical of those from a later period of Haripunchai art. Clearly influenced by the northeastern Indian 9th-10th century Pala-Sena mode of dress, these seated images are of Buddha meditating with both hands in his lap and his feet in the vajrasena position (with both soles pointing upwards) and with the robe covering both shoulders. Like other Haripunchai images, his head is covered in large curls and is topped by a low ushnisha ending in a smooth conical ornament.

Some of the best stucco work is seen in the standing Buddhas which occupy the niches of the octagonal chedi at Wat Chamatewi. The striking heads are nearly triangular in shape, similar to the 12th century Lop Buri style. The head even features the small curls of a Lop Buri image. The smooth knob crowning the ushnisha, however, is a precursor of the ushnisha treatment found in U Thong Type A images. The robe covers both shoulders and falls in symmetrical pleats suggesting both Dvaravati and early Lop Buri influence.

It is in terracotta sculpture that Haripunchai artists display their true genius. The praying disciples are some of the most splendid statuary in Thailand's art and reveal features without precedent. Well-proportioned bodies rise to square, flat heads bearing prominent eyes, curved Dvaravati-style eyebrows, incised mustaches and incised neck wrinkles. The effect is wholly un-Thai and looks more like a demon or an Indonesian drama mask. Terracotta and baked clay were also employed in small, solid votive tablets, exquisitely-molded and normally portraying Buddha meditating under a Bodhi tree.

The Kingdom of Lanna

The Lanna Kingdom, encompassing the area from the Mekong River on the north and east, Lamphun on the south and the borders of Burma on the west, flourished between the 13th and 16th centuries. Initially influenced by the Pala tradition of northeastern India, its artists subsequently developed their own iconography and created a distinct school of Thai art.

Its art is also known as Chiengsaen after the northern city which served as its first capital. On the major trade routes between China and the regions to the south, Chiengsaen may have emerged as an important city as early as the 7th century. It remained quiescent until the 10th to 12th centuries when it gained great prominence. In the late 13th century, Chiengsaen was superseded by a new force just to the south at Chiang

Mai which would dominate the politics of the northern region for six centuries.

Towards the latter half of the 13th century, King Mengrai, an energetic monarch, began taking over some of the weaker principalities of the North and founding new cities of his own. Having earlier established Chiang Rai, he founded the city of Fang in 1273 and in 1292 conquered Haripunchai. In 1296 he moved Lanna's capital from Chiengsaen to a city he built on the banks of the Ping River. He called his new capital Chiang Mai or "New City" and imported the artisans from Haripunchai to build its monuments.

In 1287, the grandson of Kublai Khan had captured Pagan in northern Burma and threatened Lanna's stability. Mengrai began by paying him tribute as a vassal but soon halted his gifts, and the next year went so far as to wage war against the Mon king of the Burmese city of Pegu and bring back 500 craftsmen to labor in his own kingdom; neither move was challenged by the Mongols.

After a long and fruitful reign marked by the construction of a sizable city and numerous wats, King Mengrai died in 1311 (some say 1317), struck by lightning at a crossroads near Wat Chedi Luang. Of all his descendants, the only one to match his energy and foresight was King Tiloka (1442-1488).

The Lanna kings were involved in constant warfare with Ayutthaya after the new power in the Central Valley captured Sukhothai in 1378. In 1556, however, Chiang Mai was subjugated not by Ayutthaya but by a lightning raid by Burmese armies. It regained its freedom for a short period but then fell once again to its captors. In 1775 Chiang Mai's resources were so depleted that its entire population moved to Lampang where they stayed for 20 years, leaving the "New City" deserted. For the next century, Chiang Mai was ruled alternately by its own princes and by the courts of Burma. Late in the 19th century, however, it was firmly incorporated into the Thai kingdom.

Architecture

Chiengsaen sits on the western bank of the Mekong River in the northernmost part of Thailand near the junction of the Thai, Laotian and Burmese borders. Its strategic position decreed early that it would be a gateway controlling trade with China and on the Mekong River.

In ancient times the city was defended by an eight-kilometer rectangular laterite wall and a moat, parts of which can be seen today. Chiengsaen's two most famous monuments, however, lie outside its walls. Wat Pasak, built by King Mengrai's grandson, King Saen Phu (1325-1335), is just beyond the western moat. On a hill to the northwest of the city is Wat Phra That Chom Kitti, the older of the two. Its chedi, dating from before the founding of the city in the 7th century, sits atop a square base and is decorated with stucco reliefs of Buddha and a single bronze plaque, also of Buddha, one of dozens that once clad the chedi.

Below: *The brick chedi of Chiengsaen's Wat Pasak, built in the 14th century has niches around the base and the upper tier to hold standing Buddha images.*

Below: The chedi of Doi Suthep in Chiang Mai, contains a precious relic said to have been taken to the hilltop site by an elephant in the 14th century. The chedi is made of gilded brick and is the most famous structure in the North.

Nearby is a smaller chedi decorated with now-ruined terracotta figures. Inside the city is the brick Wat Chedi Luang, a 12th century structure also once covered in bronze sheets. Wat Pa Kao Pan near the river still has its bronze sheets intact on its upper portion.

The main buildings of Chiang Mai were originally clustered around its oldest wat, Wat Chiangman. The city wall originally measured two kilometers by 1.8 kilometers but was enlarged and its configuration considerably altered by later kings; the most recent change occurred in 1801. Wat Chiangman was built in 1297, shortly after the founding of Chiang Mai and, like most wats of the city, has been extensively restored so that one has little idea of how it originally looked. Behind it is a chedi surrounded by 15 elephants serving as buttresses; its upper portion is sheathed in gilded bronze.

Wat Phra Singh, at the head of the city's principal street, was erected in 1345 but most of its components have been built in recent centuries. Similarly, Wat Suan Dok, directly west of Wat Phra Singh but outside the walls, has undergone major renovations. Its chedi, rebuilt in the Bangkok period, contains a famous relic of the Buddha which has been credited with numerous miracles. According to legend, Sumana, a Sri Lankan monk living in 14th century Sukhothai, was directed in a dream to dig up a relic buried beneath a ruined wat. He found several boxes within boxes made of gold, coral, silver and bronze, the last containing a very small relic that glowed. He took it to Sukhothai, but when the king tried to utilize its miraculous powers for his own purposes, it stopped glowing. It was then entrusted to Sumana for safekeeping. When Ku Na, the king of Chiang Mai, heard of it, he invited the monk to his city and built a chedi in his flower garden (suan dok) to contain it. The moment before it was to be placed in the crypt, the relic split in two. One half was put in the chedi and the other half was transported to Doi Suthep. Another story relates that in 1337, King Lu Thai of Sukhothai, wishing to honor Sumana's wisdom, ordered the construction at Wat Suan Dok of a chedi in Sinhalese style with a lotus bud spire, perhaps the last of the lotus bud chedis ever built by a Sukhothai king.

Wat Chedi Luang in the center of the old walled city is one of Chiang Mai's oldest wats and contains a beautifully decorated vihan with a tall standing Buddha. The Chedi Luang behind it was built in 1373 and in 1454 raised to 90 meters by King Tiloka. An earthquake in 1545 reduced it to its present height of 60 meters.

Three other Chiang Mai wats deserve mention. Wat Ku Tao to the north of the city was built by a Burmese ruler of Chiang Mai. While the vihan itself is recent and of no particular interest except for the image it contains, the chedi beside it is unique in the annals of Thai architecture. It was built in the shape of five globes approximating the form of inverted monks' bowls placed one atop the other in decreasing order of size. The stucco-covered brick structure has been decorated with ceramic tiles shaped into the individual petals of flowers.

Left: The chedi of Wat Rampoeng in Chiang Mai is a 16th century structure resembling a Chinese pagoda.
Below: Chedi Chet Yot in Chiang Mai was built in 1455 to celebrate the 2,000th anniversary of Buddha's death in 543 B.C.
Bottom: One of 70 stucco divinities on the walls of Chedi Chet Yot. The figures are said to resemble relatives of King Tiloka, who built it.

Below: *Bronze Buddha 71 cm. tall seated in the maravijaya position from the royal collection, probably dating from the 14th century, now in the Bangkok National Museum.*

The second is Wat Rampoeng south of Chiang Mai, whose principal attraction is a 16th century Chinese-style pagoda unlike any in Thailand. Shaped like a cone, it rises in seven tiers from a high base and ends in a slender spire. Niches for Buddha images ring each tier. Each niche is framed by geometrical columns and capitals and capped by a decorated arch that resembles a northern Thai dancer's naga diadem.

To the west of Wat Suan Dok is Wat U Mong (Underground Wat), one of the first wats built by King Mengrai in 1296. Nothing remains but the ruins of a large chedi whose brick base rests on a rock. Beneath the rock is a maze of meditation cells, a unique feature found nowhere else in Thailand, understandable because of the high water table in most section of the country. Judging by the quality of the stucco decorations on the chedi base, it can be assumed that the wat was once an important religious center.

Two of the most important of the Lanna kingdom's architectural achievements lie some distance from its main cities. The oldest, Chedi Si Liem, was built by King Mengrai at Wiang Kum Kuan, a point halfway between Chiang Mai and Lamphun, around the year 1300. A copy of Wat Chamatewi, it has retained its slender pointed spire which gives the viewer a fuller impression of the pyramidal shape of the original. Its slightly concave sides give it particular grace and beauty. Its decoration has also been copied from its predecessor but has been restored so frequently over the years as to give little idea of the skill or concept of its original sculptors.

In 1455 King Tiloka, wishing to build a monument to celebrate the 2,000th anniversary of the Buddha's death, sent a team of 30 architects and craftsmen to the northeastern Indian city of Bodhgaya where Buddha was said to have reached Enlightenment. There, they studied the plans of the Mahabodi Temple, the most famous of the shrines built to commemorate the seven sites at which Buddha meditated in the first seven weeks after gaining Enlightenment. They returned to a place just outside Chiang Mai and began construction of a high laterite base to support a main chedi surrounded by six smaller chedis, hence the seven spires (Chet Yot) of its name, Wat Chedi Chet Yot. Its most remarkable features are the 70 celestial deities in Sukhothai style rendered in stucco relief along the walls of the chedi's base. These beings, dressed in Lanna court costumes, are thought to be depictions of Tiloka's family. They float among flowers with their hands clasped palms together in a wai, a gesture of respect thought to celebrate the Buddha's victory over Mara.

Many of Lanna's most famous wats were built in teak wood cut from the vast forests which once covered the northern hills. Most wooden structures have been destroyed by insects and humid weather and only those constructed in the past two centuries have survived.

Sculpture

Despite the contiguity of their borders and chronology, Lanna sculptors developed a style quite distinct from that of Sukhothai though later Sukhothai styles would show some of its influence. Lanna art has been given the name of "Chiengsaen" though little was produced in Chiengsaen. Further, the style is divided into two periods: Early Chiengsaen dating up to the 13th century and Late Chiengsaen (or Chiang Mai) commencing with the founding of Chiang Mai in 1296 and extending into the 16th century.

Lanna sculptors preferred to work in bronze and to a lesser extent in wood. Though they produced a few statues of Hindu deities, they concentrated primarily on Buddha images. The Buddhas are most often portrayed in the seated position. They have pointed ushnishas reminiscent of the late Lop Buri period topping a broad face with bulging eyes. The most noteworthy features are the very large hair curls. Many Late Chiengsaen images, especially those of the late 14th and early 15th centuries, have eyes whose whites are inlaid with mother of pearl and/or whose pupils are inlaid with glass, a convention seen by some to suggest Burmese influence.

Early Chiengsaen images generally have a great suppleness to them by contrast with the stiffness of the Late Chiengsaen period. The Early images also betray a debt to the Pala school of northern India which flourished between the 8th and 12th centuries and whose iconography is thought to have been taken to northern Thailand by Buddhist missionaries who traveled from India via Burma taking Indian images with them. Pala images are characterized by a knob on the ushnisha which some have likened to a lotus bud but which others see only as a smooth, bulbous ornament. They also have heads with round faces, large curls, arched eyebrows, and prominent eyes and chins emphasized by lines. Like them, the Early and Late Chiengsaen images have thick, very solid bodies.

While both Early and Late Chiengsaen sculptors preferred seated Buddhas, they differed in their placement of the feet and in their attire. With both, the torso, when viewed from the side, is exactly perpendicular to the ground and the right arm is separated some distance from the side of the body. Early sculptors chose the vajrasena position with the soles of the feet pointing upwards. Later sculptors placed the legs in the virasana mode. Both chose the same hand gestures: the Bhumisparsa (Calling the Earth to Witness) and others associated with the Maravijaya (Victory over Mara) attitude. Both styles wear their robes open and covering only the left shoulder but with the Early period the shoulder flap ends above the nipple while with the Late it falls to the navel.

Whereas on Early images the finial on the ushnisha is a smooth bulb, on the Late images it is a flame, pre-dating the U Thong B and C images in which the flame is pronounced almost to exaggeration. The faces are marked by delicately molded and separated eyebrows, a treatment similar to that accorded by Sukhothai sculptors. The mouth is small with somewhat thickened lips and the nose is well shaped with flared wings. A further distinguishing feature of some of the Late images is that the dates of their creation were imprinted on their bases during casting.

Below: *This bronze Buddha, cast in 1492, called the Phra Singh, is not only a stellar example of late Chiengsaen image, but is also the most venerated image in the North of Thailand.*

Lanna sculptors carved several small Buddha images from gemstones and quartz but their appeal is more in the nature of novelty than of artistic merit. The Phra Keo Morakot or Emerald Buddha (actually carved from jasper) in Bangkok's Wat Phra Kaew, is often identified as a Chiengsaen creation but it has few of the attributes of that style and may actually have been brought to Thailand from India or Sri Lanka. Its true origins are a mystery that has never been satisfactorily resolved.

Stucco was used as architectural decoration and to create small figures but in general they lack the plasticity of those made by Sukhothai artists. It is also difficult to gain a true appreciation of their original form because many have been restored and in the process ruined. The finest examples of Lanna stucco craftsmanship are the 70 deities of Wat Chedi Chet Yot which reveal an artistry the equal of any period or locale. The images, rendered in larger-than-life-sized relief and with oval faces set with prominent eyes and noses, convey an aura of peace. Wat Pasak in Chiengsaen also has some good stucco and terracotta pieces, notably the figures placed above and adjacent to the niches reserved for Buddha images. Here, beasts and demons of remarkable vitality stare down from the heights on worshipers below. Good stuccos are also found on the stupas of Chiengsaen's Wat Ku Tao and Chiang Mai's Wat U Mong.

The Lanna kingdom had a long-established pottery industry but its output was undistinguished. When King Tiloka conquered Sawankhalok in 1459, he sought to improve the craftsmanship of Lanna pottery by taking Sawankhalok's potters back with him to Chiang Mai thereby halting forever production in the Sukhothai area. His attempt to introduce outside expertise failed, however, and Lanna pottery never reached the heights of that of the Sukhothai region.

Lanna sculptors also produced a number of votive tablets cast in terracotta which were either baked or sun dried. In varied styles and devoted to a variety of Buddhist themes, they lack the crispness and energy of their Haripunchai counterparts.

Painting

The principal examples of Lanna painting date from the 17th century, some time after the Lanna school of sculpture ceased as a functioning entity. The representative examples of the style were painted in the 18th and 19th centuries so are treated in the section of the Bangkok chapter concerned with northern Thai painting since the 16th century.

The best example of late Lanna painting is on the walls of the reliquary beneath the ruined chedi of Chiang Mai's Wat U Mong. Badly damaged by moisture, they are concerned with Buddhas of the Past who sit in meditation beneath Bodhi trees or Call the Earth to Witness. The figures are arranged in tiers and isolated from each other by decorative lines. They resemble the painted Buddhas in Ayutthaya's Wat Ratburana but the iconography is that of Sukhothai as modified by the Late Chiengsaen school. No precise date can be assigned to them, however.

Ayutthaya

In the 14th century, a new kingdom arose in the Chao Phya Valley which would complete the work begun by the Sukhothai kings before their momentum flagged. Through conquest and the wise rule of able rulers, a revitalized Thai nation centered at Ayutthaya evolved into one of the most powerful kingdoms in Southeast Asia. Except for a short period in the 16th century, it would dominate the politics and trade of the region for 400 years. Its monumental capital was filled with glittering wats and palaces that reflected the pre-eminence it enjoyed in Asia. Though not of the high order of Sukhothai, its sculpture steadily developed, reaching its height of technical mastery if not beauty at the close of the period in the 18th century.

Early Ayutthayan history is the subject of considerable debate. Some claim it begins at the small town of Ayodhya located either to the east of Ayutthaya or in the vicinity of U Thong. Other historians contend it began in U Thong, which may have been the name of a kingdom located at U Thong itself or at Suphan Buri or Kanchanaburi. In the mid-14th century, it was ruled by a monarch named U Thong, said to have been the son-in-law of U Thong's governor who was distantly related to Chiengsaen royalty. Ayodhya's prosperity depended on a small river which flowed through it, but around 1347 it silted up or dried up causing a water shortage and possibly an outbreak of cholera. These disasters prompted King U Thong to move his capital to the south bank of the Lop Buri River at the site now occupied by Wat Buddhaisawan. Three years later, he moved across the river to an uninhabited area soon known as Ayutthaya, was crowned its king and changed his name to Ramathibodi.

Ayutthaya was an excellent choice for a capital city, defended on the north, west and south by an oxbow of the Lop Buri River. Ramathibodi had only to dig a canal on the east across the neck of land to make the city an island and complete its defenses. Later, he would dig shunts to connect it to the Chao Phya and Pasak rivers. Eventually, through natural process, the shunts became the main courses of these rivers.

It was from this secure base that Ramathibodi rode out to conquer the remnants of the Angkorian empire. In 1352 he triumphed, establishing the city as the eastern outpost of his new realm, and in 1378 his successor, Boromaraja I, subjugated Sukhothai to serve as the northern boundary. In

Top: *Wat Chai Wattanaram is a late Ayutthayan wat built in 1630. Unusual are the chedis surrounding the main prang which resemble cylinders stacked one atop the other.*
Above: *Ayutthaya's two most famous wat complexes. Wat Mahathat (left) and Wat Ratburana (right).*

1431 Angkor rebelled, but Ayutthaya laid siege and sacked it after seven months. Between 1548 and 1578, the tables turned as the Burmese succeeded in overrunning and occupying Ayutthaya, a venture that ultimately proved to be a minor setback as Ayutthaya soon became the dominant force in the region.

By the 17th century, Ayutthaya boasted a population of one million, more than contemporary London. Its wealth came from rice and from serving as an entrepot in trade between East and West. In the outskirts of the city, merchant trading companies of Japan, England and Europe established profitable offices and production facilities.

Contemporary foreign accounts speak of dozens of gleaming wat roofs and gilded spires piercing the city skyline as well as the presence of more than 2,000 Buddha images clad in gold. Such wealth invited the envy of its neighbors, notably the Burmese, who attacked its ramparts time after time in the 17th and 18th centuries, finally succeeding in overpowering its defenders in 1767. The invaders looted the once brilliant city, put it to the torch and carried away its learned sages and craftsmen to practice their arts in Burmese courts.

U Thong

U Thong is the name given to a particular style of sculpture which predates the establishment of Ayutthaya in 1350. The derivation of the name "U Thong" is uncertain as the town of U Thong was largely uninhabited after the 11th century. The name may have referred to the general area which included Ayodhya.

The sculptors of the U Thong style produced a large number of statues and developed a school of art that owes much to other schools but displays its own distinct characteristics. The style of U Thong's architecture has been the subject of dispute since no complete structure has been found which can be directly attributed to the U Thong school. The bell-shaped chedis at Wat Phra Boromathat at Chai Nat have been described as U Thong and the main prang at Lop Buri's Wat Phra Si Ratana Mahathat, while ostensibly a Khmer-inspired monument, has been credited by some scholars to U Thong rather than Khmer architects. They base their attribution on the fact that it has a greater number of offsets than usual and that its stucco decorations extend much higher up the base than those on Lop Buri or Khmer monuments. It has been suggested that the wat's prang, dating from the 13th century, was a prototype for Ayutthaya style prangs.

Sculpture

Like Sukhothai statuary, U Thong output was devoted almost entirely to Buddha images, usually seated but on a few occasions standing or walking. The sculptors preferred to work in bronze but did produce a few terracotta, sandstone and gold images. The principal influences were Mon and Khmer — likely left over from early periods when U Thong had

Left: *The very elongated torso and flame ornament of a U Thong C bronze Buddha, 70 cm. tall and cast in the 14th-15th centuries. (Chao Sam Praya National Museum, Ayutthaya)*
Below: *A bronze U Thong A Buddha seated in the Maravijaya position from Wat Ratburana in Ayutthaya. (Chao Sam Praya National Museum, Ayutthaya)*

Below: *U Thong C bronze Buddha seated under a Bodhi tree on a lotus flowerbase, 31 cm. tall and cast in the 14th-15th centuries. (Chao Sam Phraya National Museum, Ayutthaya)*

Right: *Bronze U Thong B Buddha head from the 13th-14th centuries. (Praku Knanumsommanajara collection)*

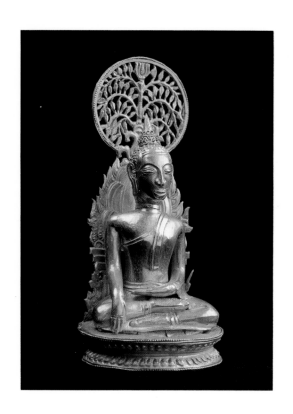

existed under their hegemony — and Sukhothai.

U Thong images are generally divided into three groups — A, B and C — but have a number of common characteristics. They are usually seated in the Maravijaya attitude with their legs in the virasana position. Their heads are marked by small curls and a small band separates the hair from the face as in Lop Buri sculpture. Like the Sukhothai and Chiengsaen images, the robe covers the left shoulder leaving the right bare and is indicated by a thickened line rather than by pleats. The robe flap falls from the left shoulder to the navel and resembles a strap or a belt. A scalloped waist is usually the only indication of a belt though a flat belt is often visible. Through the period, the ushnisha grows from a small knob to a very tall flame. Among the most distinctive features is a base shaped either like a lotus or like a thick disk deeply indented along the edge like a pulley wheel laid on its side.

The progression over 150 years from the A to the C styles is the evolution from a very square, solid figure to a taller, narrower profile, to an inordinately tall and slender form whose effect is enhanced by a very tall ushnisha and flame ornament. The U Thong A style dates from the late 13th century and betrays Dvaravati and Khmer/Lop Buri influences. The few images produced during this period display a blockiness as if they were made up of separate components welded together. The broad face is separated from the small curls of the head by a band; the ushnisha ends in a knob or lotus bud. The style is further characterized by a wide mouth with thick lips and a single eyebrow hooding both eyes, reminiscent of Dvaravati sculpture.

The U Thong B style dates from the end of the 13th to the late 14th century and demonstrates an indebtedness to Khmer styles. The face is more refined, more remote than previously. The lotus bud ornament atop the ushnisha has evolved into a flame set in a cup, a feature borrowed by Sukhothai sculptors. The very small curls give the head a surface like a rasp.

The U Thong C period which overlaps the Ayutthayan period from the late 14th to mid-15th centuries was the most prolific of all, and the least successful. U Thong sculptors seem to have made a deliberate attempt to copy the styles of Sukhothai image makers but failed to achieve the fluidity and smoothness of the masters, settling instead for figures of unpleasing awkwardness. Where the Sukhothai sculptors altered the proportions considerably yet created figures of striking beauty, U Thong sculptors only succeeded in making them look ungainly.

Ayutthaya

By digging the eastern canal, Ramathibodi created an island 2.5 km. by 4.4 km. which isolated it from attack by land. He constructed a wooden palisade and in the northern section of the city built a palace on the site of the future Wat Phra Si Sanphet. Ayutthaya's plan was not pre-ordained by symbolism like Angkor but grew according to a random

Below: Wat Phra Si Sanphet after recent restoration with its three bell-shaped chedis, porch and disk spires built in 1491 of brick of stucco.

Below: *Ruined prangs with niches for Buddha images at Wat Mahathat, Ayutthaya.*
Bottom: *Wat Phra Ram, Ayutthaya, constructed in 1369 to honor Ayutthaya's founder, King Ramathibodi. The prang demonstrates the use of vertical offsets to give the structure visual height and counter the horizontal lines of the tiers.*

pattern. The earliest wats were located to the east of the city and on the banks of the river opposite the city proper. During a spate of construction in the 14th and 15th centuries, the principal edifices and wats for which Ayutthaya would become famous were clustered in the vicinity of the palace.

In the 16th century, the wooden palisade was replaced by a brick city wall 12 kilometers around surmounted at 17 strategic points by watchtowers and breached by dozens of gates, including watergates through which boats could pass from the river into the city. At its height, Ayutthaya boasted 550 major buildings and monuments, more than 400 of them wats. As befits a riverine people, the principal mode of travel and transportation was by boats which plied 140 kilometers of canals in the city and the immediate suburbs. The nearly 53 kilometers of brick-paved streets stopped at the city walls; beyond the river/moat there were only dirt paths. The city was populated by Thai officials and merchants and included a Chinatown. Unlike the Chinese, the Europeans were classified as "foreigners" and were required to live outside the walls in the outskirts of the city. The great animosity and competition among the various European nationalities decreed that they would group themselves into ethnic neighborhoods around the offices and warehouses of their respective trading concerns.

Architecture

Ayutthaya was a society of builders rather than sculptors. As with most emerging empires in the flush of success, it was preoccupied with building monuments to impress outsiders by sheer immensity. In a tremendous burst of energy, it erected a major portion of its 400 wats in Ramathibodi's reign and completed most of its major monuments in the first 150 years of its existence. Today, even in ruins, the shattered buildings convey a grandeur and mystery.

Ayutthaya had three palaces for its rulers. The Wang Luang (Royal Palace) occupied by the principal king was on the northern rim of the city. The Wang Na (Palace to the Front) built for the Second or Vice-King was in the northeastern corner and the Wang Lang (Palace to the Rear), later occupied by princes of the royal blood, was in the western part of the city.

Ramathibodi's palace was built of wood and defended by mud walls in accordance with the ancient belief that only religious buildings and monuments should be made of more durable materials. The wooden buildings of the Wang Luang, of which only the brick foundations remain, were built by King Boroma Trailokanat (1448-1488); the brick walls of the city date from the reign of King Chakraphat (1549-1565). The first royal buildings built entirely of brick date from the time of King Narai (1657-1688). A scale model now to the south of Wat Mahathat shows the palace to be more prosaic than the exotic ruins would suggest: a city of smooth, whitewashed stucco walls gleaming in the bright sunlight and resembling the crenelated walls around Bangkok's Grand Palace and Wat Phra Kaew.

The main buildings of the Wang Luang palace complex include the Suriyat Amarin Hall built by King Narai as his residence. The Vihan Somdet, a large building crowned by a prang and used for state ceremonies, was erected in 1643 by King Prasat Thong to replace an earlier building destroyed by a lightning bolt. The vihan, also known as Prasat Thong (Golden Palace), was the first building in Ayutthaya to be clad in gold plates, a common practice in the latter part of the period when the city had become very wealthy.

Many of the early wats resembled Khmer structures with their central prangs ringed by open courtyards enclosed by smaller prangs or walls. Wat Mahathat, Wat Ratburana and Wat Phra Ram are good examples of this type. Later wats were similar to those of the Bangkok period. Made of stucco-covered brick, their plain whitewashed walls were topped by overlapping roofs of red tiles. Most were lit by slivers of light pouring into the interior through narrow slits in the walls — a mode of illumination similar to many Khmer and Sukhothai wats. Many bots were entirely without windows, being lit by whatever light entered through the doors. While a darkened interior would serve to enhance an aura of spirituality, a lack of structural engineering knowledge may account for the absence of windows and for the thick walls and very stout columns necessary to support the roof.

Columns were surmounted by lotus bud or water lily capitals, and each of the entrances flanking the main door had its own roof. One of the finest examples of this style, Wat Na Phramane, has been extensively renovated but conveys the essential character of a later Ayutthayan wat. Near the close of the Ayutthayan period, architects employed the boat-shaped base, originally a Mahayanan concept likening the bot to a ship carrying the Buddhist faithful to salvation, but by this point used simply for decorative purposes.

Ayutthayan architects borrowed the chedi forms developed by other schools but modified them according to their own aesthetics. The Sri Lankan bell-shaped chedi adapted by the Sukhothai school was used extensively in Ayutthaya but was given a new elegance. In the trio of narrow-based chedis at Wat Si Sanphet, the bell base was capped by a colonnaded hamika porch and crowned by a slim spire that imparted an airiness not seen previously. Ayutthayan architects played with this form, squaring its shoulders and elongating it to create one of Thai architecture's most graceful expressions of soaring weightlessness. The Chedi Si Suriyothai monument, honoring a brave queen who died while defending her husband in battle, is one of the finest examples of this type.

One of the most important contributions to Thai art was the Khmer-influenced prang which resembled an upended cucumber with deep vertical striations. Generally marked halfway up by four Buddha image niches facing the cardinal points, it was girded by a series of plaques

Below: *Wat Phu Khao Thong to the northeast of Ayutthaya was built by a Burmese prince in 1569 to celebrate a victory over Ayutthaya. It was rebuilt in its present form over the original spire in 1745.*

Below: *A prime example of the slender squared chedi at Wat Yanasen which closely resembles the Chedi Si Suriyothai.*

depicting Buddha in meditation. The monument's peak was crowned by a bronze vajra or thunderbolt. Developed in the early years of the period, the prang began as a heavy, almost squat form and gradually grew thinner and lighter. Towards the end of the period, it had been elongated past attractive proportions and lost much of its beauty. It was employed as the central prang in wats like Wat Mahathat, Wat Ratburana and Wat Phra Ram and in some instances was placed at the peak of a wat roof or important palace building as an indication of royal patronage. The Ayutthayan prang would later find its way south into Bangkok architecture in such complexes as Wat Phra Kaew, Wat Arun, and Wat Rakang.

Ayutthaya's oldest wat predates the founding of the city by 26 years. Wat Phra Chao Phananchoeng, across the river from the southeast corner of the city and near the mooring area for foreign merchant ships, was built in 1324 to house a 19-meter-high seated Buddha image, the Phra Chao Phananchoeng, said to have wept when Ayutthaya was overrun by the Burmese.

The first wat Ramathibodi built after ascending Ayutthaya's throne was Wat Buddhaisawan, across the river to the south. Erected in 1353 on the site of his first residence, its large prang is surrounded by cloisters sheltering long rows of Buddha images which face the prang. A vihan holds a reclining Buddha and the courtyard to the west contains a chedi built in late Ayutthayan style.

Four years later, Ramathibodi ordered the erection of Wat Yai Chai Mongkon to serve a group of monks recently returned from Sri Lanka after studying Buddhism under a famed teacher. Originally called Wat Pa Keo, it was given its present name by King Naresuan in 1592 to commemorate his great victory (chai) over the Burmese invaders led by a prince, whom he killed in single-handed combat on elephant back. Built to the east of the city walls, the wat is dominated by a very tall chedi set on a square base with four smaller chedis at the corners.

One of the first wats built in the city center was Wat Phra Mahathat, erected in 1384 by King Ramathibodi's brother-in-law, King Boromaraja I (1370-1388). It is said that the king was meditating in his palace in the pre-dawn hours when he perceived a glow from the ground to the southeast. Deciding it emanated from a Buddha relic, he decreed the construction of a wat on the holy site. One of the most impressive of all the Ayutthayan monuments, its center was a 38 meter high laterite prang surmounted by a six meter tall spire. In the following century, the top portion collapsed, perhaps the target of a lightning bolt, and was rebuilt by King Prasat Thong in 1633. Brick and plaster were used to increase its height to 50 meters. At the same time the sides were augmented by additional layers to thicken it in proportion to its new height. In later years it collapsed once again; today only the base remains.

Before it is a bot which once contained a large seated Buddha image and surrounding it are numerous prangs and chedis of varying sizes. In

Below: *The vihan doorway frames
the main prang of Wat Ratburana,
built in 1384 in the center of
Ayutthaya.*

Below: *The mango seed shaped chedi at Wat Mahathat, Lop Buri dating from the early Ayutthayan period.*

the courtyard to the east are several smaller vihans constructed like the bot of the large (35 cm. by 15 cm.), very hard bricks which were the principal building material of Ayutthayan masons. Traces of stucco decoration can still be seen on the chedis of Wat Mahathat which, even in ruins, conveys the splendor of the massive original.

As often happened in Thai architecture, a prang was built on the site of a royal cremation, and soon after it became the centerpiece for a new wat. Such was the case with Wat Phra Ram, built in 1369 by King Ramesuan on the spot where his father was cremated. Rebuilt in the 15th century by King Boroma Trailokanat and again in 1741 by King Boromakot, it now bears little resemblance to the original.

Wat Ratburana, one of the most famous Ayutthayan monuments, stands just to the north of Wat Phra Mahathat. It was constructed in 1424 by King Boromaraja II (1424-1448) on the cremation site of two princes who killed each other during single-handed combat on elephant back to determine which one would rule the kingdom. He later added a long vihan and, behind it, a large prang. Like Wat Mahathat, Wat Ratburana was severely damaged by fire in the aftermath of the 1767 Burmese invasion. The looters overlooked a large crypt beneath the prang however, and in 1957 it was opened to reveal a wealth of superb gold statues and other gold art objects.

Wat Na Phramane, directly across the river from the Wang Luang palace, is the most complete example of late Ayutthayan wat architecture. Built in the mid-15th century, its bot, with its thick walls, slit windows, pilasters, and thick columns crowned by water lily capitals, was one of the largest in the city. Bangkok's King Rama III constructed the small vihan which now shelters the famous Dvaravati limestone Buddha image seated on a throne which was found at Nakhon Pathom by King Rama IV. Its walls were covered by fine murals, most of which have faded badly in the damp air. Among the glories of its bot are the beautiful red ceilings with gold star clusters, and beautifully worked gold and lacquer entrance doors.

Rounding out the wats built in the first century and a half of Ayutthaya's existence, and completing the triumvirate of Wat Mahathat and Wat Ratburana, is Wat Phra Si Sanphet. Erected in 1491 on the site of Ramathibodi's first palace, it stood within the confines of the Wang Luang much like Wat Phra Kaew is situated within the walls of Bangkok's Grand Palace. Its patron, King Ramathibodi II began by erecting two large chedis, one on the east to hold the ashes of his father Trailokanath and one on the west to hold those of his elder brother Boromaraja III, who had died after ruling for only three years. In 1499 he added a vihan. King Ramathibodi II's ashes are enshrined in a third chedi of the same style built to the west by King Boromaraja IV. It has been renovated twice, once in 1631 and again in 1742. In the year 1500, Ramathibodi II had a 16 meter tall standing Buddha cast in bronze, one of the largest bronze works ever attempted. He covered it in gold and then built a vihan around it, which failed to protect it from marauding Burmese armies and in 1767 it was virtually destroyed.

Adjacent to Wat Phra Si Sanphet is another building erected to protect an enormous Buddha image. The Phra Mongkon Bopit was originally cast to stand in the open air as was a common practice in Ayutthaya. In 1603 a vihan was erected to shelter it, but in 1706 it was struck by lightning and burned to the ground. Moreover, when the roof collapsed in flames, it broke off the image's head. A new head was fashioned and a new vihan was erected. It burned again in 1767 and was rebuilt in 1931 and again in 1956, the latter reconstruction in the style of the original. Six rows of columns support a very graceful roof which is low in proportion to its width. The overall effect is that of a giant bird settling down after flight. The pediment is painted red and on it are bas reliefs in gold leaf of the tables on which holy relics are placed; to the sides are devas in prayerful attitudes.

Wat Chai Wattanaram dates from the latter part of the period. Constructed in 1630 by that prolific monument builder, King Prasat Thong, it is thought to have been conceived on the plan of an Angkorian temple but modified to less ambitious dimensions as a variation of a Lanna structure. The central prang is Ayutthayan in style but the smaller chedis resemble columns of barrels stacked in descending order of size. Wat Chai Wattanaram suffered heavy damage in 1767 and was not rebuilt.

Two other late Ayutthayan wats are noteworthy for their decoration. Wat Maheyong's centerpiece is a large chedi supported on the backs of stucco elephants in the style of several Si Satchanalai and Sukhothai chedis; it was the only Ayutthayan wat to be treated in this manner. To the east, the bot is made up of brick walls broken by three stucco-decorated windows and reinforced by pilasters. Wat Khudi Dao, on what is presumed to have been the site of Ayodhya, is a 1711 renovation of an older building. Despite its present decrepit state it is possible to discern its extremely fine workmanship. Especially interesting is the treatment of the doorways and windows. The tall, slender openings terminate in ogees of particular grace and beauty.

Northeast of Ayutthaya is Phu Khao Thong, the Golden Mountain. An impressive structure, it is the largest example of the square bell-shaped chedi which is associated with the Ayutthayan school. King Ramesuan built the bot which stands next to it in 1387. In 1569, while the Burmese were occupying Ayutthaya, the Burmese king ordered that a Mon-style chedi be built to celebrate his victory over the Thais. In 1745, King Boromakot rebuilt it in its present form.

Many of the best examples of Ayutthayan architectural genius lie in far corners of the kingdom. The chedi of Wat Phra Si Ratana Mahathat, built in Phitsanulok during the Sukhothai period, was changed to a prang by King Boroma Trailokanat (1448-1488). Wat Phra Kaew in Sankhaburi, built by King Boromaraja II's elder brother, Chao Yi Phraya,

Below: An old photograph, taken at the turn of the century, showing the Phra Mongkon Bopit before the reconstruction of the vihan which shelters it. (Hamilton King Collection)
Bottom: Town plan of Lop Buri drawn by a 17th century European artist. (Courtesy of White Lotus, Bangkok)

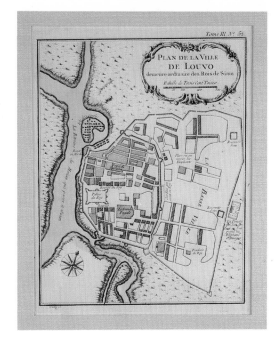

may have been patterned on Wat Chedi Sung in Sukhothai. Sankhaburi boasts another attractive Ayutthayan prang in Wat Song Phi Nong, an early 15th century complex. Built in the Ayutthaya period, Wat Sai in Thon Buri has one of the finest sala kanprien known. King Phra Chao Sua (1703-1709) added a beautiful wooden library decorated in lacquer and gold.

Wat Yai Suwannaram in Phetchaburi is not only one of the best and most complete examples of the Ayutthayan style of architecture but has fine mural paintings. Except for its courtyard, which was extensively restored during the reign of King Rama V (1868-1910), it has remained essentially as it was originally built.

The most complete example of Ayutthayan royal architecture is the Narai Raja Niwet Palace in Lop Buri. As its name suggests, it was built by King Narai in the 17th century on the banks of the Chao Phya River to protect Ayutthaya's southern flank. Its stout, well-preserved walls and stucco-covered brick buildings provide a comprehensive picture of Thai palace design combining practical defensive considerations with a certain lightness and grace one does not normally associate with military structures. Its fine museum contains numerous relics of the period.

Sculpture

The spirituality of Sukhothai statuary was replaced during the Ayutthayan period by an art which betokens a rational, practical people cognizant of the importance of religion in their lives but very much rooted in the here and now. These were monument builders with an eye for whatever conveyed a sense of purpose, of a people to be reckoned with. This concern with authority and power is evident in Ayutthayan sculpture. It is not so much a reminder of a spirit but a symbol of greatness, a monumental sculpture depicting a man more than a god. As the period progressed, the Buddha image became increasingly remote and devoid of charm. In large part, it reflected the mode of kingship adopted by Thai royalty after the fall of Angkor in 1431. From that time onwards, Thai monarchs took for themselves the Khmer concept of the deva-raja (god-king) and sequestered themselves in their palaces, forbidding their subjects to look at them or even mention their names.

The Ayutthaya school can be divided into three periods:

14th-15th centuries: The Ayutthayan sculptors, still very much influenced by Lop Buri and Sukhothai styles, begin to develop their own aesthetic.

16th-17th centuries: As the kings become more remote from their people, the images become less humane. There is greater concern with massive size to overwhelm the viewer. The delicacy formerly evident is missing.

18th century: There is a preoccupation with intricate detail and decoration to the detriment of expression. Faces and poses are alternately bland or cold, a triumph of style over content.

Opposite: *Bronze Buddha head of the 15th century.*
Below: *A giant bronze Buddha head cast in the 15th century. (Chao Sam Praya National Museum, Ayutthaya)*

Below: *The bronze Crowned Buddha in Wat Na Phramane's bot is a late Ayutthayan image.*
Bottom: *A stone Bodhi tree from the 17th-18th centuries found in a canal in Ayutthaya. The 48 cm. piece is extremely rare. It probably stood behind a meditating Buddha image.* (Bangkok National Museum)

The principal activity of Ayutthayan sculptors was the creation of Buddha images. Their primary contribution was to depict a wider range of incidents in which the Buddha was involved, choosing to portray episodes in his life other than the standard meditation or Maravijaya modes. They also made greater use of the pedestal on which the Buddha sits or stands, etching on it intricate patterns or making it a stage for a group of characters with whom the Buddha interacts. A prime example is the cluster of Mara's demons struggling to claw at the Buddha's feet or fleeing before the flood issuing from the goddess Toranee's hair. Hindu deities were also depicted but with a few notable exceptions they, too, suffered from a lack of spirituality which characterized statuary of former periods.

Bronze was the principal medium and in its casting, Ayutthayan sculptors were technical masters. This is ably demonstrated in the colossal seated Buddha that now occupies the Vihan Phra Mongkon Bopit adjacent to Wat Phra Si Sanphet. Stone, especially sandstone, was a popular material. Stone statues were often carved in sections and then covered with stucco. Gold was also highly favored as evidenced by the huge cache of gold-cast objects, including several gold Buddha images, found in a crypt beneath Wat Ratburana in 1957-1958 and lesser discoveries beneath Wat Mahathat and Wat Phra Si Sanphet. Ayutthayan sculptors were consummate carvers of wood; numerous teak doors remain as tribute to their skill in creating finely-cut dvarapala or door guardians. The sculptors also used stucco-covered brick to fashion gargantuan images of the Buddha, the 28 m. reclining Buddha at Wat Lokayasutha being a prime example.

Early Ayutthayan sculptors were influenced primarily by the Sukhothai school and by the school of Lop Buri via U Thong, but trod a middle way between the extreme spirituality of Sukhothai and the naturalism of Lop Buri. The main pose they chose for seated Buddhas was the Maravijaya with the feet in the virasana position but they favored the samaddhi or meditating position to a far greater extent than previous schools. The Buddha was also seated with his feet on the ground in "European fashion" which had been used by Dvaravati sculptors.

Standing Buddhas were very popular and displayed a greater variety of poses than before. They were shown holding alms bowls or with their hands in the vitarka mudra or abhaya mudra gesture. The Ayutthayan penchant for gigantism is amply displayed in the standing Buddha cast in 1499 ordered by Ramathibodi II to stand in Wat Phra Si Sanphet. Sixteen meters high on an eight meter tall pedestal, its bronze core was sheathed in 360 kilograms of gold plates. Unfortunately, it was destroyed by the Burmese in 1767 when they fired it to remove the gold and succeeded in cracking the bronze. Later, a portion of the wat wall collapsed shattering what remained of it.

Perhaps emulating their Sukhothai preceptors, early Ayutthayan sculptors created a number of walking Buddhas but with the weight resting on the right rather than the left foot, and the right rather than the left hand displaying the abhaya mudra. As the period progressed, the pose lost favor.

Reclining Buddhas are few in number, the aforementioned brick and stucco image at Wat Lokayasutha being the principal work.

The attire worn by the Buddha depends on his pose. Seated Buddhas are garbed like those of Sukhothai with the robe covering only the left shoulder and with a long, almost belt-like flap falling over the left shoulder. Standing images wear robes covering both shoulders in the manner of Lop Buri images. Down the front of the lower torso, a gathering of pleats falls to the lower hem of the robe. The robe is worn wide like bat wings and with the Sukhothai "hooks" at the meeting point of the leading edge and lower hem. With the reclining Buddha, the robe covers only the left shoulder and defies gravity by clinging to the body exactly as if the image were upright. This style image usually wears a belt as well.

With the passage of time, adorned or ornamented Buddhas, usually in the standing position, became increasingly popular perhaps as a reflection of the pomp and glory with which Ayutthayans regarded personages of power. The number and complexity of decorations are valuable guides to dating the images. They begin with simple diadems, and as the centuries pass add necklaces, bracelets, belts, embroidery on the robe and other jewelry. So, too, the mukuta headdresses become higher and higher.

Ayutthayan image faces are usually broad, often ovoid, resembling the U Thong C style. The eyebrows are like two flat arches meeting at the top of the nose, giving the impression of a gull in flight. The eyes are very prominent and appear half closed as if contemplating the ground. There is the barest hint of a smile on a mouth whose size lies halfway between the very narrow Lanna mouth and the very wide Dvaravati mouth. There is also a defining line around the lips almost like a second set of lips framing them. On sandstone images, a thin mustache is often etched above the lips. Ayutthayan images have strong chins often emphasized by two incised curved lines, with a line starting at the nose and passing through the lips.

The head is covered in small curls that climb the sides of the ushnisha to a flame ornament. The ushnisha treatment is unusual in that it is not portrayed as a separate protuberance but rather the head slopes to the flame without delineation of the division between skull and ushnisha. This technique gives the head an odd cone shape.

The pedestals mentioned before are stepped and tiered and decorated with demons and other figures, a treatment which would carry over into the Bangkok or Ratanakosin period. The Buddha is also depicted seated on a lotus flower.

Ayutthayan artists delighted in exploring new situations in which to portray the Buddha. Buddha footprints little different from those of previous periods were very popular. The Chadok tales served as another rich trove of new themes.

Ayutthayan sculptors created Hindu images but not in the numbers of their predecessors in Sukhothai. Among the most outstanding is a huge Siva 2.8 meters tall and with a goatee like a plowshare. His costume is intricately wrought with multiple pleats covered by a long leaf-like

Below: An adorned seated Buddha, 98 cm. tall, cast in bronze in the late 17th century. The image is seated on a lotus flower and displays the bhumisparsa mudra. (Bangkok National Museum)

Two of the many gold images done in the respoussé technique, found in the crypt of Wat Ratburana in Ayutthaya.
Right: A 90 cm. tall early Ayutthaya standing Buddha displaying the abhaya mudra dates from the late 13th-early 14th centuries. (Chao Sam Phraya National Museum, Ayutthaya)
Below: A late Ayutthayan Buddha maravijaya of superb execution.

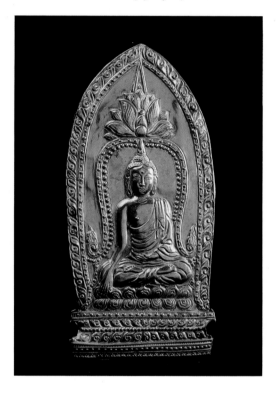

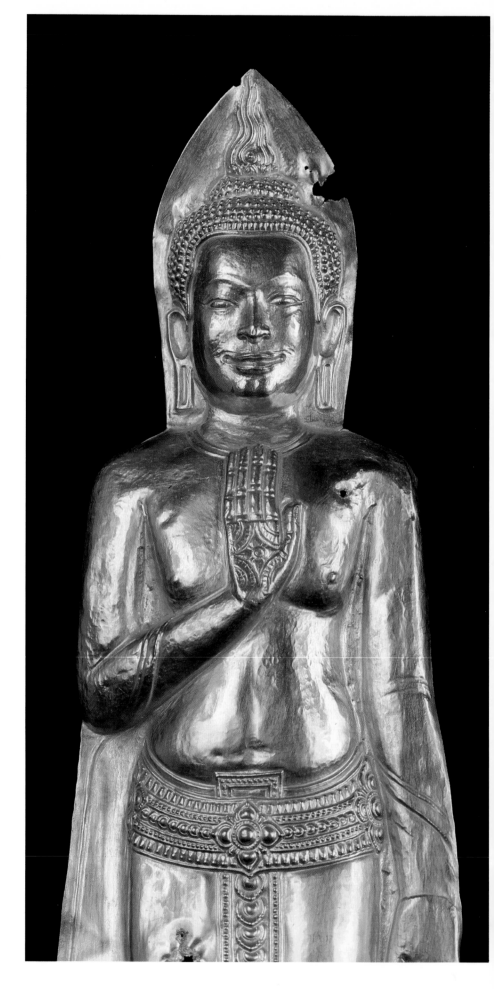

ornament and with a naga crossing his chest diagonally.

Stucco was used to cover the huge brick Buddha images and to decorate the exterior and interior walls of wats. Most of the stuccowork in Ayutthaya was destroyed in 1767. Many provincial wats, however, were spared and provide good examples of the style of decoration used in the mother city. Among Phetchaburi's wealth of examples is Wat Khao Bandai It, dating from the late Ayutthaya period, whose gable demonstrates supreme craftsmanship. Wat Sa Bua in the same town has beautiful stucco figures on the bases of its bai semas.

Wood carvers were employed in great numbers to decorate doors, windows and ceilings. Again, some of the best examples are found outside Ayutthaya. The carved and painted ceiling of Wat Sa Bua is a late Ayutthaya work depicting the cosmos. The doors of the sala of Phetchaburi's Wat Yai Suwannaram are some of Thailand's finest works.

While Ayutthaya potters produced terracotta Buddha images as well as human and animal figurines, the craftsmanship is not of the high level of its northern neighbors. Votive tablets fashioned of terracotta, pewter or baked clay portray Buddha in the Maravijaya position under a Bodhi tree or standing with his right hand in the abhaya gesture.

Painting

Ayutthaya painting has suffered considerably from the ravages of fire and water, the first at the hands of Burmese invaders in 1548 and 1767 and the second from the technique employed by Thai artists which left the paintings vulnerable to the country's damp climate. As a result, the finest examples of the period's painting are found in areas far from the capital, notably in Phetchaburi, Uttaradit, and Nonthaburi.

Little is known about the first 75 years when the majority of Ayutthaya's monuments were erected. It is probable that their interior walls were painted but not even traces of paint remain to indicate the style of their decoration. A later burst of activity was interrupted by the Burmese occupation and partial destruction of the city in 1548. It resumed after that only to be halted forever in 1767. Many of the remaining murals were considerably altered when they were restored in later centuries.

Ayutthayan murals depict the Tosachat, the life of Buddha, the Ramakien and a few local stories. Fine strokes drawn by sure hands outline brightly-colored figures, a practice that carried over into the Bangkok period. Ayutthayan murals are somewhat monochromatic by comparison with Bangkok paintings. Moreover, the backgrounds are generally cream or light-colored perhaps to compensate for the gloom of the dimly-lit, often windowless bots. Notable is the introduction of zigzag lines to compartmentalize individual scenes. In some instances, the line serves to create a series of diamonds in which various elements of the composition are placed. Ayutthayan artists were fond of incorporating nature motifs into their paintings, a practice which had largely disappeared by the 19th century. Flowers appear singly or in bouquets and animals, mythical and

Below: *The principal image at Wat Yai Suwannaram in Phetchaburi; this bronze seated Buddha was probably created in local workshops in the 17th century.*

Below: *Detail of a worshiping deity in Phetchaburi's Wat Yai Suwannaram, painted in the late 17th or early 18th centuries.*
Right: *A guardian, one of a pair carved on the wooden doors that once were part of Wat Phra Si Sanphet. Measuring 1.96 m., they were carved late in the 15th century or early in the 16th. (Chao Sam Phraya National Museum, Ayutthaya)*

real, cavort in a tangle of foliage on both the murals and on the gold and lacquer book cabinets which Ayutthaya excelled in producing. Chinese, Arabs and even Europeans appear in various episodes. Chinese influence can be seen in the vermilion that covers vast areas of the murals, alternating with the cream color of the walls themselves. There was also a decided preference for gold leaf to create ornaments, a practice which would continue into the Bangkok period.

Two examples of early painting remain in Ayutthaya itself. The earliest, the reliquary crypt of Wat Ratburana, dating from 1424, has paintings in two different styles. In the upper chamber there is strong evidence of a Chinese artist painting in the style of the Middle Kingdom. The paintings of the lower crypt, however, are similar to the engravings of Wat Si Chum. Episodes of the Tosachat cover the bottom half of the wall while above them is a single band of the 80 major disciples. These are surmounted by a wide band representing events in the Buddha's life, including 30 miracles he performed. Just under the vaulting are portraits of 24 Buddhas of the past each meditating under the species of tree (each different) whose branches sheltered him as he attained Enlightenment. Sharing the panels are mythical animals and disciples with the remaining space filled with ornate floral motifs. Also at Wat Ratburana is a prang whose inner walls are decorated with Buddhas under Bodhi trees separated by floral motifs. The whole is rendered in muted shades of white, yellow, rust and black.

The niche walls in Wat Mahathat's chedi have been lavishly decorated. Intended primarily as frames for the Buddha images, the walls feature elaborate ogee arches as nimbuses with the remaining space devoted to leaves and flowers. What remains today are the heavy outlines of individual elements and faint traces of the colors used. The other extant example of early Ayutthayan painting is found at Ratchaburi's Wat Mahathat. The walls here are covered with Buddhas of the past rendered in yellow, rust and black hues.

Only one example of late Ayutthayan painting has survived: the Somdet Phra Buddakhosachan pavilion in Wat Buddhaisawan, said to have been built by King Phra Petraja (1688-1702). The paintings cover the interior walls of the upper storey and represent a cross-section of the most important religious and secular Thai literary works. Vying for attention are scenes from the Tosachat, the Three Worlds (Heaven, Earth, Hell), Buddha's Enlightenment, the Ramakien and the voyage to Sri Lanka of the abbot for whom the pavilion is named. The outline of each figure is executed in a thin, concise line of unvarying thickness as if drawn with a pen.

The best examples of late Ayutthaya painting are found in distant cities. In the bot of Phetchaburi's Wat Yai Suwannaram are 17th century paintings of theps paying respect to Buddha who is seated in the Maravijaya posture. The worshipers are depicted in horizontal bands characterized by the predominance of white space and the liberal use of red

Below: *Pale deities against a vermilion background in the 18th century murals of Wat Chompoowek, Nonthaburi.*

Below: *The Life of Buddha mural in the lower crypt of Wat Ratburana makes heavy use of vermilion and gold leaf to ornament the figures' costumes.*
Painted in 1424.
Bottom: *The deities decorating the walls of Wat Ratburana's upper crypt show strong Chinese influence and may have been painted by a Chinese artist in 1424.*

pigments. Filling the spaces between the figures are floral motifs.

Also in Phetchaburi is the bot of Wat Ko Keo Suttaram whose paintings date from 1734. Here the zigzag lines do more than separate individual elements, they are part of the composition. The subject is the Life of Buddha and while overall it appears a bit disorganized by comparison with Wat Yai Suwannaram, it is distinguished by a highly original and realistic approach far removed from the more static or stylized figures of later painting. Visitors to 18th century Thailand have been included among the worshipers: Arabs, Europeans in wigs and beards and dressed in the fashions of the times. In the Miracle of Savatthi in which Buddha spouted fire and water to terrify the unbelievers, the horrified viewers are depicted as Arabs. Uttaradit's Wat Phra Boromathat marks the northernmost extent of the Ayutthayan school. In its vihan luang are episodes from the Life of Buddha and scenes from the Tosachat.

Providing a contrast to the classicism of Ayutthayan painting is the rustic simplicity of the Nonthaburi school north of Bangkok. Like Ayutthayan painting, Nonthaburi murals are characterized by the use of light-colored backgrounds and a predominance of reds. The composition, however, is more random and often lacks harmony, with too many figures crammed into too small a space. Zigzag lines are employed erratically and often without regard to the overall effect; a panel may be divided diagonally from top to bottom by a zigzag line. Simply drawn and with a disregard for proportion, the figures are not without a certain charm, making up in spontaneity what they lack in skilled execution. Their saving grace is that they have been created by artists unfettered by aesthetic constraints but free to paint as they pleased.

Of the three representative examples of the Nonthaburi school, the paintings at Wat Pho Bang Oh are the best preserved. Eschewing the normal subjects, the murals concern the various evils which confront man and offer the broad hint that the way to avoid them is to join the monkhood. The figures are crisply drawn with very thin strokes outlining them against the light background. The bot of the late Ayutthayan Wat Prasat is windowless, giving uninterrupted space for murals of the Tosachat in a predominance of reds and whites. Wat Champoowek's bot portrays the Tosachat and the Battle with Mara. The wat's vihan contains murals of the Life of Buddha which are characterized by the use of free-standing rather than grouped figures and by the very heavy weight of its palaces and halls.

Ayutthaya also produced a number of excellent lacquer and gold art objects as well as beautiful manuscripts devoted to a variety of religious themes including the Three Worlds and the Tosachat. These are discussed in the chapter on the Minor Arts.

Below: Buddha confounds the heretics, in this case looking much like foreigners, a bit of wry humor since the foreigners were doing their utmost to convert the "heathen" Thais to Christianity. The scene appears at Wat Ko Keo Suttharam, Phetchaburi and was painted in 1734.

Left: Bands of praying deities are framed by zigzag lines and the remaining space is devoted to bouquets of flowers. Wat Yai Suwannaram, Petchaburi, late 17th-early 18th century.

Bangkok

Barely afloat in the wake of the catastrophe that swept over Ayutthaya in 1767 were a shattered people who had seen their capital city and most of their culture, art and literature destroyed overnight. Rallying from defeat, they routed a Burmese garrison force, then sat down in their smoldering city to decide what to do next. The outlook was bleak. The capital was in ruins; to rebuild it would require dismantling and then reconstructing it, an impossible task to undertake with vastly depleted manpower. Mindful that Ayutthaya was indefensible and that there was a strong possibility the Burmese might return, the Thais decided to move downriver and start anew. The site they chose was Thon Buri, an old town on the western bank of the Chao Phya River which had been the customs port for ships moving upstream to Ayutthaya.

For the next 15 years, Thon Buri served as Thailand's capital. Preoccupied with repulsing fresh Burmese invasions, the king had little time for building a proper city. In 1782, a new king came to the throne, a man of vision who kindled in his people the desire to create a kingdom to rival Ayutthaya. Deciding that Thon Buri was difficult to defend and too constricted by canals and wats to permit future expansion, King Rama I moved his capital across the river to the small village of Bangkok.

To invest the new city with the spirit of Ayutthaya as well as economize on its construction costs, Rama I ordered that bricks from the ruined buildings of the former capital be transported to Bangkok and incorporated into thick defensive walls and a system of 14 watchtowers be erected. He then engaged in a vigorous construction program, building the city's main wats and palaces and spawning a major metropolis.

While the first three reigns were characterized by a look to the past in an attempt to recreate a lost heritage, the ascension to the throne of King Rama IV in 1851 marked an about face to gaze into the future. Rama IV (1851-1868) began a determined drive to modernize Thailand and bring it to the level of development enjoyed by Europe. New political ideas were introduced and a new scientific approach was taken toward remedying social problems. In art, there was an endeavor to emulate the spirit if not the content of Western art. New subjects and themes were explored and a new generation of artists with an interest in worldly as well as otherworldly concerns was born.

Below: *Detail of columns, pilasters, wall and embrasure of the Phra Thepidon at Wat Phra Kaew.*

The next turning point occurred in 1932 with the revolution that overturned 700 years of absolute monarchy, replacing it with a constitutional monarchy. In art, there was a wholehearted absorption of Western modes to the virtual neglect of all that had come before, a trend which only recently has begun to be reversed.

The period from 1782 to the present is called the "Bangkok" or "Ratanakosin" period, the latter being the formal name for the city which translates as "the city of the Emerald Buddha". The art of the years since 1900 is treated in the Contemporary Art chapter.

Architecture

Like Ayutthaya, Bangkok was conceived of as a water-based city. Boats traveled waterways which branched off from Klong (Canal) Lawd and Klong Banglampoo, dug as the main arterials and as the city's defensive moats in times of attack. The city was centered on the artificial island now known as "Ratanakosin" defined by the bend of the Chao Phya River and Klong Lawd, an area roughly the shape of a conch shell. Here the principal buildings of the city were erected. The area not reserved for wats and official buildings was occupied by the palatial homes of the nobility. The houses of the populace, raised on stilts against the annual invasion of the monsoon floodwaters, filled the districts east of the city walls.

The original city was spacious, with wats occupying small corners of vast, tree-filled courtyards. Where feasible, they were built to face water in accordance with ancient architectural tenets. Viewed from canal level at a leisurely pace, their beauty could be appreciated to the fullest. As the city grew, however, there was a need for bituminous roads to replace the dusty elephant paths. In response, King Rama IV ordered that New Road, Bamrungmuang Road and Fuang Nakhon Roads be constructed. At the same time, royal architects built shophouses which were leased to merchants. Ethnic neighborhoods sprang up complementing the already established Chinese section. The Europeans built along the riverbank around the present Oriental Hotel, the Vietnamese and Kampucheans chose the area along Samsen Road and the Indonesians settled in the environs of Makkasan, named for the Indonesian town of Makassar. At the beginning of the 20th century, King Rama V built a country villa called Amporn Palace in the Dusit district and a sizable community of well-to-do gentry grew up around it. King Rama VI added to the neighborhood by building the Chitrlada Palace where the present royal family resides.

Increased prosperity, the desire to replace wooden houses with concrete structures and rising land values decreed that the city would become more and more densely populated as the years passed. Today, it is difficult to imagine that Bangkok was once regarded as a garden city of wide boulevards passing through sparsely populated neighborhoods.

Wat Architecture

Bangkok wat plans were similar to those of Ayutthaya as would be expected in a city dedicated to recreating the architecture of its predecessor. One deviation was that, except for Wat Arun, the prang-centered wat disappeared entirely. Favored were the rectangular bots and vihans. Windows with shutters replaced the slit windows of Ayutthaya and water lily capitals were chosen to the virtual exclusion of lotus bud capitals.

The heavy look of Ayutthaya was replaced by an airier, lighter design that substituted height for mass with slender columns and roofs more sharply peaked. By contrast to Ayutthaya's grandly ornate decoration, Bangkok's buildings and wats were subdued. The walls of the principal wats were covered in a wider variety of materials like ceramic tiles, mirror tiles or marble slabs which clad them from ground to roofline. Doors and window shutters were elaborately decorated in gilded reliefs, gold and lacquer, painted dvarapala guardians or mother-of-pearl scenes and the embrasures now framed full figures of guardians. During the reign of King Rama III, the vogue for Chinese art resulted in a number of wats with tympana of ceramic tile flowers and bai sema enclosed in stone Chinese lanterns. In the North, architects continued to build in wood and only gradually adopted brick and stucco as their principal material. To their credit, they built wats according to their own dictates rather than to a standardized design as most of the capital city's wats seem to have been planned.

The first building ordered by King Rama I was a repository for the Emerald Buddha. While Wat Phra Kaew was being erected, the king lived in a rude wooden building at the southwest corner of the grounds. In 1785, the bot of the new wat was consecrated in a solemn ceremony recalling the glorious days of Ayutthaya. The bot, 55 meters long and 24 meters wide, was built with the three doors of the entrance facing the rising sun and another three doors facing the setting sun.

Flanking the steps leading to the main doors are three pairs of bronze singhas, while around the baseboard on the two long sides and portions of the western and eastern sides are garudas rampant in bronze and covered in gold leaf. The exterior walls are covered in gold mirror tiles in leaf shapes. The interior space is free of columns and the exterior corridors are framed by rows of columns tied together by a balustrade.

The eastern and western doors are sheltered by a raised porch. The tympanum is dominated by a figure of Phra Narai mounted on a garuda; nagas in gold mirror tiles run down the bargeboards of the three overlapping roofs. The bai sema are enclosed in elaborate mondops.

In a row to the north are three of the most important structures in the kingdom. On the east is the Prasad Phra Thepidon built in 1855; a fire destroyed the original structure and it was rebuilt in 1903. It was converted by King Rama VI to serve as the pantheon and now holds the statues of the first eight Chakri dynasty kings. The graceful building is

Below: Wat Phra Kaew from the west with the chedi (front), library and Prasat Phra Thepidon. The trio represents the principal styles of Thai architecture: the bell-shaped chedi, the multi-tiered mondop and its predecessor, the prang, used here to crown a roof.
Bottom: The tiled roof of the bot and surrounding phra rabieng of Wat Phra Chetupon, Bangkok. (See also, illustration on Page 16).

covered in blue and red tiles and topped by a prang that rises above an orange and green tiled roof. The entrance is flanked by a pair of gilded chedis whose lower portions are guarded by demons. In the courtyard are gilded bronze kinnaras and kinnaris.

To the west of the Prasad Phra Thepidon is a delicate jewelbox in the shape of a mondop ringed by slender columns and crowned with a tiered roof like a mongkut. Designed in the same style and by the same architect as the mondop of Phra Buddhabhat at Saraburi, it was erected as a library to hold the Tripitaka, the sacred scriptures of Thai Buddhism. The original was accidentally burned down by fireworks during a celebration marking its completion and was rebuilt in a slightly different style shortly thereafter. The last structure of the trio is a tall gold-sheathed chedi called the Phra Si Ratana Chedi built on the exact design of those at Wat Chedi Si Sanphet in Ayutthaya.

South of Wat Phra Kaew is Wat Phra Chetupon, known popularly as Wat Po. Formerly an Ayutthayan wat called Wat Bodharam (Monastery of the Bodhi Tree), it was rebuilt by King Rama I between 1789 and 1801 and restored in 1831 by King Rama III. The bot is surrounded by a courtyard bordered by a phra rabieng connecting four vihan thits set perpendicular to the bot at the cardinal points and serving as entranceways. Another set of walls compartmentalize eight smaller courtyards ideal for meditation. A second courtyard encompassing the first is defined by four vihan khots at the corners.

The bot is one of the most beautiful in Bangkok. It sits on a platform reached by a short stairway guarded by singhas. The base of the platform is covered in superb bas reliefs of Ramakien scenes and represents some of the best stone carving ever done by Thai sculptors. The bot doors are also devoted to Ramakien scenes and are considered to be among the finest examples of mother-of-pearl craftsmanship in the kingdom.

To the west of the bot, galleries that once sheltered a series of paintings of daily life in each Thai province enclose four identical chedis, three in a row running north to south and the fourth to the west. They honor the first four kings of the Chakri dynasty. The green-tiled chedi in the middle is dedicated to the memory of King Rama I and contains fragments of the ruined bronze image that once stood in Ayutthaya's Wat Phra Si Sanphet. In the northwest corner is the vihan built by King Rama III to protect the 45 meter long, 15 meter high gilded stucco Reclining Buddha. Three other structures complete the complex. To the west of the four royal chedis is a library; to its north is a Chinese style pavilion and to its south is a European style pavilion.

Wat Mahathat is another example of an Ayutthayan period wat restored to serve the new city. Situated between the Grand Palace and the Palace to the Front, it was rebuilt by the younger brother of King Rama I in 1802 after its vihan had been destroyed by fireworks. It developed into an important meditation center where, in 1824, the future King Rama IV began his 27 years as a monk. It was completely reconstructed between

1844 and 1851.

The wat consists of an identically sized bot and vihan set side by side and a mondop on the east, all crowded into a very tiny courtyard. Like the vihan, the bot, the largest in Bangkok, is undistinguished. Its interior columns run down both sides and across both ends forming a central rectangle surrounded by a corridor encompassed by the exterior walls. The bot is unusual in that it has only four bai sema and they are affixed to the inner walls at the four cardinal points, perhaps because there was so little space to place them in the courtyard. The mondop containing the relic which gives the wat its name ("Great Relic") is one of the few in Bangkok with a cruciform roof.

Wat Suthat stands to the east halfway between the palace and the city wall. Bangkok's tallest wat, it was built by King Rama I to hold the eight meter tall by six meter wide 14th century bronze Phra Sri Sakyamuni Buddha image he had moved from Sukhothai's Wat Mahathat to Bangkok. The vihan is an impressive structure with teak doors that stand 5.5 meters high and 1.5 meters wide.

Just across the city walls to the east was an old wat named Sake built in Ayutthayan times. On returning from wars in Kampuchea in 1782, General Chakri paused there for an old royal rite known as the lustration of the hair, prior to entering the city and being crowned King Rama I. Later he rebuilt the wat, renaming it Wat Saket ("Sa" meaning "cleaning" and "ket" from the Pali "kesa" or "hair"). In its courtyard, King Rama III decided to erect the greatest chedi in the kingdom. The structure collapsed and it was left to King Rama IV to heap the rubble into a tall artificial mountain. He crowned it with a golden chedi and a platform overlooking the city. In 1897, this Phu Khao Thong (Golden Mount) was invested with relics brought from the Buddha's birthplace in Nepal.

Wat Rakang, directly across the river from the Grand Palace, was the last major wat rebuilt by King Rama I. The Ayutthayan style bot is unremarkable except for an unusual pair of windows high on its front wall. What is noteworthy are the three wooden houses which sit behind it. Superb examples of Thai house architecture, they belonged to King Rama I while he was still a general serving under Thon Buri's sole monarch, King Taksin. He donated them to be used as monks' residences and when he ascended the throne in 1782, he had them converted to a library for religious texts. The complex, together with its window panels and murals, was restored in 1982 primarily by noted Thai painter Fua Haripitak.

King Rama III is known for four wats he built or restored in the Chinese style. Wat Chalerm Phra Kiat, Wat Raja Oros and Wat Thong Nophakhun in Thon Buri and the Sala Geng in Bangkok's Wat Bovornivet are examples of the fad that swept the kingdom to emulate the styles of Chinese architects and artists. Ceramic tiles grace the pediment. The roof peak does not have a chofa, and the murals inside as well as the decorations on the window shutters are all in the style of the Middle

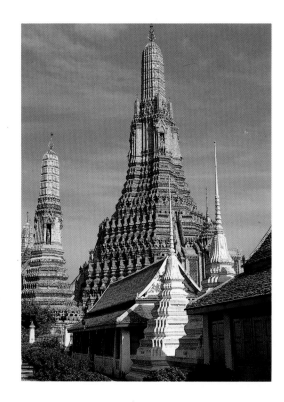

Below: *The prang and two of the four corner prangs of Wat Arun on the Thon Buri bank of the Chao Phya River. Built by Rama IV.*

Below: *Wat Rajabopit's circular phra rabieng connects a bot and three vihan khot all of which surround a central chedi.*
Bottom: *Wat Benjamabopit with its walls clad in Carrara marble.*

Kingdom.

Wat Bovornivet was founded in 1827 by the Deputy King of Rama III. Later, King Rama III erected the Phra Panya vihan for his half brother, the future King Rama IV, who was its abbot and spent several years there revising the Buddhist scriptures. The wat has served subsequent kings as well. Ramas VI and VII were ordained at Wat Phra Kaew but resided at Wat Bovornivet. The present monarch, King Rama IX (Bhumibol) was ordained there and resided in its monks' quarters.

Perhaps the most unusual building constructed by King Rama III is the Lohaprasad in the courtyard of Wat Theptidaram. The structure is modeled on an ancient monastery with 1,000 cells erected in Sri Lanka in 161 B.C. The pyramidal structure measures 38.6 meters on a side and rises in six tiers to a height of 33.5 meters. The ground floor, made of laterite and brick is made up of 15 corridors with vaulted ceilings that run from one side of the building to the other on a north-south axis and another 15 on an east-west axis. The intersections of the corridors form small rooms which were used by monks for meditation.

Spiral staircases lead to the second story which is identical to the first. The third and fourth stories are considerably indented with only seven vaulted corridors per side. The fifth level has three corridors and is surmounted by a tower which is crowned by a mondop. On the outer rim of each level are iron spires which give the wat its name ("Loha" means "Metal").

Wat Arun (the Temple of Dawn), a huge prang which sits on the Thon Buri bank of the Chao Phya River, has a long and venerable history. Originally known as Wat Cheng, it was a small structure when in 1780 King Taksin (1767-1782) placed in its vihan the Emerald Buddha which resided there until King Rama I moved it to Wat Phra Kaew in 1785.

King Rama II began raising the 15 meter tall tower to its present height, a project completed by King Rama III. Today, the vajra-crowned 67 meter tall prang stands atop a 37 meter high base. Built in Ayutthayan style, it represents Mount Meru whose upper portion is guarded by a ring of demons. At the top of stairways which climb it at the four cardinal points are niches containing figures of Indra riding a three-headed elephant. On the first terrace at the foot of each of the stairways are four pavilions containing images depicting the four most important events in Buddha's life: birth, meditating sheltered by a seven-headed naga, preaching to his first five disciples and in death attended by his followers.

At the four corners of the complex are smaller prangs each with four niches containing statues of Phra Pai, the god of the wind, astride a white horse. The four prangs and the massive central tower are decorated by pieces of broken Chinese pottery donated by Buddhist devotees. The pieces have been shaped into petals to form flowers, many with seashells at their centers. A prasad to the west of the prang is similarly covered in ceramic tiles of Chinese design.

King Rama IV is credited with the construction of Wat Rajapradit, a small but charming bot clad in white and gray Chinese marble. The bot's doors and windows are topped by bas reliefs of mongkuts. Behind the bot is a Sinhalese style stupa; to the east is the Khmer style Traipidok prang and to the west is a prang reminiscent of the Bayon at Angkor Thom.

By far the most astounding piece of architecture and engineering is the gigantic Phra Pathom Chedi at Nakhon Pathom. While still a monk, King Rama IV discovered an ancient chedi which he surmised had once had great importance in Thai Buddhism. When he became king, he assigned the architect who built the Prasat Phra Thepidon to design a massive chedi over the ruins of the original. The architect created a 127 meter tall structure regarded as the tallest Buddhist chedi in the world.

Wat Rajabopit was built by Rama V in 1870 when Thailand was becoming increasingly infatuated with Western ideas. Its centerpiece is a tall chedi built over a crypt with a niche containing a Lop Buri Buddha meditating under the outspread hood of a naga. Encircling the chedi is a phra rabieng covered in Chinese ceramic tiles and broken at the four cardinal points by three vihan khots and on the northern side by a bot. The bot is an ornate building whose pride is flawless mother-of-pearl doors with the insignias of the five royal ranks, a motif which is repeated in the same material on the windows. Like the phra rabieng and the vihans, the bot is clad in ceramic tiles but its pediment depicts a seven-headed gilded elephant beneath a crown. The pediment on the porch is decorated by a Phra Narai atop a garuda decorated in gilt and red and blue mirror tiles.

Its most stunning architectural feature, however, is its interior. One feels he has stepped into a European chapel. Bearing no resemblance whatever to typical Thai bots, it has a vaulted ceiling like a miniature Gothic cathedral rendered in brown with gold leaf on the ribbing.

King Rama V's other main contribution to Bangkok period architecture is Wat Benjamabopit. An old structure dating from the late Ayutthayan period, it was called Wat Lem and later Wat Sai Thong. In 1827, it served briefly as the headquarters of an expeditionary force led by a son of King Rama II against the Prince of Vientiane. When he returned victorious from Laos, the young man and his four brothers built a chedi in Wat Lem's forecourt. King Rama IV later changed its name to Wat Benja (five) Bopit (princes) in honor of the five brothers. In 1899, King Rama V assigned the well-known architect Prince Naris to design a new bot. When the wat was completed, the king added the syllable "ma" to its name so it became Benjamabopit or "ruler of the fifth reign" of the Chakri dynasty.

Prince Naris designed Wat Benjamabopit according to an old plan that called for a cruciform bot capped by a series of overlapping roofs. He clad the building in Carrara marble imported from Italy, an innovation which gave the building its other name, "the Marble Wat".

Below: *The Lohaprasad at Wat Theptidaram was built by Rama III as a replica of an ancient temple in Sri Lanka.*

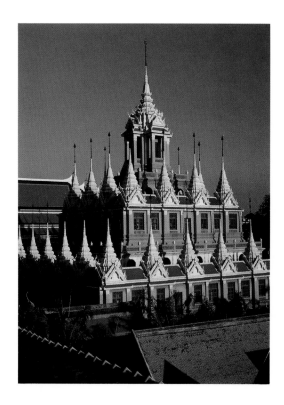

Royal Architecture

The principal royal building in Bangkok is the Grand Palace, a complex of buildings which has been constructed over a period of a century. Shortly after the consecration of Wat Phra Kaew in 1785, King Rama I began work on the Amarindraphisek Audience Hall near the western wall. When completed, the royal throne was installed and the king began to hold audiences. The building was struck by lightning in 1789 and burned to the ground. Among the firefighters was the king himself, who helped carry his throne to safety. On the site, the king built the Dusit Mahaprasad, a dignified building whose roof is capped by a gilded mongkut with corners supported by four garudas. To the present day, the building has served as the royal audience chamber.

To the northeast of the Dusit Mahaprasad, King Rama I built the Aphon Phimok pavilion. Here, kings would dismount from their elephants, change their robes and proceed to the audience hall.

Further to the east is the Maha Montien, an edifice comprising of three buildings connected along a north-south axis. At the entrance to the northernmost building, the Amarinda Vinichai, are the gold-topped red poles at which royal guests could tether their elephants. The building itself served as a receiving hall. The two buildings beyond it, the Paisal Taksin and the Chakrabardibiman Hall, were used by King Rama I as his throne hall and royal bedchamber. King Rama III was the last to live in it full time, but it has been customary for each king to spend the first night after his coronation in it.

The most important building of the group is the Chakri Mahaprasad. Built by King Rama V, it was designed by a British architect in Italian Renaissance style. The king had originally intended that it have an Italian roof, but conservative elements in the court demanded a Thai-looking building so it was given its three mondop spires. Thais responded to the building's somewhat schizoid personality by dubbing it "the farang (foreigner) wearing the chada (Thai dancer's headdress)". Beneath the central spire are ashes of the eight Chakri kings, while those of principal members of royal houses are under the other two.

The outer courtyard contains the Borompiman Hall, a building almost completely Western in style, which is used as a residence for foreign royalty and state visitors. The Sala Sahathai, also in Western design, is used for royal banquets.

Rama I's younger brother, who served as vice-king, built his own Palace to the Front, north of the Grand Palace, a site which today is the National Museum. Most of the buildings he erected have since been torn down but one of its most beautiful edifices, the Buddhaisawan chapel, remains as testament to the buildings which once occupied its spacious courtyard. The chapel houses the second most revered image in the kingdom, the Phra Buddha Sihing, but is best known for the fine mural paintings on the Life of Buddha which cover its lower walls.

Opposite: *The Aphon Phimok Prasad Pavilion where monarchs dismounted from their elephants and changed their robes before proceeding to the Dusit Mahaprasad, the Audience Hall which stands behind it. The hall was built on the site of the fire-ruined original, both built by King Rama I. It is in the cruciform shape that its name, Prasad, suggests.*

Above: *One of the 12-month Ceremony murals at Wat Rajapradit.*
Top: *The Chakri Mahaprasad, the principal building in the Grand Palace. The late 19th century structure was begun as an Italian Renaissance building, but in its latter stage of construction a Thai roof was added. At right is the Aphon Phimok Prasad Pavilion.*

Below: A pair of guardian yaksas made of painted stucco face the bot of Wat Phra Kaew.

Sculpture

Bangkok period sculpture is not a shining star in the annals of Thai art. Technical virtuosity has not been matched by sensuous expression, with the result that while most statuary is superbly crafted, it is lifeless. The Bangkok school, however, does not entirely deserve the drubbing it has received from art historians. While its artists were not as prolific as those of previous ages, they demonstrated an admirable willingness to explore new themes. The inspiration is no longer entirely religious. Sculptors of the period between 1782 and 1851 delved into old literary and Hindu texts to find new themes and new ways in which to depict the Buddha, and created a variety of pieces without precedent.

There is a preoccupation with monumental representations, an attempt blindly to emulate Ayutthayan modes and thereby to regain the past. What has been achieved, however, has been the form and not the substance. The Reclining Buddha at Wat Chetupon is one example. Some 45 meters long and 15 meters high, the gilded brick and stucco image is highlighted by enormous feet on which the 108 auspicious signs identifying a Buddha have been beautifully crafted in mother-of-pearl. While the image overwhelms the viewer it fails to touch him.

Early Bangkok sculptors preferred to work in bronze, wood and stucco. There are almost no stone images but there are numerous fine examples of marble bas reliefs, notably those on the base of Wat Chetupon's bot. Bangkok sculptors display a fascination with drapery and ornamentation; adorned Buddhas have become jewel-encrusted Buddhas. While the workmanship in some of the robes, notably that on a statue of Phra Malai, is excellent, it detracts from the impact of the piece. At the same time, the faces are often badly proportioned and vacuous.

The problems facing King Rama I were enormous, but nowhere more so than in art. Artisans were valuable war booty and undoubtedly a large number were marched west across the mountains to serve Burmese kings after Ayutthaya's fall. In order to fill Bangkok's many new wats with Buddha images, Rama I brought from Sukhothai and Ayutthaya those statues which had not been smashed by looters. By doing so, he accomplished a number of objectives. He established Bangkok as the new center of the Buddhist religion in Thailand, in part giving it legitimacy as a national capital. He provided comfort to those still mourning the loss of Ayutthaya by compelling them to focus their eyes on the city in which the country's future would take place. Finally he provided sculptors with examples of various styles enabling them, like court poets, dramatists, artists and religious scholars, to recreate the works lost in Ayutthaya's destruction.

One of the first images transferred from Thon Buri to Bangkok was the Emerald Buddha, which Rama I had captured from the King of Vientiane. He then set to work encouraging sculptors to create new works. Typical is the Gandharattha Buddha now kept in the Grand Palace and taken out only for the Plowing Ceremony and Songkran. It rests in the virasana position with the right hand in the "Calling Down the Rain" mudra and the left hand in the "Catching the Rain" mudra. Despite its grand inspiration, it is a somewhat insipid piece. Another work of Rama I's sculptors is the Phra Chai Lang Chang (Victory Buddha on Elephant Back). It sits in the Maravijaya attitude and its eyes are inlaid with porcelain. Rama I carried it with him on his elephant when he went to war.

King Rama III (1824-1851) was an active patron of the arts. One of the outstanding creations of his reign are two standing Buddhas, each three meters tall and clad in 84 kg. of gold. They were dedicated to the king's father and grandfather and placed in the bot of Wat Phra Kaew. Among the most remarkable creations of his sculptors is a series of 33 small bronzes, one for each of Ayutthaya's 33 kings, depicting the main events of Buddha's life. These mini-tableaux are angular and semi-abstract lending them a particular charm.

Bangkok artists created numerous statues of disciples and hermits, far more than earlier periods. One of the finest is one entitled Phra Malai Visits Hell. Reminiscent of Ayutthayan approaches, the base is utilized to help tell the story, being encrusted with odd creatures representing the damned of the nether regions. Phra Malai wears an ornate brocaded robe which seems far too rich for a penniless monk. Similarly, in 1836, Rama III commissioned statues of 80 rishis to depict all the yoga exercises. Cast in lead, they display great vitality and variety.

After 1851, the government espoused new ideals based on modern thought. While a monk, King Rama IV had revised the Buddhist canons, ridding them of their fantastic elements by applying the yardstick of pragmatism and rationality, a more scientific orientation than hitherto followed. As king, he looked at the institutions of government and social codes in similar manner and made his reforms accordingly. To a major extent, the same approach was taken in art. A new rationalism stripped art of its otherworldliness. One of the images created under Rama IV's auspices was the Sambuddhabarni, which wears a simplified robe and whose head bears a flame but no ushnisha. A second image, the Phra Nirantaraya, also lacks a ushnisha. It sits in the samaddhi position and wears a very realistic looking robe. Despite these bold new steps, there were no emulators and the styles died with the king.

King Rama V ordered a number of copies of famous images, Phitsanulok's venerated Phra Buddha Jinnarat now in Wat Benjamabopit being the best known. He also commissioned a number of original works. In 1871, his sculptors cast a bronze standing image as an amalgam of old styles. The image wears a Sukhothai robe with its hem hooks but it is embroidered in Bangkok fashion. The fingers are of equal length, recalling late Sukhothai iconography, but the ushnisha and flame are both Ayutthayan. In the end, despite its fine craftsmanship, the face is unappealing and the statue as a whole is lackluster.

Rama V also undertook the creation of several bronze Hindu deities. These images were inspired by the Tamra Devarupa, a Hindu

Below: An Adorned Buddha displays the abhaya mudra. The gilded bronze image dates from the 19th century and is in the Sala Geng of Wat Bovornivet. Bottom: One of the 152 marble panels devoted to retelling the Ramakien. The 45 cm. tall slab was carved in the reign of Rama III and placed along the base of the Wat Chetupon bot.

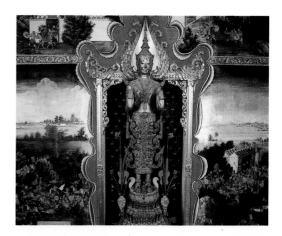

Below: A guilded bronze kinnara in the forecourt of Prasad Phra Thepidon at Wat Phra Kaew.
Right: Adorned Buddha in bronze alloy with red and green enamel ornaments, gems and pendants is typical of early 19th century decorated Buddhas. The robes of the 40 cm. tall image are like those worn by monarchs of the period. (Bangkok National Museum)

iconological treatise written during the reign of Rama III as a guide for artists. The resultant statuary is surprisingly traditional, however, in sharp contrast to the modern modes being pursued during the rest of the mid-Bangkok period. At the other extreme, Rama V caused to be molded in terracotta several realistic portraits of living people. One of the best examples is that of Princess Yikheng, an elderly lady of the court. She is portrayed in a simple panung sarong with loose blouse and with cropped hair, and appears as she would in life without embellishment or refinement.

Of the many decorative sculpture works, the most outstanding are the 152 marble bas reliefs of scenes from the Ramakien created during the reign of Rama III to decorate the base of Wat Chetupon's bot. The figures cavorting in foliage suggest the sculptor's good eye for composition and steady hand in execution. Highly detailed, they flow in a way seldom duplicated by the statuary of the period. Stucco statues covered in ceramic tile were also popular. The giant six meter tall yaksas which guard the entrances to Wat Phra Kaew, Wat Chetupon and Wat Arun are good examples of this genre but, again, size seems to be more important than artistic delicacy.

Wood carving was accorded scant attention by Bangkok sculptors, but one area merits special consideration if for no other reason than that it conveys the grandeur of the Thai monarchy in a way that almost overshadows all its other artistic achievements. The Royal Barges in their grand progress down the Chao Phya River during state ceremonies are marvels of engineering and of decorative sculpture. An aquatic people, Thais have always depended on their waterways to move goods and people swiftly. During the Ayutthayan period, an estimated 100,000 boats cruised the rivers and canals of the Central Valley. Long, slim, and low to the water, they ranged from tiny sampan-like skiffs to regal vessels whose size, decoration and number of oarsmen declared their owner's rank and status. The most magnificent of all belonged to the king.

When King Rama I built his new capital, he decreed the construction of a new fleet of royal barges, the largest being 36.15 meters long. Over the years, the barges fell into disrepair and King Rama V ordered that new ones be built. The longest, the Sri Suphannahongse, was 44.9 meters from stem to stern and was carved from a single teak log. Today the fleet numbers 51 barges and is propelled by the arms of 2,100 paddlers. The prow of each of the principal barges is intricately carved in elaborate patterns covered with gold leaf and inset with mirror mosaics. The subjects include the Sri Suphannahongse with its graceful swan-like prow, the Anantanakraj with seven semi-ferocious nagas, and lesser boats with figureheads of demons, monkeys, crocodiles, and tigers.

Below: *Detail of one of the gilded wooden doors carved by Rama II for Wat Suthat. The nature motif is an inheritance from the Ayutthayan period. (Bangkok National Museum)*
Bottom: *A gilded wooden singha. (Bangkok National Museum)*

Below: *Prince Siddhartha cuts his hair and begins the life of an ascetic in this episode from the Life of the Buddha murals in Buddhaisawan Chapel. The murals, painted in the reign of Rama I, are considered some of the finest in Thailand.*

Opposite: *The annual festival at Phra Buddhabhat in Saraburi is the subject of a mural in the bot of Phetchaburi's Wat Mahasamanaram. Painted by Khrua In Khong, it is especially interesting for its portrayal of the vehicles of transportation in the reign of Rama IV.*

Painting

While architecture and sculpture failed to evolve and perhaps even regressed after the Ayutthaya period, painting flourished as artists expended their creative talents on the brilliant murals which decorate the inner walls of vihans and bots of wats. Indeed, if Sukhothai was an age of sculpture and Ayutthaya an era of architecture, then Bangkok must be characterized as an age of painting.

The formalism evident in sculpture is found in painting as well, but what saves them from being static are the observant eyes of the artists that have recorded small details of life, often with a wry and even slightly risqué humor. Personality quirks are conveyed and body positions are natural, not contorted or contrived. They are portraits that even in two dimensions convey a human quality.

The principal difference between city classicism and the rural simplicity of up country wat painting is in the formal expressions on the subjects' faces. The figures in city murals wear composed miens; they smile in adversity even when they are playing the roles of avenging deities. Serenity and detachment prevail as if nothing will be permitted to disturb their tranquility. In one of the Tosachat episodes, the demon Punnaka rides a swift horse to whose tail the wise sage Vitoon clings. The demon tries his best to brush the sage against the mountaintops as he flies, hoping to kill him. Through it all, Vitoon smiles. By contrast, in rural wats, the expressions, while restrained, convey the subject's emotions and in many cases are more appealing.

The penchant for rich color and decoration is evident in architecture and costume. The cream backgrounds of Ayutthayan murals are exchanged for darker hues. Splendid palaces, fabulously appointed, are inhabited by princes and princesses dressed in beautiful raiment. As the period progresses the muted hues become brighter and gold leaf adorns royal bodies, an addition which interferes with composition and renders the murals less pleasing. The increasing strength of the colors is one of several changes which affected the quality of Bangkok paintings as the period progressed. It came hand in hand with the mid-19th century fascination with the West and was accompanied by the introduction of three dimensions, perspective and modeling of the figures through play of light and shadow. Except for some celebrated exceptions, the new techniques were detrimental to painting as a whole.

The medium of painting includes murals, manuscripts and to a certain extent lacquer and gold work used principally to decorate manuscript cabinets, wat doors and windows and some utensils; the latter two aspects are treated in the Minor Arts chapter. As with architecture and sculpture, painting began by trying to emulate the works of Ayutthaya but soon branched into new areas, discovering new themes and subjects and exploring them to the fullest. The period divides roughly into the years of adherence to past art styles during the reigns of Kings Rama I and II followed by a delving into new, principally Chinese themes

during the reign of King Rama III and succeeded under the leadership of Ramas IV and V by a determined attempt to look westward and adopt a European approach to art. Thai art after the death of King Rama V in 1910 was to take a radically different turn, a process explored in the chapter on Thai Art Since 1900.

Many of the early works have been restored, which in reality means that whitewash has been brushed over the old paintings and completely new creations bearing only slight resemblance to their predecessors painted on top of them. The Bangkok era begins in Thon Buri at the library of Wat Rakang directly across the river from the Grand Palace where in 1788 anonymous artists painted scenes from the Ramakien and the Traiphum (Three Worlds) in a style somewhere between the hard edges of Chinese painting and the soft pastels of primitive works. It continued in the Palace to the Front with one of the finest works to emerge from any age: the brilliant murals of the Buddhaisawan Chapel. In lush colors, artists rendered 28 scenes from Buddha's life along the lower portions of the four walls while, above the windows, five bands of theps kneel in silent respect to the Phra Buddha Sihing image which occupies a position just back from the center of the room. The paintings, executed between 1795 and 1797, are evocations of the greatness of Ayutthaya but are rendered with a vivacity and sensitivity that makes them superior works in their own right. Thousands of figures populate the murals, yet each is painstakingly painted as if it were a portrait meant to stand on its own. The palaces depicted are so detailed and precise, they could serve as architects' perspective drawings. The details of a single event are compressed into a small space as if the artist was loath to let any of the area allotted to him go to waste. Yet there is a freedom and lack of tension that belies their compactness. As such, the Buddhaisawan Chapel murals set the standard for future works, few of which surpassed their model.

One of the earliest works of Bangkok period painting relates in two dimensions the fabulous Ramakien tale of the god-king Phra Ram (Rama) and his rescue of his beautiful wife Nang Sita from her abductor, Totsakan, king of the demons. The story, a favorite of Thais and the principal theme of its masked dance/drama presentations, runs the entirety of the cloisters around the compound of Wat Phra Kaew. Repainted several times during the 19th century and again in 1932 and 1982, the murals have lost their original form but none of their appeal. If one can suspend his recognition that the present-day murals are inferior to their predecessors, he can delight in the vivid, never dull legend as millions have before him.

For many art historians, King Rama III's reign marks the high point of classical Thai painting. It was as though the artists had turned a full 180 degrees. Satisfied they had recreated all that had been lost in Ayutthaya, they were anxious to explore new topics. Their new endeavor was to depict traditional subjects in manners reflecting Bangkok aesthetics and times rather than those of eras long dead. At the same time, and wholly without contradiction, they began looking toward a wider world beyond the horizon. Not only did this include incorporating figures, ships, costumes, architecture and accouterments of Chinese, Europeans and Arabs into their paintings but also painting entirely in these foreign modes. Thus, in addition to borrowing Chinese motifs, Thai artists rendered entire scenes in the Chinese style, a good example being the Tosachat murals at Thon Buri's Wat Rachasitharam. In Wat Raja Oros, on a Thon Buri canal bank, the paintings are completely Chinese without any reference to Thai or Buddhist tales. The new eclecticism included introducing Hindu figures into Buddhist wats; Ganesha peers from the window shutters of the Wat Suthat vihan while Chinese still lifes decorate the embrasures of walls that are covered in Thai and Buddhist paintings. Despite the contradictions, the interior is a composite whole.

The interior walls of Wat Suthat's vihan demonstrate the exploration of new themes with a depiction of the last 24 rather than last 10 Chadoks. A further departure is that none of the paintings is a straight-forward telling of the tales but is a romp through the imagination to portray heaven, hells, mountains and seas populated by fantastic mythical creatures. The same mood prevails in Wat Suthat's bot where the lives of the Pacheka Buddhas (Buddhas who do not teach) are depicted. The Buddhas sit quietly in pavilions or caves while mythical animals cavort in complete abandon, their playfulness compellingly infectious, or, like the elephants, pluck lotuses from a pond and carry them to the Buddhas. The scenes are light-hearted and utterly charming, as if the artists were determined to enjoy themselves to the fullest while engaged in their very exacting task.

Wat Phra Chetupon (Wat Po) was conceived of as a living university where every branch of learning could be pursued. In 1832, King Rama III attempted to carry forth that ideal by engaging artists to paint a wealth of instructive and edifying scenes in every space available. His objective was that the most illiterate person be able to "read" everything worth knowing with minimal help from the monks. The murals covered the bot and vihans, the cloisters around the bot and the cloisters surrounding the western courtyard. Subjects included the Life of the Buddha, the 10 stages of knowledge, the 10 stages of bodily decomposition to instill in monks a recognition of the impermanence of flesh (much like the ghoulish slides in the monastery school in Wat Bovornivet), portraits of Buddha in Tavatimsa Heaven, the Traiphum or Buddhist cosmology, the story of the Hair relic and famous Buddhapadas (footprints), medical treatises, acupuncture charts, illustrations of life in the provinces, military treatises, pictures of the inhabitants of other Asian countries, the key works of Thai literature such as the Ramakien, the Chinese classic tale "The Romance of the Three Kingdoms", the Persian "Duodecagon" (translated in Thai as Sibsong Liem or 12-sided figure), famous nuns, the history of Sri Lanka, depictions of hells and of ghosts and more. Unfortunately none of them has survived, and our knowledge

Below: *A scene rendered in Chinese style in the Sala Geng of Wat Bovornivet during the reign of King Rama III.*

of them comes from descriptions of their contents.

Across the river in Thon Buri is one of the finest examples of Bangkok painting and one of the only examples of which the identities of the artists are known. Kru Khong Pe, a Chinese, and Luang Vichit Chetsada, a Thai, were engaged to decorate the interior of Wat Suwannaram. The theme chosen was the Tosachat. The Vessandan, the tenth and most popular tale, covers the entire left-hand wall as well as a major portion of the front wall. Tales numbers one through eight are on the right-hand wall with the ninth appearing in the right corner of the front wall; dominating the upper part of the wall is the Traiphum and on the back wall is the Maravijaya. The area above the windows is devoted to four bands of celestial deities paying respect to the Buddha image. The colors are well preserved and even in dim light convey the vividness of the artists' imaginations. Nearby is Wat Dusidaram with its superbly-executed Traiphum, Hell visited by Phra Malai, Maravijaya (with Europeans among Mara's hordes of soldiers), events in the Buddha's life, and worshiping deities.

The final stage of classical Thai painting occurred in the second half of the 19th century and was marked by the introduction of western perspective and modeling in a third dimension. There was also a greater realism in keeping with Rama IV's application of rationality to all aspects of life and to his experiments with sculpture. At the same time there was a plunge into surrealism.

In certainly the most novel experiment of the 19th century, King Rama IV patronized an artist who represented a most radical departure from the classical norm both in theme and treatment. Khrua In Khong was a master of mysticism rendered in somber, almost midnight ethereal tones which he and his students applied to the murals of a number of Bangkok and rural wats.

The artist's work is marked by the use of perspective, three dimensions and the incorporation of often bizarre elements into soft, quiet compositions which, despite the use of European architecture and subjects, was designed to illustrate Buddhist and moral tenets. Though he never traveled outside of Thailand, he was familiar with Western architecture and painting styles through postcards and views which found their way to Thailand. It would appear from his style that he was also cognizant of the 16th century Venetian school. Early in his career he was befriended by the abbot of Wat Bovornivet, the future King Rama IV, who was intrigued by his iconoclastic approach and invited him to spread his vision over the interior walls of the wat's bot.

The bot murals are Khrua In Khong's most famous work. They appear in two parts: the portion between the windows and the area above them. The lower section is devoted to a detailed depiction of a monk's life done in somewhat traditional manner, as if he and Mongkut were concerned that conservative courtiers might object to anything more radical. The murals are characterized by a tonal gradation that begins with

Opposite: *King Sanjaya travels on elephant back to the hermitage to take Vessandan back to the capital. (Wat Suwannaram, Thon Buri)*
Below: *A thep in a detail from the Nemi Chadok also at Wat Suwannaram.*

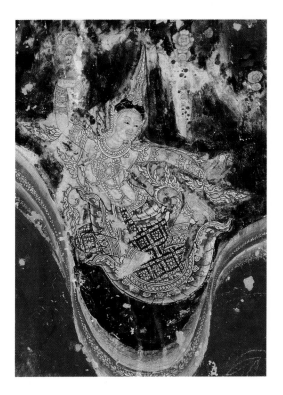

180

Below: A portrait of Rama IV viewing an eclipse of the sun in 1868 painted in a mural in Rama V's ordination pavilion in Wat Benjamabopit.

dark hues at the bottom and lightens as it reaches the tops of the windows. The technique is in keeping with the painter's concept of an upward progression from evil to goodness.

It is in the upper registers, barely discernible in the dim light, that he gives full rein to his imagination. Here, in the gloomy light, are racecourses, southern U.S.A. antebellum mansions, steamboats, clipper ships in raging seas, and other Western subjects combined in a morality play of the virtues of a good Buddhist in a style which presages Thai painting of the 20th century. Crowds dressed in European fashions gather in silence at the edge of a lake to observe a gigantic lotus in full bloom. Elsewhere, in a prosperous European town, folk go about their daily business while floating high above them in the sky are two theps in all the regalia and color of traditional Buddhist paintings.

Khrua In Khong was not a precise painter — his buildings are slightly atilt and the proportions sometimes jar — and he often seems more of a primitive painter than a polished craftsman, but his boldness and fresh eye are apparent in every instance. Most of the blank space is rendered in murky tones, but the depiction of forests is done with a sure hand and is extremely pleasing, as if he were more at home with figures and nature than with architecture. The mood of the walls is repeated in a series of scenes that decorate the twin rows of five columns that run down the interior of the hall. Beginning at the back in dark tones and ending at the front with white backgrounds, the evocative paintings show the evolution of man from a barbarous state to one of perfection in accordance with Buddha's doctrine.

Khrua In Khong and his style continued to enjoy Mongkut's favor in later years. He was invited to paint the walls of the Ratchakoramanuson Pavilion and the Ratchaphongsanuson Pavilion just inside the western entrance to Wat Phra Kaew. He chose as his subjects the epic wars with the Burmese and other historical events. Both were restored in the 1930s and have lost some of their original flavor. When Mongkut, after being crowned King Rama IV, built Wat Rajapradit in 1864, he asked one of Khrua's students to paint its walls. They show the Royal Ceremonies of the 12 months in much the same manner as the Wat Bovornivet murals. Included is an eclipse of the sun and moon, a thinly-veiled reference to Rama IV's passion for astronomy and, ironically, a prognostication of his death four years later from malaria contracted while observing a solar eclipse.

Other works credited to Khrua In Khong's school are Wat Pathumawanaram, whose lower walls are covered with the adventures of Sithanonchai, a hero of Thai literature. The upper register is devoted to the entire Royal Barge fleet which floats majestically in a continuous procession around all four walls. The school's style is also found in Wat Mongkut, Wat Protketsachettharam in Paknam and Wat Boromnivat where the gigantic lotus appears once again.

Khrua In Khong's unique style contrasted sharply with the classical school but never entirely supplanted it. Both schools would continue to function, often side by side in the same wats, until the beginning of the 20th century. Wat Thong Thammachat in Thon Buri, for example, includes views of Bangkok presented in perspective and the Life of Buddha rendered in the traditional two-dimensional manner. Nearby is Wat Thong Nophakhun, all of whose paintings are done with perspective. Some of the murals of Wat Saket, which date from late in the 19th century, show the tenacity of the classical school in that they are done in the traditional mode.

The last major wat built in Bangkok was also King Rama V's experimental ground for carrying forward the objectives of his father. The Song Panuat Chapel at Wat Benjamabopit contains a series of paintings on the life of King Rama V including his experiences as a monk and his trip to Europe. Treated in much the same manner as the Life of Buddha but marked by the use of perspective, they include the only known portrait of King Rama IV, painted with depth and a vanishing point.

Bangkok period art of the provincial workshops contrasts considerably with that of the royal capital but shows that the westernized approach extended into the outlying areas. Rural art shows not the staid classicism of the royal houses but the freshness and vitality of country people. The paintings are generally cruder but are livelier, combining a deep piety with a certain childlike quality and leavening it with good humor which often crosses the borderline into bawdiness. In them, one finds the naturalism of farm life with village scenes like cockfighting or fishing included among otherwise lofty subjects.

Among the best examples of provincial art are the murals at Wat Yai Inthararam in Chon Buri. The Tosachat are presented with a liveliness which restoration has failed to mute. Wat Na Prathat in Pak Thong Chai near Korat is typical of a northeastern proclivity for painting the outside as well as the inside walls. The area over the door features a painting of the Adoration of the Chulamani Chedi reliquary. Inside is the Nemi Chadok and the Four Great Kings who protect the world of man from harm. Their appeal lies in their naiveté and the inclusion of overt eroticism, an element rare in classical art but found in provincial painting, perhaps as a test of a monk's ability to concentrate during meditation. Only one example of early Bangkok period painting has survived in the South: the depiction of Rusis performing yoga exercises at Songkhla's Wat Machimawat, built by Rama III.

Khrua In Khong also painted the bot of Wat Mahasamanaram. Rendered in warm tones with perspective and European buildings and ships, they portray pilgrims on their way to holy sites. One of the master's students is responsible for the Life of Buddha murals in the mondop of Wat Phra Ngam in Ayutthaya. The story is told in a Western setting with Sino-Portuguese buildings.

Bangkok period artists also produced cloth banners. Often three or more meters tall, they are dominated by earth colors.

Below: *Buddha's doctrine seen as a lotus flower is the work of Khrua In Khong in the upper portion of the Wat Bovornivet bot. Painted in the reign of Rama IV, it was restored in the 1950s.*

The North since the 16th century

Previous pages: *Two 17th century seated Buddhas in gilded stucco in Nan's Wat Phumin have the bat ears attributable to Lao influence.*
Opposite: *The Lai Kham Vihan at Wat Phra Singh in Chiang Mai was built in the 18th century. It is a stellar example of northern architecture with the "eyebrow" spandrels between the columns of the front porch and the wooden shake roof.*

Above: *The library of a northern wat showing Burmese influence in the roof construction.*

Northern architects built according to aesthetic principles that allowed a far wider latitude for individual interpretation than the strict orthodoxies of the Bangkok school. The result is a rich variety of styles, each unique in its own way. In general, wats are wide in relation to their height, have lower side walls, and seem more compact than their Central Valley cousins. They are built entirely of stucco-covered brick or have stucco and brick bases on which wooden walls and roofs are set. Often with raised floors, the stairway leads from the ground to roofed porches built to protect one or three sets of entrance doors. The stairway balustrade is frequently capped by nagas, a popular decorative element used with great flair by northern architects. Like the main roof, the porch roof is supported by round or square columns. Gently arched spandrels connect the four columns, those between the central pair being much higher off the floor than the outer pair. The arch is meant to represent eyebrows hooding the invisible eyes of Buddha watching over the community often placed between the two central posts is a pendant decoration which some see as the Buddha's nose.

Northern architecture is highly ornate with finely carved wooden tendrils and foliage creeping over the columns, facade and pediments. Despite their exuberant decoration, northern wats seem more introverted than those of Bangkok due perhaps to the use of quieter, darker hues. The wooden pediments are the glory of both the stucco and the wooden wats. Exquisitely carved and gilded, they display superb craftsmanship and often reflect proximity to the styles of Burma. Even the chofa of a northern wat is different; having more the look of a wild bird than those of Bangkok wats. In contrast to the continuous sweep from top to bottom of Bangkok wat roofs, it is divided into two sets of roofs, a steeply angled upper roof overlapping a more acutely angled lower roof and separated either by a short wall, windows, or an air space which permits ventilation. The roof is normally tiled in wooden shakes.

Inside, the framework of short posts and beams that supports the roof is usually visible, covered only in red paint with gilt decorations. In several wats, such as Wat Phra That Lampang Luang, the ceiling is coffered and decorated by beautiful gilded stars or lotus clusters. One element unique to northern wats is the ku, a brick and stucco-covered pedestal enclosing the

Below: *The wooden library of Wat Phra Singh stands atop a stuccoed-brick base. Notable are two examples of sculpture at which northern artists excelled: the carved wooden pediment and the stucco deities on the base.*

Right: *The ku at Wat Phra That Lampang Luang, is made of brick and stucco which have been gilded. The structure holds the principal Buddha image.*

Buddha image and clad in gold leaf. The ku in Wat Phra That Haripunchai is a fine example of this structure.

In many of Chiang Mai's oldest wats, only the chedis have survived since the Lanna period; all other buildings have been added in the past three centuries. Wat Phra Singh sits at the head of the city's main street. Its chedi was built in 1345 but equally well known is its beautiful library and Lai Kham Vihan.

In a similar vein, the elaborately decorated vihan at Wat Chedi Luang shelters a standing Buddha. Lacking side walls, the interior of the huge wooden hall at Wat Suan Dok is flooded with light, enabling one to appreciate its immense size and the intricate work of its ceiling. In ranks on either side of the nave, two rows of mirror-tiled columns lead one's eyes to the large Buddha images at the far end. Recently restored, the hall has lost some of its former beauty.

One of the more interesting wats is Wat Mahawan, which contains a Burmese style chedi bearing singhas on its upper level and holding a standing Buddha in its niche. It is elaborately decorated with stucco floral patterns, a motif repeated in similar structures over the doorways leading from the street. Impressive in a different way are three wats famed for their supreme carved wooden decorations. Wat Phantao contains two wooden chapels, one of which has a gorgeous peacock on its pediment. Over the bird is an elaborate reliquary and flanking it are exquisitely-rendered twin nagas. Wat Saenfang also has a vihan every exterior surface of which is covered in carved wooden panels. Wat Duang Di's gables are equally impressive.

Lampang claims one of the most beautiful wats of the North in Wat Phra That Lampang Luang. Surrounded by a massive wall, it is entered via a stairway with naga balustrades. In the outer courtyard is the Ho Phra Tham library. The inner courtyard is dominated by a chedi with bronze plaques. On each side of the chedi are the Vihan Nam Tem, with its beautiful woodwork, and Vihan Phra Phut in carved wood containing two famous Chiengsaen Buddha images. It is rivalled by Wat Phra Keo Don Tao's brilliant coffered ceiling and the carvings at Wat Si Rong Muang.

The cruciform Wat Phumin in Nan, built in 1596 and restored between 1865 and 1873, is an example of an architect's flight of fancy being turned into a very respectable building. Unusual in that a single structure contains both the bot and vihan, the theme is set by two enormous nagas running parallel to each other straight through the structure, their sinuous bodies forming a balustrade that leads to the road. In another example of the North's fascination with nagas, Wat Phra That Chae Heng in Nan has a pair which slither a great distance to the street.

The North is also dotted by Burmese style wats with their multiple roofs and fairy-tale architecture. The best examples are Wat Nantaram in Chiang Khan, Wat Huad in Ngao and others in Lampang and Mae Hong Son.

Below: *A gilded brick and stucco Buddha displays the bhumisparsa mudra at Wat Phra Chao Thong Luang in Phayao. Phayao developed its own school of northern art, its distinguishing feature being the unusual shape of the mouth.*

Below: *A bronze Adorned Buddha dating from the 18th-19th centuries. (Wat Phra That Haripunchai Museum, Lamphun)*

Sculpture

Once the Lanna school died out at the end of the 16th century, the remaining sculptors began producing in the styles of the kingdoms further south. They did make one last contribution. Cast in the waning days of Lanna rule, a group of Buddha images of the 17th and 18th centuries were heavily influenced by Laotian styles resulting in statues of somewhat rude craftsmanship but with the distinguishing mark of pointed ears like those of bats. Not the finest examples of Lanna art, they provide an interesting anomaly not duplicated elsewhere. Late Lanna artists were also fine stucco sculptors, the library at Wat Phra Singh being a prime tribute to their skill.

Painting

Northern paintings of recent centuries have, for the most part, failed to stand up to the damp climate. Phitsanulok's Wat Ratburana, however, has a bot with superb paintings of the Ramakien. The scenes are delicately rendered, with an admirable depiction of landscape containing a host of delightful monkeys.

In Chiang Mai, paintings were brushed onto the walls of Wat Phra Singh's Lai Kham Vihan early in the 19th century. Redone in 1863, they relate the story of Suwannahong from a collection of 50 chadoks which were subsequently proven to be fictitious. The Suwannahong is done in Central Thai style and provides an interesting contrast to the story of Sang Thong, the Prince of the Golden Conch, done in Lanna style on the opposite wall. The latter contains buildings constructed in northern style and with figures wearing garments and jewelry quite unlike those of Bangkok. Moreover, the faces are northern and are individualized rather than stylized as in Bangkok paintings.

The paintings in Nan's Wat Phumin, though in bad condition and with several problems in composition and proportions, display a certain appeal. The subject is life in the North but includes several Europeans garbed in 19th century costumes.

Found at Wat Chedi Dok Ngon was a cloth banner similar to the tankas of Tibet. The 3.4 meter high by 1.8 meter wide painting is divided into five horizontal bands, the largest one of 2.15 meters dominating the central portion of the banner. The theme is the Buddha Descending from Tavatimsa Heaven so popular among Thai artists. The central ladder/stairway is flanked by two narrower stairways which are occupied by vertical ranks of deities witnessing the event. A number of curious figures are in attendance, including the Panchasikha god who plays a harp-like instrument whose sounding board bears a pair of penetrating human eyes which stare at the viewer. Through the background float fruits, vegetables and flowers. Warm earth colors predominate and a soft glow seems to emanate from the painting, one of the few instances in which time seems to have enhanced rather than destroyed the beauty of an original work.

Left: Detail of a cloth wall banner found at Wat Chedi Dok Ngon depicting the Panchasikha god playing a harp-like instrument.
Below: Detail from the Sang Thong Tales in the Lai Kham Vihan of Wat Phra Singh.

Contemporary Art

The drive toward westernization that began in earnest during the reign of King Rama V (1868-1910) had a profound impact on Thai art. By the turn of the century, the fascination with Western modes of architecture had reached such heights that the king had employed a British architect to design his palace in Italian Renaissance style. Similar developments were taking place in other arts, with foreigners being imported to undertake important commissions with the object of transforming Thailand into a first-rate modern country. A few talented Thai artists continued to produce works, but without the royal patronage of previous ages and without the public acclaim they had once enjoyed. They were men of the past, caretakers of a dead classical school. Thai eyes, at least those of the men in power, were focused on the future.

The trend continued into the 20th century. Thailand's leaders wanted European-style buildings, and since Thai architects had not been trained in Western techniques, Europeans were invited to design them. Many of Bangkok's bridges, like those along Ratchadamnoen Avenue, are graced by Italian decorations, testament to the engineers who drew their plans. German architects were engaged to train Thai architects and stayed to design some buildings of their own. When the Ananda Phiman Hall, which until the 1970s served as the national Parliament building, was built, Italian artists were hired to paint the interior of its dome in neo-Renaissance scenes. The bronze statue of King Rama I which stands at the foot of the Buddha Yodfah (Memorial) Bridge was designed by Prince Naris but was cast in Italy by an Italian sculptor, Corrado Feroci, because it was felt the piece was too large to be made locally, even though Thai sculptors in the past had produced far larger statues.

Feroci's contribution to Thai art was much more enduring than the few sculptures he created at various points around the city. A man with a passionate interest in modern art, he devoted his life to teaching its principles and encouraging budding students, so much so that he is regarded as the Father of Modern Art in Thailand.

Invited to Thailand in 1924 by King Rama VI (1910-1925), he initially concentrated on producing bronze statuary to celebrate the exploits of Thailand's past heroes. In 1933, one year after the Revolution which established a constitutional monarchy, he was asked to found an

Below: *Painting by Preecha Thaothong (acrylic on canvas).*
Bottom: *"Bencharong", acrylic and oil on canvas by Uab Sanasen.*

institute of fine arts within the Department of Fine Arts. Its purpose was to instruct a new generation of sculptors and painters in modern art, a task to which Feroci devoted his energies up to the time of his death in 1962. The school was eventually elevated to the status of a university and changed its name to Silpakorn (Fine Arts). Feroci's own name was to be changed to Silpa Bhirasri, the name by which the country's only modern art museum is known, an institution which was built by Bhirasri's grateful students.

The period between 1932 and the mid-1950s was characterized by a pursuit of European ideals to the exclusion of Thai subjects or themes. Realism was the order of the day, quite literally since the matter of taste in all areas of social life was dictated by the country's new military/civilian government which issued "state-approved norms" for art that held sway throughout World War II. It was only after the war that artists would begin to seek their own norms, but still in the realistic vein. Two major works of sculpture were undertaken during the pre-war period: the Democracy Monument, which was designed by Feroci and finished in 1939, and the Victory Monument, completed in 1941, in which Feroci was aided by the Fine Arts School's first graduating class of 1937. Each is a solid geometric monument decorated in the first case by friezes and in the second by free-standing sculptures. Both are in the mode of Heroic Realism of the type popular in Germany and Italy at the time, depicting muscular men of noble ideals toiling to advance the cause of the state be it in industry or in war. The period saw the emergence of two fine sculptors, Piman Mulapramuk and Sitthidet Saenghiran, and of a painter, Fua Haripitak, who would evolve through Impressionism and by the late 1970s be a leading proponent of a return to traditional themes and treatments. One noted architect dabbled with Art Deco but produced only one building reflecting its tenets.

In the 1950s, Sawaeng Songmangmee and Sitthidet Seanghiran took the bold step of sculpting nudes while Paitoon Maungsomboon created flawlessly crafted bronze statues of animals which were marvels of detailed observation, capturing not only their anatomy but their idiosyncrasies as well. The pre-eminent sculptor of the period, however, was Khien Yimsiri, an artist who would continue to dominate the field in the following decade. His models were the ceramic figures of 14th and 15th-century Sukhothai but modified to reflect his own era. Another sculptor who worked in the same mode was Chit Rienpracha, who carved wooden figures of young village boys playing flutes or engaged in other boyish pastimes.

While sculptors continued to hew the Realist line, painters began experimenting with Impressionism and, to a much lesser extent, Cubism. As the decade closed there was a drift toward abstract impressionism and even emulation of artists like Van Gogh. Thai painters chose nature themes or depicted rural scenes, usually devoid of people. Some painted scenes of village celebrations which eventually became formalized into what came to be called "tourist art" with happy, smiling villagers light-heartedly engaged in rural rituals rendered in bright colors. Fua Haripitak continued to experiment, venturing into monochromatic planes of Cubism, while others like Prayoon Ulushata painted rolling landscapes or village scenes in warm earth tones.

During this time, Angkarn Kalayanapongsa looked closely at nature, drawing flowers and plants in charcoal and pen to reveal their inner beauty. Angkarn would eventually become better known for his poetry than his painting, but would continue to serve as a polar star to new artists. Another who began as a painter but who became better known in a related field was Misiem Yipintsoi. An accomplished painter in the 1950s, she turned to sculpture and in 1963 began producing the first of her many welded metal statues. She was the first Thai sculptor to experiment with this new medium and continues to excel in it today, producing numerous pieces of children at play.

Chamras Kietkong painted superb portraits of famous and not so renowned personalities while the end of the decade saw the emergence of Damrong Wong-Uparaj, who would gain prominence in the 1960s. Damrong chose rural and seaside village life as his subjects, producing colorful evocative paintings filled with geometric shapes but in the Impressionistic vein. Uab Sanasen has progressed from abstracts to portraits and still lifes rendered in soft pastels and misty backgrounds, paintings which because of the strong detail emerge as firm renderings of their subjects' personalities.

The 1960s saw a further fragmentation in painting, one which suggested a quest for a new direction. Numerous Western modes — figurative, non-representational expressionism, abstract expressionism — were attempted but it was as though the styles were too foreign to be absorbed properly or to be internalized and emerge as something distinctly Thai. A multitude of genres were pursued but it often seemed to be a conscious mimicking without a message to convey. There were notable exceptions and evidence of embryonic talent which would discover paths in later years and become potent forces in Thai art. One of these was Pichai Nirand, who began as a painter of forms expressing a despair with society and the direction it was headed. In the 1970s, Pichai would emerge as a powerful painter of Buddhist themes rendered in exquisite detail and conveying a crystal clear message of serenity through truth. Two more potent voices began to be heard during this period, those of Thawan Duchanee and Prateung Emjaroen, both, like Pichai, exponents of truth through Buddhism and the purity of purpose demonstrated in nature.

As the decade closed and the 70s opened, artists were using acrylics to produce hard-color, hard-edged works with a great deal of force but less impact than they would have had had the same themes and treatments not already been explored to their fullest potential in the West. Many of these artists would continue in these modes and in the process begin

Below: *Painting by Thawan Duchanee (ball point on paper).*

Below: *Footprint of Buddha (oil and sand on canvas) by Pichai Nirand. (Courtesy of the Visual Dhamma Art Gallery, Bangkok)*

creating their own styles. Their numbers would be augmented by an influx of new Thai artists who had studied in art schools in the West and evolved their own aesthetics. During this period sculpture, for the first time, received little attention. Thai painting, however, was beginning to move in new directions.

The 1970s were characterized by political and social ferment which culminated in the uprising of 1973. The tumultuous experiment with true democracy was brought to an abrupt halt by the late 1976 suppression of all dissent. For artists, it was a period of self-examination, of exploration of their proper role in society and of social responsibility. Many took the challenge seriously, producing paintings of social protest which depicted society's downtrodden. The treatments were either realistic or abstract but were intended to implode in the viewer's eyeball and force him to take action. After 1976, many of these artists found other outlets for their artistic talents but a few persisted, notably the artists of the Vane Group.

Of the artists who pursued their own directions during this period, one of the most outstanding was Chakrabhand Posayakrit, a painter of people in the vein of Andrew Wyeth. A superb portraitist, Chakrabhand has also ventured into other areas, interpreting classical themes in soft colors and giving them new life. In addition to portraying characters from the literary and dramatic classics, he has created the faces for a series of "hun krabok" puppets reviving an antique art and placing it firmly in the 20th century.

The 1970s also saw a resurgence of interest in sculpture, but this time the realism of the 1950s was almost entirely supplanted by abstract forms. Among those showing great promise is Cheewa Komolmalai, who works in stone and papier maché and tends to shapes and forms that parallel those found in nature.

While artists like Prinya Tantisuk continue to pursue graphic art and Kiettisak Chaenonart social protest, Thai painting in the 1980s has entered a new phase, one which in a sense harks back to the religious art that opened the era of Thai art a millennium ago. These new artists are reinterpreting Buddhism and its iconography to seek a more mature understanding of man's role in the cosmos. In the process, they are for the first time creating a style of modern art that is unique to Thailand and one which is beginning to attract widespread interest from outside the country.

A master of line and iconography of all religions, Thawan Duchanee is considered one of the doyens of a school of representational art called "Visual Dhamma". "Dhamma" is a Pali term meaning "truth" or "law", but refers to laws of physics and existence rather than moral edicts. The subjects of Thawan's paintings are muscular men who take a visceral approach to life. These men are composites of all their animal instincts tempered by rationality. Painted in bold black brush strokes or in ballpoint pen against a stark white background, these men struggle with their inner selves and against their bestial natures to achieve perfection. The figures, one or two to a canvas, dominate the space, their tension and anger conveyed admirably to the viewer by the snarling wild animals and the multitude of beasts which stare Argus-like into the viewer's consciousness, compelling him to react. The figures have been used in depictions of the Tosachat and in a representation of the Battle of Mara whose Buddha is a man who stands resolute against the forces of evil which assail him.

Like many of his compatriots, Thawan comes from the rural areas of Thailand but displays a cosmopolitan grasp of the world. Though trained abroad, he returned to Thailand to claim his roots, returning to his native Chiang Rai where, among other projects, he has created a spirit village of 10 houses built in his version of northern style architecture and decorated with wood panels he has carved himself. One of the very few Thai painters who has achieved international recognition, Thawan has been influential in inspiring new painters to seek their own paths and not mimic foreign modes or heed popular trends.

In contrast to the iconoclastic, confrontational stance taken by Thawan is the quiet approach of another seeker, Prateung Emjaroen. Entirely self-taught, Prateung probes into nature's mysteries to produce bright canvases suffused with an ethereal light and the freshness of creation. Ensconced in a fruit plantation in Thon Buri Prateung has for a number of years been exploring man's place in the cosmos and his responsibility to the society in which he lives. In contrast to the bombastic demands made by earlier, younger painters that people take an active part in reforming society, Prateung asks that improvement begin within oneself. By quiet contemplation, one can perfect his own being and, through helping others to achieve the same goals, make a meaningful contribution. This is apparent in his paintings which invite con-templation of nature. The rays of light that shoot through the works hint at the flashes of understanding one experiences when fully immersed in nature's beauty.

Midway between Thawan and Prateung is Pichai Nirand, a painter whose spiritual evolution can be grasped by a study of his past works, perhaps more so than with his peers. From the despair over mankind's suffering which pervaded his earlier works, Pichai has arrived at a resolution of his dilemma through an internal purification and a concentration on a realm beyond the material world. Employing bold yet soothing colors like Prateung, he explores the symbols of Buddhism — principally the lotus and the Buddha's Footprint — like Thawan but with a style of his own.

Two painters who work in similar veins are Surasit Souakong, a painter from the northeastern town of Roi Et, and Preecha Thaothong, both of whom evoke the stillness of life in a wat. Surasit's works have a softness that borders on monochrome. He prefers to depict wats and the people in them in the dim light of dawn or the glow of candlelight. With

Below: "Symphony of the Universe", oil on canvas, by Prateung Emjaroen. (Courtesy of the Visual Dhamma Art Gallery, Bangkok)

an unerring eye, he captures the paraphernalia of a monk's room or the muting effect of low light which blurs objects and softens contours.

Preecha also depicts wat interiors but his delight is in playing with contrasts between light and shadow. An otherwise brightly painted wall is hidden in shadows while a sliver of light floods through a window to illuminate one corner of the painting, giving it far more impact than it would have were the wall lit evenly. Another painter of considerable promise is Arunothai Somsakul whose works are filled with hidden images. A work that on the surface appears innocent is, on closer examination, found to be pregnant with deeper meaning.

Two of Thailand's most talented and promising young painters are engaged in completing a circle which began in Sukhothai 700 years ago. Chalermchai Kositpipat from Chiang Rai and Panya Vijinthanasarn, from Prachuap Khiri Khan, come from opposite ends of the country, and though their styles differ considerably they are united in their objective of portraying the futility of pursuing material pleasures. In their works they offer an alternative path through Buddhist contemplation.

Like many Thai painters, Chalermchai began his career at an early age by painting the giant posters that cover the marquees of movie theaters. He graduated to painting village scenes and then capturing laymen worshiping at wats on holy days. After a period of examining the chaos of city life, he began exploring Buddhist themes. Working either in black and white with accents in gold leaf or blocks of solid color, Chalermchai's paintings are characterized by precisely detailed figures. Carefully balanced, there is a bi-symmetry to his works and a sense of great depth, the mastery of perspective which plagued artists in the past. His works convey both a sense of philosophical insight and of peace which resonates, rather than a static serenity devoid of movement or life.

Panya's works are marked by bold use of color, primarily reds and midnight blue. His leitmotifs are the fantastic mythical beasts to symbolize the struggle between good and evil. The beasts are mutations of those found in sculptures and wat decoration, but Panya's exquisite detail and command of color has rendered them as fierce creatures similar in impact to those of Thawan but with a power all their own. Through them, Panya can be viewed as a visionary of the ilk of William Blake and others who have attempted to portray man's struggles against his animal nature through the use of phantasms of compelling beauty.

Despite the disparity in their technique, Chalermchai and Panya have joined their talents in an endeavor which links them to the artists of ancient Thailand. In a departure from the stance taken by artists who see themselves in opposition to society, the two painters have elected to paint the interior walls of a new Thai Buddhist wat, Wat Buddhapadipa in London. Their venture marks the first time in over half a century that noted artists have been engaged to transfer their visions to the walls of a wat. Whether it marks a return of the artist to the mainstream of Thai life remains to be seen.

Below: "To the Heaven" sketch of
mural painting at Wat Buddha
Padipa, London, by Chalermchai
Kositpipat. (Courtesy of Luca
Invernizzi Tettoni)

The Minor Arts

Though most of the interest in Thailand's art has been focused on the major classical arts, craftsmen have also produced numerous minor arts which equal the beauty of the country's better-known creations. They provide further evidence of the broad range of artistic creativity and variety of mediums that has characterized the kingdom's creative endeavors throughout its long history.

Gold and Gold Leaf

Gold is not found in abundance in Thailand. A few small mines in scattered locations have produced small amounts of the precious metal but not in sufficient quantity to explain the wealth of gold artifacts which have been discovered, particularly in Ayutthaya. More probably, the revenues from agriculture and trade as well as the spoils of war have accounted for the major portion.

As gold is considered a valuable commodity, its use was generally reserved for religious or royal objects. Several sizable gold Buddha images have been found beneath stucco skins applied during times of war to hide them from marauding armies. The most famous is the 5.5 ton gold image at Wat Traimit, discovered in 1957 when, while being moved, it slipped from a sling and broke its concealing layer of stucco. Others have been found but none on such a colossal scale.

The majority of antique gold pieces now extant from early history were discovered in 1957 in Ayutthaya. They had been placed in the crypt beneath Wat Ratburana's prang in 1420 by King Boromaraja II in honor of his two elder brothers who killed each other in an elephant-back duel over who should inherit the kingdom. The treasure exhumed from the crypt included superbly-executed Buddha images in the U Thong style, votive tablets and gilded lead votive tablets. In addition to sacred objects there were more prosaic items like spittoons, necklaces, a jewel-encrusted sword, bracelets, a hairnet, crowns set with semi-precious stones and an elephant, all rendered in fine detail. Among the more delicate objects were trees made of gold which were presented as tribute or placed at the base of Buddha images in wats as reminders of the Bodhi tree under which Buddha sat while meditating.

One of the most notable objects from the South is a gold and silver

Previous pages: Detail of a lacquer screen with scenes from the Ramakien created in the early 19th century, now in the Buddhaisawan Chapel, Bangkok.
Opposite: A gold elephant, hong and shoe encrusted with semi-precious stones. Created in the 15th century, they were found in the crypt of Wat Ratburana in Ayutthaya. (Chao Sam Phraya National Museum, Ayutthaya)

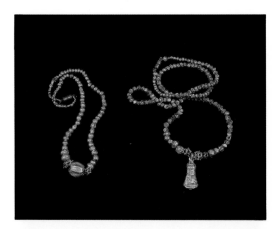

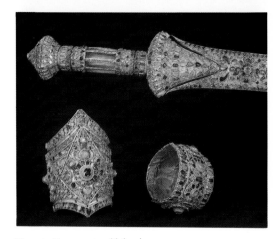

Top: A Dvaravati gold bead necklace found at Nakhon Pathom. (Bangkok National Museum)
Above: A gold sword and sheath, bracelet and armband dating from the late 14th-early 15th centuries and found in the Wat Ratburana crypt. (Chao Sam Phraya National Museum, Ayutthaya)

Below: *Detail of the furnishing of a royal barge made for Rama V at the turn of the century, executed in niello. (Nakhon Si Thammarat Museum)*

reliquary in the form of a stupa. Designed in Sinhalese style in the area of Narathiwat, it dates from the 11th-13th centuries and is a superb example of the supreme heights which gold crafting attained.

The popular use of gold is in the form of gold leaf which Buddhist devotees apply to Buddha images they regard as particularly beneficial to their spiritual well-being. The gold leaf is also pressed into a lac base to decorate chedis or any of a dozen highly regarded objects which require embellishment to enhance their beauty.

The gold leaf is created by sandwiching small bits of the metal between layers of rice paper. A thick bundle of papers is wrapped in deer hide and placed on a low pillar. Two workers wielding brass-tipped hammers alternate in striking the bundle until the gold is beaten to the appropriate thinness. The original bit of gold, now a sheet the size of a pancake, is cut into 2.5 cm. by 2.5 cm. squares with a knife made of bamboo, the only material to which the fragile material will not adhere as it is being cut. The squares are placed in individual packets and sold. Artists applying gold leaf to objects can use a brush, "painting" with it as one would a liquid.

Nielloware

Nielloware is the art of applying an amalgam of dark metals to etched portions of a silver receptacle to create silver patterns against black backgrounds. The process has been known in Europe for at least 2,000 years and seems to have been brought via India to Thailand by early merchants. It first appeared in Nakhon Si Thammarat some time before the 12th century, and from there made its way north to Ayutthaya and also to workshops in Ubon and Chanthaburi. Royal laws during the reign of King Boroma Trailokanat (1448-1488) decreed that a nobleman of a certain high rank was entitled to govern a city and to demonstrate his exalted position by owning a nielloware pedestal and tray. It is also recorded that King Narai (1657-1688) sent a nielloware gift to King Louis XIV of France.

The object to be decorated must have a silver content of at least 95% for the niello mixture to adhere properly. Artisans of old used chisels to etch the designs; today they resort to acid to accomplish the same purpose. The niello amalgam is made of lead, copper and silver which have been heated until they form a compound. Sulphur is added and the mixture is allowed to cool and harden.

The compound is then crushed to a powder and mixed with soldering flux which is pressed into the etched areas. A blowtorch is used to anneal the mixture to the silver taking care not to leave any "ant eyes" or small holes. The object is smoothed with sandpaper and polished by rubbing it with soft charcoal either imported or made from the sano plant which grows in swampy lowland areas. Fine details like eyes, smiles or thin lines are entrusted to special artists known for their delicate touch. Once completed, the piece is given a final polishing.

Gold may also be wiped on to silver areas or lines of a nielloed piece such as gold flowers on silver vines. Lime juice is wiped over the surface to remove any oil. An amalgam is prepared by mixing quicksilver with 99% pure gold which has been crushed to a powder. This "wet gold" is applied with cotton wool onto the silver surface. The object is placed in the sun for several hours until the quicksilver evaporates leaving the gold behind. The process is repeated three or four times until the required density of color is reached. The piece is then given a final polishing.

Niello is used to decorate trays, receptacles, betelnut boxes, teapots, cigarette cases, vases and valuable art objects.

Ebony and Gold

The art of overlaying black lacquer with gold leaf to create intricately detailed figures and scenes dates from the late 17th or 18th centuries. Then, as now, gold was regarded as a precious metal to be used to decorate sacred objects. The holiest items were Buddha images which devotees covered in gold leaf in acts of adoration. So, too, were the cabinets holding Buddhist manuscripts regarded as holy and deserving of special treatment, as were the tall doors and windows of the wats which served as repositories for both the images and the manuscripts.

The technique used by Thai artisans involved brushing three layers of untreated lacquer from the sumac tree (Anacardiaceae family) over wood, and polishing each coat with charcoal after it dried. Over this was laid a final coat of a darker lac thickened by boiling it. This was then polished to a high gloss with soft charcoal.

The artist drew his design on a separate sheet of paper the exact size of one panel. With a needle, he perforated the paper along the lines of the pattern. The paper was then laid on the panel and a small bag containing chalk dust or ashes was pressed on it so the dust penetrated the needle holes. When the paper was lifted off, the pattern appeared on the lacquered panel as lines of dots.

The artist worked in reverse, much as a photographer works with a negative or a batik craftsman paints a cloth with wax. The areas to be left black were covered with a water-soluble gummy yellow paint composed of "ma khwit" juice and orpiment. When it was dry, the panel was covered with a layer of gold leaf applied in microscopically thin 2.5 cm by 2.5 cm. squares until the entire surface was a single sheet of shining gold.

Thin sheets of blotting paper were laid over the panel and sprinkled with water until the moisture soaked through and loosened the yellow paint. When the paper was pulled off, the gold leaf over the yellow paint area came with it, exposing the ebony areas beneath it and leaving the adjacent gold decoration in high relief against the jet black background. The technique required great skill; the artist had to be precise the first time as there was no opportunity for corrections or touching up.

In Thailand, the art progressed through three stages. It commenced in the Ayutthaya period with gold figures on broad uninterrupted black

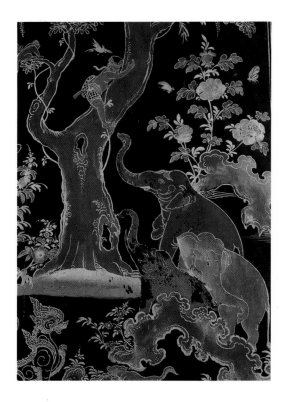

Below: *A similar motif in lacquer on the back of a cabinet of Ayutthayan period. (Bangkok National Museum) This particular technique of introducing red and gray colors into a gold and black scene is of Chinese origin.*

Below: *Buddha and his disciples cross the Iraniya River in this scene from the Lacquer Pavilion at Bangkok's Suan Pakaad Palace.*

backgrounds. In the second phase, the background gradually gained importance in the overall composition. By the late Ayutthaya and early Bangkok periods, the panel was covered with complete scenes. There was also a change in the manner in which nature was portrayed. In the Ayutthayan period, an entire panel would be devoted to a single, very Thai tree with birds and squirrels romping through its branches. By the Bangkok period, the trees and stones had become Chinese, repeating a style of decoration found in contemporary mural paintings.

One of the most stunning creations is a library known as the Lacquer Pavilion resting on stilts and comprising an inner and outer section. Found between Ayutthaya and Bang Pa-in, the pavilion, now in Bangkok's Suan Pakaad Palace, dates from the late Ayutthayan or early Bangkok period. The outer walls encompass a corridor which runs around all four walls of an inner cell which once contained the manuscripts. The exterior and interior sides of both the inner and outer walls are covered floor to ceiling with brilliant gold and lacquer scenes which appear in two bands and depict scenes from the Ramakien, Traiphum and the Life of Buddha. Among the panels are several portraits of phlegmatic 17th century Europeans with tall plumed hats and riding horses, undoubtedly inspired by the European merchants living in the old capital.

Because they held the Buddha's words, manuscript cabinets were originally decorated with scenes from the Buddha's life or the Tosachat, but by the Bangkok period scenes from the Ramakien might cover their fronts and sides. Those in Bangkok's Buddhaisawan Chapel are prime examples of the art.

In the Bangkok period lacquer and gold was reserved for important objects made of wood, usually teak. Northern artists preferred to apply the gold over a red lacquer background and adopted the Burmese technique of etching the surface of small items and dropping in colors after which the piece would be polished to a high sheen. While lacquer techniques were used on a wider range of objects, the artistry never rivalled that of Central Valley studios.

Mother-of-pearl

The technique of setting pieces of mother-of-pearl to glow moonlike in an ebony sky of lustrous lacquer may have been pursued in earlier ages but it is associated primarily with the Ayutthayan and Bangkok periods. Initially it was applied only where one wanted to convey a sense of grandeur and majesty, the marvelous Ramakien scenes on the doors of Wat Chetupon's bot or the royal decorations on the doors of Wat Rajabophit being superb examples. Later it came to be used on more prosaic items like furniture and utensils, usually intended for royal use.

Thai mother-of-pearl is only distantly related to its Chinese cousin. The Chinese method involves gouging patterns or figures into a slab of wood and then dropping precisely cut pieces of the nacreous material into the empty spaces, like putting together pieces of a puzzle where each bit fits snugly into the space provided for it. Over the entire panel a film of black lac is brushed. When dry, the surface is polished with fine, wetted sandpaper leaving the mother-of-pearl to glow lustrously in the jet black sheen of the surrounding lac.

Thai artists invented their own technique, one which made better use of the art's basic ingredient. Whereas the Chinese used a bivalve shell in which each layer had been laid down one atop the other (which accounts for its peeling in old age), the Thais used the Turban shell which had been built up by minute accretions secreted gradually along the outer rim. The result was a more solid shell which lasted for years, as attested to by the Wat Chetupon doors.

The outer skin was first removed and then the shell was cut into small pieces. Because the shell contour is curved, each piece was slightly bowed. Thus, the craftsman had to patiently sand both sides to remove this curve and allow the piece to lie flat against the wooden panel. The pieces, only one millimeter thick, were then cut to proper shape and glued down. The spaces between the pieces were filled with lac and the whole was sanded and polished.

Lac, the filler material, is a somewhat frustrating material to use. A thick, rubber-like liquid which flows from the sumac tree, it was painted into the empty spaces with a brush. It took seven layers of lac to fill the spaces to the desired height. Complicating the process was the fact that lac has decided weather preferences. It doesn't like summer's heat or winter's cold but prefers the high humidity of the monsoon season. Even then, it will take one week for each coat to dry and two weeks before the final coat can be polished.

The late 17th and 18th century Ayutthayan period is regarded as the zenith of the art. Evidence of the artisans' skill can be seen in three sets of doors which were created sometime after 1695 for Ayutthaya's Wat Borom Buddharam and, after Ayutthaya's destruction, were transported to Bangkok. One set was installed in the Phra Montien Dham in Wat Phra Kaew, a second was set in the walls of Wat Benjamabopit and the third is in the National Museum.

Two masterpieces of mother-of-pearl art are concerned with the same subject: the Buddha's footprint. One, in Chiang Mai's Wat Phra Singh, is two meters high by one meter wide and shows some Chinese influence. The second pair, six meters long, are on the feet of the Reclining Buddha in Wat Chetupon and also display the 108 auspicious signs in intricate, marvelously crafted detail.

By the mid-19th century, much of the delicacy of the 18th century works had been lost. Bangkok period mother-of-pearl pieces are characterized by a greater amount of clutter in the background and a formalization of elements. Thus they lack the warmth and life of earlier works.

Below: A *food container (Lung)* decorated with a singha, 19th century, Bangkok. *(Bangkok National Museum)*
Bottom: A *food container (Tiep Muk)* with a singha among kranoks. *(H.R.H. Princess Chumbhot Collection)*

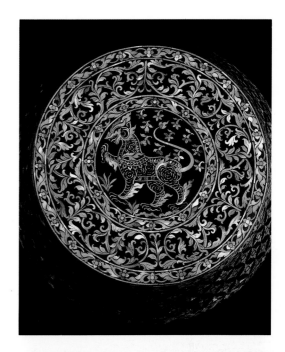

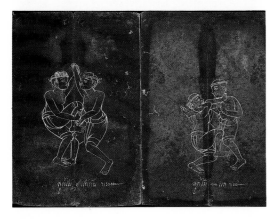

Manuscripts

Long before the introduction of processed paper, Thai scholars were writing books on materials found in nature. In the early Ayutthayan period the sole subject of the manuscripts was religion. Later, manuals were prepared on a wide variety of subjects ranging from anatomy to warfare.

In former times, there were two kinds of materials on which Thai characters were written: palm leaf and khoi. Each was reserved for a specific type of text. The individual leaves of palm fronds were dried and trimmed to flat sheets between 35 and 45 centimeters long and 5 to 7.5 centimeters wide. The calligrapher wielded a sharp needle like a pen to scratch the surface. When the text was completed, the surface was rubbed with ink to fill in the engraved area and make the letters visible. The palm leaf books were used only for religious texts and were rarely illustrated.

Like the monks of medieval Europe, "khoi" manuscript copyists and their patrons regarded their work as a holy task which would gain them merit. In an Ayutthayan manuscript dated 2286 B.E. (Buddhist Era, beginning with the death of Buddha in 543 B.C. and corresponding to A.D. 1743), a man who introduces himself as "Nai Bunkham" (who may be the patron since artists rarely identified themselves) writes "I made this manuscript so that my father and mother might attain Nibhan". He notes further that he intends that the reader or chanter may gain merit by reading its pages.

Khoi manuscripts took their name from the paper on which they were written. The paper was prepared according to an ancient formula. The paper-thin bark was stripped from the khoi tree and soaked in water. It was then beaten with wooden mallets until the bark separated into fibers. These fibers were laid on a flat surface and dried in the sun until they gained the consistency of cardboard. The edges were trimmed and the sheet was folded accordion like into 70 to 80 panels, 30 to 60 cm. wide, to form a book which, when opened, could be up to 50 meters but was usually around 18 meters.

The "pages" of the manuscript are read horizontally. In the earliest example which dates from before the 17th century, the illustration occupies the center of the panel. Others of the period may cover an entire panel or even a double spread. In some later manuscripts, the illustrations are placed along one or both edges of each panel with the text separating them.

The ink with which the words were written was made from lampblack which coated the ceiling above a cooking fire. The best quality lampblack was made from the soot of a burnt pine tree. This was then combined with a number of liquids (reputedly including the liqueur of fish kidney extract) to give it consistency and left to dry into a hard block. When he wished to write, the artist would rub the block against an inkstone and add water.

Left: A treatise on military tactics created in 1815. (Bangkok National Museum)
Below: Ganesha, God of Knowledge and the Arts, is depicted in this page from a manuscript dating from the reign of King Rama II. (National Library, Bangkok)
Bottom: Another page of the same manuscript showing a mythological elephant, composed of the bodies of 26 deities.

Below: *Khon masks, of a Rusi.*
(Bangkok National Museum)

Illustrations were considered an important part of the manuscript. They were rendered in natural pigments mixed with the sap of the krating tree to make them adhere to the paper. The painters' brushes were traditionally made from the inner hair of a cow's ear. Fine details were painted with a single whisker from a cat.

The khoi manuscripts which survive from the Ayutthaya period are devoted solely to religious topics such as the Traiphum and Tosachat. Two of the stellar examples of the art were produced in the Thon Buri period. Both were commissioned by King Taksin in 1776. The longer of the two, 50.9 meters of 272 leaves including 109 illustrations, is in the Berlin Museum. The second, now in Bangkok's National Museum, is 34.7 meters long. Half is devoted to the Traiphum; the rest depicts events from Buddha's life, the Tosachat and, interestingly, the geography of Southeast Asia. The panels include stones, water and trees in the Chinese style as well as figures dressed as Muslims, Chinese and Europeans.

Bangkok period manuscripts cover a number of subjects. There is a treatise on military strategy, another on elephants and yet another on horses. Manuscripts were also produced as aids to astrologers, the Brahma Jati being one example. Invaluable to artists were the khoi manuscripts known as Tamra Thepharup (Devarupa) which were iconographical treatises. In white lines against a black background were detailed sketches of mythical animals, heroes of the classics, poses of the Buddha, architectural elements and decorations, floral motifs like the popular kranok which resembles a flame or a head of rice. These were guarded closely and consulted by artists who regarded them as their link to the ancient masters who had originally prepared them.

Theater Arts

Thailand's many drama forms have provided craftsmen with a number of art mediums all of which they have exploited to the ultimate. The three theatrical arts most highly regarded are Khon (masked), Puppet and Nang Yai (giant hide figures).

Khon Masks

Khon, or masked drama, is one of Thailand's supreme classical arts. It arose during the Ayutthaya period and was a popular entertainment in the royal courts. Refined over the centuries, it has come to be regarded as the epitome of Thai grace and artistic excellence.

It takes its subject matter from the Ramakien and is performed like a Greek drama wherein the actors wear masks and a chorus and orchestra provide their voices in rhyme and song. The dramas provided the impetus for a new art form: the molding and decoration of the hundreds of masks required for a khon performance.

The masks are made on plaster molds whose dimensions and contours were determined ages ago by masters who consigned them to large Tamra Thepharup copybooks. Khoi paper is laid over the mold and

Below: *Hun Lek puppets perform the Ramakien. Created in the reign of Rama V. (Bangkok National Museum)*

Below: *Hun Lek puppets of Rama and Sita made in Rama V's reign.* (Bangkok National Museum)

fixed in place with a glue made of rice flour. Fifteen layers of paper are required for a mask. When the mask is dry, it is removed from the mold, trimmed and augmented where necessary by a few additional layers of paper. Lac is heated to make it malleable and is then rolled into long rods which are used to thicken the ridges of the brows, lips and ears.

For ornaments on the characters' crowns, more lac rods are pressed into soapstone molds carved with stylized flames, highlights and other motifs. Buffalo hides are cut into tiaras for the heroines. The lac ornaments are affixed to the tiaras and brushed with gold leaf. Facial details are then painted on with gouache. Teeth and eyes are usually made of mother-of-pearl.

Some masks are reputed to have magical powers and are treated with great respect. The mask for the Rusi, or holy hermit, whose benediction is necessary for a successful Khon performance, is entirely covered in gold leaf with the facial details overlaid in gouache. It is kept in a safe place and propitiated each time it is taken out for a performance.

Among the most famous masks are four which were created in the 19th century. The masks — all of the albino monkey god Hanuman — were made of mother-of-pearl on a papier mache base, the nacreous shell with its irridescent colors suggesting the giant simian's creamy coat.

Thai Puppets

Thai puppets are not only a form of drama but an art form as well, calling upon the skills of artisans to build the puppet bodies, fashion the costumes, paint the faces and create their jewelry. Puppet theater dates from Ayutthayan times, though the first record of a performance is the account by an envoy of France's Louis XIV to the court of King Narai in the late 17th century. Puppet theater was essentially a palace art which found its way into popular theater in much simplified form. It reached its height between the reigns of Kings Rama II and VI. Because of its slow pace, it lost favor and today only a few troupes perform it.

Down the centuries, Thai artists have evolved four types of puppets, each less sophisticated than the one before. The first was the Hun Luang or Hun Yai (Royal or Large) puppets which performed up to the reign of King Rama II. One meter tall, they had hollow bodies which were fitted with a complex arrangement of control strings that could make them dance, move their fingers and even roll their eyes. They were costumed and painted to resemble real people and performed episodes from classical dramas like the Ramakien and Unarut. Because of their large size, two to three puppeteers were required to operate them, usually standing up for the entire performance. Only one of these puppets has survived and it is now in Bangkok's National Museum.

The Hun Lek (Small) puppets date from the reign of King Rama V. Around 1870 one set of puppets were adapted from the Chinese theater by the Second, or Deputy King, and used to perform Chinese dramas. The 30 cm. tall puppets were less complex and required only one puppeteer each to operate. Later, a second set was created to perform the Ramakien. This second set and 51 of the Chinese puppets are now in the Bangkok National Museum.

Hun Lakhon puppets date from the end of Rama V's and are a modification of the Hun Lek. A central rod supports the body and two sticks attached to the hands are used to manipulate the arms. The final type, the Hun Krabok (Rod Puppets), are the simplest of all. The 30 cm. tall puppets have no legs or arms. Instead, a central rod supports the body and is hidden by a capacious robe. There are no arms or legs, only hands which are attached to the robe and operated by two sticks hidden within the cape.

The heads of the puppets are carved of wood and tiny details are made of lac which is either covered with gold leaf or painted. The Hun Krabok used by Thailand's few remaining troupes date from early in this century. In the past decade, one of the country's foremost artists, Chakrabhand Posayakrit, has created an entirely new set whose expressions and costumes have been rendered in exquisite detail that rival the finest puppets ever created.

Nang Yai

Shadow puppets are one of Asia's oldest forms of theater. The antique Buddhist text, the "Therigatha" dating from 400 B.C., tells the tale of a young man who tries to induce a woman to leave the nunhood by describing the beauty of worldly life. She spurns him with the words, "Blind man, thou enthuse over a thing which is unreal ... as a tree of gold seen in a dream, as a shadow figure exhibited to a crowd of people".

Shadow puppet theater seems to have come to Thailand and Kampuchea from India. By the 15th century, Nang Yai (Giant Hide) figures as tall as a man were being used to perform the Ramakien and were a popular nighttime entertainment in the royal courts. As time passed, interest in the art form died and today only a few puppets remain.

Magic and ritual play an important part in the creation of Nang Yai puppets. The figures are carved from the skins of water buffaloes or cows. Soaked in salty or chalky water for two weeks, they are dried and scraped clean of hair. They are then rubbed with charcoal to darken them or with herbs and berries to tint them faintly. Finally, they are carved in intricate detail to represent a character or group of characters.

Ancient tradition prescribes special preparations for three of the key actors. The hero Phra Ram and his brother Lak must be made from the skins of buffaloes which have died while giving birth, been struck by lightning or which were partially devoured by a tiger. The Rusi (rishi) or holy hermit who possesses magical powers to protect the troupe and ensure the success of the performance, must be made from a tiger's skin so that beast's reputed magical power will automatically be transferred to the leather figures.

Below: *Detail of a painting on cloth dating from the middle of the 19th century showing a Nang Yai performance. (M.C. Piya Rangsit Collection, Bangkok)*
Following pages: *Rama is killed but will come back to life. Here, Sita in a chariot thinks him is dead, an illusion created by Totsakan so she will marry him. Two of the giant Nang Yai figures belonging to the Wat Khanon troupe in Ratchaburi.*

Map of Thailand

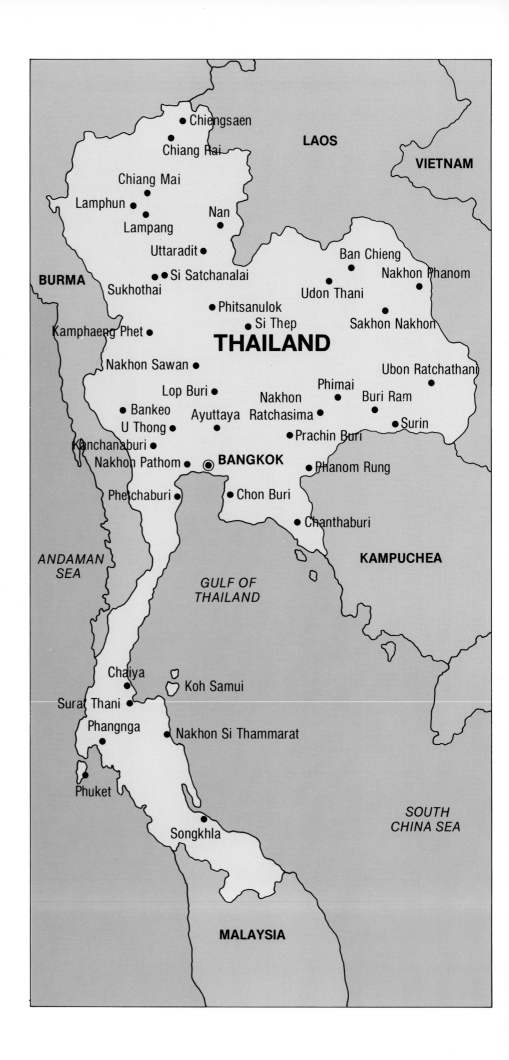

Glossary

Abhaya mudra: The gesture of dispelling fear, protecting or calming. The upper arm is held tight against the body while the forearm is held in front of and at a right angle to the body with the palm facing forward. May be performed with both hands but usually with the right only.

Amithaba: The "Infinite Light" Buddha, one of five transcendental or Dhyani Buddhas in Mahayana belief. This, the Buddha of the western paradise, is usually depicted in meditation. Avalokitesvara is his emanation.

Apsara: Celestial female who dances to please the gods. She is usually seen floating in the skies of murals.

Avalokitesvara: One of the most popular of the five Boddhisatvas of Mahayana Buddhism, he is portrayed with as many as 11 heads and 22 arms. On his tall chignon, he wears the emblem of Amithaba from whom he emanates. His body is heavily ornamented and he may be portrayed with an antelope skin over his left shoulder or a tiger skin tied at his waist. The arms of a "Radiating Avalokitesvara" are fanned like a nimbus around him and his body is covered with tiny images of the Buddha. One of the most popular Boddhisatvas, he is regarded as a personification of compassion.

Avatar: An incarnation of a god, specifically of Vishnu. Phra Ram is an avatar of Vishnu.

Bai sema: One of eight leaf-shaped stones placed at each of the corners and cardinal points around a bot to demarcate sanctified ground; even a king may not give orders within the limits they define. Only a bot has bai semas, they being the singlemost feature distinguishing it from a vihan.

Bhumisparsa mudra: The gesture of Calling the Earth to Witness performed by a Buddha image seated in the Maravijaya position. The right hand is laid on the right knee with the fingers pointing to the ground. While Buddha was meditating, he was challenged by Mara to name those who would testify to Buddha's goodness. By pointing to the ground, he signified that the earth itself would bear witness to his store of merit accumulated by doing good deeds in past lifetimes.

Boddhisatta: In Theravada Buddhism, a Buddha-to-be, one of 550 noted in the Chadok tales.

Boddhisatva: An emanation of the five Dhyani Buddhas, four of the cardinal points and one of the zenith, in Mahayana Buddhism. A Buddha-to-be who has postponed his passage into nibhan to help others reach Enlightenment.

Bodhi tree: The tree beneath whose branches Buddha meditated when he attained Enlightenment.

Bot (also **Ubosot**): The congregation and ordination hall of a wat, reserved solely for use by monks. It is denoted by eight bai sema; otherwise it is virtually indistinguishable from a vihan.

Brahma: The "Creator" in the Hindu trinity of principal gods. Depicted with four faces.

Brahman: A devotee of Brahmanism prior to the creation of Hinduism. After that point, the term describes a member of the highest rank in the Hindu caste system. In Thailand, the Brahmans have been responsible for conducting ceremonies of state and rites of passage for the royal family.

Brahmanism: The religion of India out of which Hinduism and Buddhism grew.

Buddhapada: A footprint left by the Buddha in his travels and venerated as a reminder of his doctrine. Buddha Footprints are depicted in art with the sole bearing the 108 auspicious signs by which a Buddha can be recognized.

Chadok: One of the 550 incarnations in various human and animal forms which a single soul assumed in its quest for perfection before being born as the Buddha.

Chakra: A disk or wheel, one of the attributes of Vishnu.

Chakravartin: A "Universal Monarch" and one of the two forms it is said Buddha could have assumed in his last birth to lead mankind. Instead, he chose to be a Teacher and by that means to bring salvation to mankind.

Chedi: A monument originally erected over the ashes or a relic of Buddha. In later years, chedis were built over the ashes of an important religious or royal figure.

Chofa: Variously translated as "bunch of sky" or "tassel of sky", the slender finial like a stylized bird's head graces either end of the roof peak of a bot or vihan. It is thought to signify the garuda and may originally have been intended to render Buddhism more appealing to Vishnuites, the garuda being Vishnu's mount.

Deva: Pali word for "angel". See Thep.

Dhamma: The Doctrine formulated and preached by Buddha.

Dhammachakra: Literally, the "Law Wheel or Disk", a wheel symbolizing Buddha's law. Produced in stone by Dvaravati sculptors. Usually accompanied by deer symbolizing the Deer Park at Sarnath in northeastern India where Buddha preached his first sermon.

Dhammachakra mudra: the gesture of "Setting in Motion the Wheel of the Law", symbolizing Buddha's sending his doctrine into the world at his first sermon. Performed with both hands in front of the chest held as though around the rim of wheel he is preparing to roll. Not seen in Indian art, the gesture is associated with Srivijayan sculpture.

Dhyani Buddha: In Mahayanan belief, there are five Buddhas, four of the cardinal points and one of the zenith. They are generally portrayed in an attitude of meditation. The most popular is the Amithaba.

Dhyani mudra: The gesture of meditation, also called samaddhi. Performed by a seated Buddha, both hands are placed in the lap palms up.

Dvarapala: Door guardians carved or painted on the inner and/or outer leaves of a pair of wat, bot or vihan entrance doors to ward off evil spirits.

Erawan: A white elephant with 100 heads which serves as Narai's mount.

Gajasingha: A mythical lion with an elephant's head.

Gandharattha mudra: The gesture of Calling Down the Rain performed with the right hand, and Catching the Rain with the left hand cupped at waist level. Used only by Bangkok period sculptors.

Gandharva: Celestial musician.

Ganesha: The elephant-headed son of Siva and Parbati, regarded as the god of arts or knowledge.

Garuda: A giant fierce bird often with a human upper torso and human hands, who serves as Vishnu's mount. Half-brother of the naga and his sworn enemy, the garuda is often depicted fighting with or eating a naga. The chofa is considered a symbolic representation of a garuda.

Gautama Buddha: The fourth of five Great Teacher Buddhas who was born in what is now the border region of India and Nepal and who died in 543 B.C.

Hamika: The porch, often colonnaded, set between the bell-like base and the spire of the chedi.

Hamsa: Sanskrit word for a mythical swan, the mount of Brahma. See Thai word Hong.

Hanuman: The albino monkey general of the Ramakien who leads his armies against Totsakan to rescue Sita. The son of the wind, Hanuman is a magical creature, full of mischief, and one of the most popular characters in Thai literature.

Harihara: A Hindu god combining the features of Vishnu (Hari) and Siva (Hara). Revered by Khmers in the 9th century.

Hatsadiling: A mythical beast with the wings, tail and lower torso of the hong, the tusks of a kotchasi, the ears of a singha and bearing an elephant's trunk.

Hinayana: "Lesser Vehicle", derisive term applied by the Mahayana sect to the original Buddhists. See proper term, Theravada.

Ho trai: The library of a wat housing the tripitaka or holy scriptures. Usually set on stilts above a pond to protect the fragile works from insects.

Hong: The mythical swan mount of Brahma.

Indra: Foremost among the 33 gods dwelling on Mount Meru. Also known as Sakka, he is devoted to protecting Buddha.

Jataka: Sanskrit and Pali word for Thai term Chadok.

Jatamukuta: The chignon worn by many Boddhisatvas including the Avalokitesvara.

Kampaeng Keo: The wall surrounding a wat when there is no Phra Rabieng.

Khon: The principal classical dance/drama of Thailand, performed while wearing masks. Its repertoire consists of episodes from the Ramakien.

Kinnara, kinnari: Male and female children of a marriage between humans and birds, they have bird's wings and lower bodies but the upper torsos and heads of humans. They live in the forests of the Himalayan mountains.

Kirtimukha: A lion mask often with arms and horns, which spews forth foliage and symbolizes prosperity. Seen in many Khmer lintels, it has been adopted by both Hindu and Buddhist sculptors.

Khoi paper: Paper made from the bark of the khoi tree and used for illustrated manuscripts.

Kotchasi: A mythical beast resembling the singha but having an elephant's trunk and tusks.

Kranok: Ornament which appears mainly in gold and lacquer work and representing either a flame or a stylized head of rice.

Kuti: A meditation cell for a Buddhist monk.

Lakshana: A sign or characteristic. Used in reference to the marks by which a Buddha may be recognized.

Laksmi: The Hindu goddess of wealth.

Leogryph: A singha-like creature of Asian mythology combining the features of a lion and an eagle.

Linga, lingam: A symbolic phallus associated with Siva whose face is often carved upon it. It may also appear as a composite of a cubic base representing Brahma, an octagonal shaft representing Vishu and a cylindrical finial with rounded head symbolizing Siva. A Hindu symbol, it is representative of the life force and considered a symbol of potency. Its counterpart is the yoni representing the female organ.

Luk nimit: A round stone ball buried beneath a bai sema.

Mahayana Buddhism: One of the two major sects of Buddhism which arose some 300-400 years after Buddha's death in 543 B.C. Its prime tenet is that it is the duty of those who have achieved Enlightenment to refrain from passing into nibhan but to remain behind to aid others to reach their own state of perfection. Practiced in Japan, China, Korea, Nepal and Tibet.

Maitreya: In Theravada Buddhism, the fifth and last Buddha who will appear on earth 5,000 years after the death of Buddha, or in A.D. 4457.

In Mahayana Buddhism, he is one of the great Boddhisatvas.

Makara: A mythical beast combining the body of a dolphin, a crocodile's head and an elephant's trunk and frequently depicted devouring the rear portion of a naga. He is the mount of Ganga, deity of the river, and often of Varuna.

Mara: Powerful force of evil, temptation and death. In Buddhist iconography, Mara attempted to sway Buddha from his purpose of attaining Enlightenment by promising him all the delights of earth.

Maravijaya: Victory over Mara, the attitute assumed by Buddha at the successful completion of his battle with temptation and signified by the bhumisparsa mudra.

Meru: Funerary tower often of colossal proportions built for the cremation ceremonies of Thai kings.

Mondop: A square building in a wat used to house a relic or Buddha image.

Mongkut: An architectural structure comprised of tiers of disks which rise in descending order of size to a pointed finial. Used to cap important wat buildings, notably the prasad, the tiers symbolize the 33 Buddhist levels of perfection, a concept borrowed from the Hindu 33 levels of heaven represented in the prang. The term also describes the crown worn by Thai kings.

Mount Meru: The realm of the gods comprised of 33 tiers and represented in Khmer and Lop Buri architecture by the prang.

Muchalinda: A naga with seven heads who dwells in Lake Muchalinda and best known for protecting Buddha during a violent rainstorm during the fifth of the seven weeks after his Enlightenment. While Buddha was meditating by the lakeside, the naga king slipped his coils under him to raise him above the floodwaters and at the same time spread his seven hoods to shield him from the rain.

Mudra: Hand gesture, as in abhaya mudra.

Mukhalinga: Literally, "face phallus" and referring to the face, usually Siva's carved on stone lingams.

Mukuta: A diadem worn by Adorned Buddhas, Hindu deities and Boddhisatvas.

Naga: A divine serpent that dwells underground and guards rich treasures. A water symbol, it may also be found in lakes and in the sky where several may gambol, spitting water at each other which, when it misses, falls to earth as rain. In the Hindu puranas, the naga has 1,000 heads and bears the weight of the world. On stormy days, it appears as a rainbow, a link between heaven and earth. As such, a pair serve as the supports on the ladder on which Buddha descends to earth from Tavatimsa heaven. They are also incorporated into wat architecture as at Wat Phumin in Nan, as the balustrade from hilltop wats such as Doi Suthep, and on the stairways leading the few steps from the ground

to a bot or vihan entrance. Nagas also appear in pairs on the bargeboards of wat buildings, caught securely in the claws of their mortal enemy, the garuda in the form of the chofa. In rare instances, a single naga may serve as the chofa. The naga king of Muchalinda spread the hoods of his seven heads to shelter Buddha while he was meditating. The naga also has the power of appearing in human form as the sixth Chadok of the Tosachat, "Bhuridatta", and may be portrayed with his upper torso in human form.

Nandi: A white bull, the mount of Siva.

Nang yai: Literally "large hide" and referring both to the hide figures and the shadow drama in which they perform.

Nibhan: Nirvana, the state of total extinction entered after one has achieved Enlightenment and thereby escaped the cycle of deaths and rebirths to which all life is subject.

Nirvana: See Nibhan.

Nophasun: Thai term for the vajra or thunderbolt, shaped like a short rod with five prongs at both ends. Seen most often atop prangs.

Pachekha Buddhas: Those Buddhas of the past who have attained Enlightenment but have chosen not to remain on earth to preach.

Padmapani: One of the forms of Boddhisatva Avalokitesvara, so named for the "padma" or lotus he holds.

Pali: A language derived from Sanskrit and serving Theravada Buddhism as the language of texts and sermons.

Panaspati: A composite mythical figure usually composed of the vehicles of the Hindu trinity i.e. the body of Nandi the bull (Siva), the wings of a hong (Brahma) and the beak and face of a garuda (Vishnu). On the beast's back rides Buddha, the whole signifying the pre-eminence of Buddha over Hinduism.

Panung: A sarong-like costume worn by Thai women to cover the area from the waist to below the upper calf.

Phra Malai: A monk in legend who visited hell and then rose to heaven to pay respect to the venerated Relic of Buddha's Hair before returning to earth to tell of what he had seen.

Phra Pim: Votive tablet.

Phra rabieng: The cloisters or galleries that enclose the courtyard of a Thai wat. They often contain rows of Buddha images and their walls may be covered with murals.

Prajnaparamita: A goddess of Tantric Buddhism symbolizing wisdom. She is often depicted in a trinity with Buddha and the Boddhisatva Avalokitesvara, the latter representing the "male" or means of effecting the tenets of wisdom.

Prang: A tall monument with rounded top used extensively in Khmer architecture and later by Sukhothai and Ayutthayan builders. In Hindu mythology, it represents the 33 levels of heaven, the summit being occupied by Indra. In Buddhism, it was seen as the 33 stages of perfection.

Prasad: A royal edifice or religious building reserved for royal use, generally cruciform in shape and crowned by a mongkut or prang.

Rama: Also known in Thai as Phra Ram, he is an avatar of Vishnu and the hero of the popular classical tale, the Ramakien. He is revered as both the perfect monarch and the perfect husband.

Ramakien: The Thai version of the Hindu classical tale, the Ramayana, or "Tales of Rama". Rama is deprived of his throne and forced into exile by a conniving aunt. While wandering with his wife Sita, and his brother Laksaman (Phra Lak) they are seen by Totsakan, King of the demons who, smitten by Sita's beauty, abducts her to his island kingdom of Lonka. The story concerns Rama's attempts to rescue her aided by Hanuman, the albino monkey-god.

Ramayana: See Ramakien.

Rusi: A rishi or holy hermit imbued with powers of healing and protection.

Sakka: The Buddhist name for Indra.

Sakya: The clan situated in the southern section of present-day Nepal, into which Prince Siddhartha was born. Another of the Buddha's names, Sakyamuni, means "sage of the Sakyas".

Sala: A small open pavilion in a wat courtyard where monks take their midday meals.

Sala kanprien: A wat building resembling a bot but lacking walls. In it monks say prayers at midday for the Buddhist laity to hear.

Samaddhi: The attitude of meditation usually performed while sitting cross-legged.

Sanskrit: A language of ancient India which became the language of Mahayana Buddhism.

Savatthi: The site of what is known as the "Great Magical Display" at which Buddha performed miracles to confound the heretics.

Singha: A lion-like beast of which there are four types: the fierce white Kraisorningha whose roar can be heard from great distances and who terrifies most forest animals, the silver Trinnashingha that has the wings of a bird, the black Kalasingha, and the golden Pandarasingha that wears a mane. Singhas stand guard at wat entrances, especially in the North.

Sita: The beautiful wife of Rama in the classical tale, the Ramakien. She is considered the perfect wife, a model for all wives.

Siva: One of the Hindu trinity, Siva is the Destroyer. Though less powerful than the gods in the 33 heavens, he is the greatest of them on earth.

Sri: Another name for Laksmi, the goddess of beauty and wealth, the sakti or female counterpart of Vishnu. Her name is used as an honorific before the names of certain gods, high-ranking humans and geographical locations as in Sri Lanka.

Stupa: An early name given to the mound of earth heaped around a relic of the Buddha. In Thailand, it is commonly known as a chedi.

Suriya: The god of the sun.

Tantima: A mythical beast with the lower body and wings of a kinnara but with human hands. The head is that of a garuda with the addition of a small elephant's trunk.

Tavatimsa: The heaven of 33 levels where the gods dwell. Buddha visited Tavatimsa heaven for three months to preach to his mother and the gods.

Theravada Buddhism: The "Doctrine of the Elders" which was the earliest form of Buddhism. Practiced today in Thailand, Laos, Burma, Kampuchea, Sri Lanka and India.

Therigatha: Scholarly commentary on Buddha doctrine written in 400 B.C.

Toranee or **Mae Toranee:** The earth goddess. After the meditating Buddha overcame all of Mara's temptations, Mae Toranee wrung out her hair and the floodwaters that issued from it washed away Mara's army.

Tosachat: "Ten Births" referring to the last ten Chadoks or incarnations of Buddha.

Totsakan: The King of the Demons who abducts Rama's wife Sita and precipitates the grand war which is the subject of the Ramakien.

Traiphum: Literally "Three Worlds", of Heaven, Earth and Hell. Various versions of the Traiphum were assembled by King Lu Thai in 1340 in the belief that Buddhism would one day perish and no record would remain. In form, the Traiphum resembles Dante's works in that Hell is segmented into levels with punishments meted out in accordance with the crime.

Tribunga: The triple-flexion or hipshot stance given by sculptors to standing statues of Hindu gods and Buddhist figures.

Tripitaka: Literally "Three Baskets", a term which describes the Pali canon of Theravada Buddhism.

Ubosot: See Bot.

Uma: The compassionate form of Devi, the sakti of female energy of Siva.

Unarut: The story of Unarut, grandson of the god Krishna, who falls in love with the daughter of the demon-king Bana. He is imprisoned by King Bana and rescued by an army led by Krishna. Unarut marries the daughter, Princess Usa, and becomes the realm's new ruler. A popular tale which forms part of the repertoire for lakhon nai (unmasked drama normally performed by court ladies) and Hun Luang puppet performances.

Urna: A hairy mole between the eyebrows of the Buddha, and one of the lakshanas or masks by which he may be identified. Appears rarely in Thai sculpture.

Ushnisha: Protuberance on top of Buddha's head which may be likened to a topknot. It is regarded as an important lakshana and is often crowned by a flame symbolizing the fiery energy of his intellect.

Uttarasanga: The outer robe of a Buddhist monk. By tradition, the uttarasanga was the discarded robe formerly belonging to a dead man which had been left hanging on a tree, a practice replicated by the Tod Kathin ceremony in which a small tree hung with money or gifts is given to a monk. In later times, monks began to wear new robes but continued the tradition by sewing together several small pieces of cloth to form the whole robe.

Vajra: A thunderbolt. See Nophasun.

Vajrasena: Also called the Adamantine Seat, which appeared as Buddha prepared to begin the meditation which led to his Enlightenment. It refers to the seated position wherein the subject sits cross-legged with the soles of both feet facing upwards.

Vara or **Varada mudra:** The gesture of charity performed with the arm stretched full length down the side and the palm facing outward towards the viewer.

Vihan: One of the principal buildings of a Buddhist wat, the vihan is used as a worship or assembly hall by monks and laity who gather to hear their sermons.

Vihan khot: An L-shaped vihan, usually one of four placed at the corners of a courtyard of a vihan or bot and containing a Buddha image.

Vihan thit: A lesser vihan, one of four set at the cardinal points in the phra rabieng. Containing a Buddha image, it serves as an entrance gate to the wat courtyard.

Virasana: The "hero position" in which a figure sits cross-legged with one leg atop the other.

Vishnu: One of the trinity of principal Hindu gods, Vishnu is the preserver.

Vitarka mudra: The gesture of argumentation or teaching and performed with one or both hands parallel with the sides, at chest level and with the thumb and forefinger joined.

Votive tablets: Clay or metal tablets imprinted with a figure or figures of the Buddha. Traditionally, they were buried under chedis and were intended to extend the life of Buddhism should a catastrophe destroy all other evidence of its existence. Known in Thai as "Phra Pim".

Wai: A gesture of respect to a Buddha or an important monk or person or simply as a gesture of greeting. It is performed by placing the palms of both hands together before the chest in an attitude of prayer.

Wat: A term meaning both "temple" and "monastery" and describing the complex of buildings including the bot and vihan contained within a single courtyard.

Yaksa, Yaksi: Male and female giants who serve as guardians at wats.

Index

218

Selected Bibliography

Abhivijjo Bhikkhu: Wat Rajapradit. Bangkok, 1960.

Anuvit Charernsupkul: The Elements of Thai Architecture. Bangkok, 1978.

Anuvit Charernsupkul, Vivat Temiya-bandha: Northern Thai Domestic Architecture and Rituals in House-Building. Bangkok, 1978.

Auboyer, Jeannine; Beurdeley, Michel; Boisselier, Jean; Rousset, Huguette; Massonaud, Chantel: Oriental Art, A Handbook of Styles and Forms. London, 1979.

Bhirasri, Silpa: Murals of Nondburi School. Bangkok, 1963.

Boisselier, Jean: The Heritage of Thai Sculpture. New York, 1975.
— Painting in Thailand. Fribourg, 1976.

Boribul Buribhand, Luang, and Griswold, A.B.: Thai Images of the Buddha. Bangkok, 1971.

Bowie, Theodore (ed.): The Arts of Thailand. Indiana University, 1960.

Bruce, Helen: Nine Temples of Bangkok. Bangkok, 1960.

Chin You-di: Ban Chiang Prehistoric Cultures. Bangkok, 1975.

Coedes, George: Angkor. Singapore, 1963.

Damrong Rajanubhab, H.R.H. Prince: Wat Benchamabopitr. Journal of the Siam Society, Vol. XXII, Part 1, Bangkok, 1928.

Dhanit Yupho: Dharmachakra or the Wheel of the Law. Bangkok, 1974.

Doehring, Karl: Buddhist Temple Building in Siam. Berlin, 1920.

Fickle, Dorothy H.: The Life of the Buddha Murals in the Buddhaisawan Chapel. Bangkok, 1979.

Griswold, A.B.: Dated Buddha Images of Northern Siam. Ascuna, Switzerland, 1957.
— Towards a History of Sukhodaya Art. Bangkok, 1967.

Groselier, Bernard: Art of the World Series: Indochina. New York, 1962.

Hall, D.G.E.: A History of South-East Asia. London, 1964.

Hoskin, John: Ten Contemporary Thai Artists. Bangkok, 1984.

Izikowitz, K.G. (ed.): The House in East and Southeast Asia. London, 1982.

Joti Kalyanamitra: Six Hundred Years of Work by Thai Artists and Architects. Bangkok, 1977.

Le May, Reginald: A Concise History of Buddhist Art in Siam. Tokyo, 1963.

Lyons, Elizabeth: The Tosachat in Thai Painting. Bangkok, 1971.
— Thai Traditional Painting. Bangkok, 1973.

Matics, K.I.: A History of Wat Phra Chetupon and Its Buddha Images. Bangkok, 1979.

P. Phrombhichitr: Buddhist Art and Architecture. Bangkok, 1952.

Paothong Thongchua, Piriya Krairiksh, Pishnu Supanimit: Art in Thailand Since 1932. Bangkok, 1982.

Pawlin, Alfred: Dhamma Vision. Bangkok, 1984.

Piriya Krairiksh: Art in Peninsular Thailand Prior to the 14th Century. Bangkok, 1980.
— Art Styles in Thailand. Bangkok, 1977.
— The Sacred Image: Sculptures from Thailand. Cologne, 1979.
— Sculptures from Thailand. Hong Kong, 1982.

Pisit Charoenwongsa, Subhadradis Diskul: Archaeologia Mundi: Thailand. Geneva, 1978.

Stratton, Carol and Scott, Miriam McNair: The Art of Sukhothai. Kuala Lumpur, 1981.

Subhadradis Diskul, M.C.: Art in Thailand: A Brief History. Bangkok, 1976.
— (ed.) The Art of Srivijaya. Kuala Lumpur, 1980.
— Sukhothai Art. Bangkok, 1978.

Sumet Jumsai: Seen: Architectural Forms of Northern Siam and Old Siamese Fortifications. Bangkok, 1970.
— Water: Origin of Ritual, Architecture and Urban Planning. Bangkok, 1982 (in Thai).

Swearer, Donald K.: Wat Haripunjaya. Missoula, Montana, 1934.

Tri Amatyakul: The Official Guide to Ayutthaya and Bang Pa-in. Bangkok, 1973.

Wenk, Klaus: The Art of Mother-of-Pearl in Thailand. Zurich, 1980.

White, Joyce: Discovery of a Lost Bronze Age: Ban Chiang. University of Pennsylvania and Smithsonian Institution, 1982.

Wiyada Thongmitr: Khrua In Khong's Westernized School of Thai Painting. Bangkok, 1979.

Woodward, Hiram W. Jr.: History of Art. University of Michigan, 1974.
— Wat Mahadhatu and Phra Prang Sam Yot in Lopburi. Lecture in Bangkok, 1970.

Wray, Elizabeth, Rosenfield, Clare, Bailey, Dorothy, Wray, Joe: Ten Lives of the Buddha. Tokyo, 1972.